PRAISE FOR
Real People, Real Jobs

"This book is a must-read for every 21st century careermaker and should be on the desk of every career and guidance specialist."

ROBERT JAY GINN, JR.
former Director,
Office of Career Services,
Harvard University

"Offers much-needed help to anyone struggling with figuring out where to begin the often mysterious and overwhelming job search."

ANDY THOMSON
Career Planning Center,
Tufts Universit

"There is an extraordinary amount of change going on in the workplace. It is more important than ever that people know how to make smart career decisions based on thorough knowledge of who they are and how they can contribute. *Real People, Real Jobs* is an excellent book for anyone making a career change, for whatever reason, and I highly recommend it. Read it before you need it."

RICHARD A. MORAN, PH.D.
Author of *Never Confuse a Memo with Reality*
National Director, Organizational Change
Practice, Price Waterhouse LLP

"Matching holland's types to real people doing real work provides an interesting and credible approach to career decision making. Many of life's valuable lessons are embedded in the profiles."

RUTH SCHNEIDER
Director, Career Planning
and Placement Center
Stanford University

"Real people, real jobs creatively brings the Holland codes to life. The diverse career/personality profiles of real people vividly illustrate the essential elements of each code. Fascinating and instructive reading for practitioners and laypeople alike!"

VICTORIA BALL
Director, Career Planning Services
Brown University

"The extra value in this book is the description of various career options. No author could describe every occupational field. What it does do is to give a flavor of a few key areas which make it easy for the reader to extrapolate to other fields. Explorers have a methodology to employ.

"The text does a great job of describing Holland's Themes and relating real-world orientations back to the *Strong Interest Inventory*. But the fun begins when the interviews with practitioners start. The interviews are very personal and warm. The credibility really comes through far more effectively than a description of these careers could ever do. Students need it, especially freshman and sophomores. How do we force them to read this? Everyone needs it."

C. RANDALL POWELL, PH.D.
Assistant Dean and Director of Placement
School of Business, Indiana University

"Finally, a book about careers that is educational AND entertaining! Real People, Real Jobs is great for teenagers beginning to explore their futures and college students who need to choose a major and focus their career interests. Parents will love this book…before my daughter graduates from high school, I want her to read this book."

LINDA K. GAST, PH.D.
Director, Career Center
University of Maryland

"This is must reading not only for all the students who head off to college each year without a sense of what to do with the rest of their lives but also for the college professors, counselors, and administrators who help these students find the answers. Even students and recent graduates who think they know what they want to do often end up in quite different fields and could benefit from the advice and guidance this book offers. Don't hesitate to read and use this book to help you make some of the most critical decisions affecting your future."

MARION L. OLIVER
Former Director of
Wharton Undergraduate Division
and Manager of Recruiting
for Mobil Oil Corporation's
Marketing and Refining

Real People, Real Jobs

Real People Real Jobs

REFLECTING YOUR INTERESTS IN THE WORLD OF WORK

40 People Tell Their Stories

David H. Montross

Zandy B. Leibowitz

Christopher J. Shinkman

Davies-Black Publishing • Palo Alto, California

Published by Davies-Black, a division of Consulting Psychologists Press, Inc., 3803 E. Bayshore Road, Palo Alto, CA 94303; 1-800-624-1765.

99 98 97 96 95   10 9 8 7 6 5 4 3 2 1
Printed in the United States of America
Printed on recycled paper

Library of Congress Cataloging-in-Publication Data
Montross, David H.
    Real people, real jobs : reflecting your interests in the world of work : 40 people tell their stories / David H. Montross, Zandy B. Leibowitz and Christopher J. Shinkman.
      p.   cm.
    Includes bibliographical references and index.
    ISBN 0-89106-077-4
    1. Vocational interests.   2. Vocational guidance.   I. Leibowitz, Zandy B.
  II. Shinkman, Christopher J.   III. Title.
HF5381.5.M568 1995
331.7' 02--dc20   95-8818
                                                                      CIP

First edition
   First printing 1995

To our children

▰▰▰ CONTENTS

~~ ~ PREFACE

HOW IS IT THAT SOME PEOPLE CAN FIND tremendous satisfaction and pleasure in their worklives, while others are seemingly miserable? If you are someone who is seeking a good match between your interests and the range of jobs out there, then this book is for you. Whether you are a student who has yet to make an initial career choice or someone already in the workplace feeling that you are ill-suited for what you are doing, you will find answers to your questions in this book.

We have written this book because we are career development professionals who for many years have worked with and helped people like you. We have often wished we had this book as a resource. In our professional work as career counselors, as consultants to organizations on career issues, and as human resource development practitioners in Fortune 500 companies, we have long realized that a book such as this is needed to help those who are seeking to express their interests in their work in a satisfying way. We know from our experience that career choice is a difficult decision for many people. We have worked with many who made poor initial decisions and who quickly realized the importance of work in their lives. For those in need of assistance, both present and future, we feel this book will provide invaluable insight.

We are well positioned by our experiences to write this book. Among us, we have worked as career counselors and directors of career services offices at Stanford, Georgetown, Holy Cross, and Trinity; as human resource development professionals at companies, including Digital Equipment Corporation, Houghton-Mifflin, and Stratus Computer; and as internationally known consultants. We have helped numerous Fortune 500 companies design career systems for their employees. In our experience in these various settings, we have repeatedly seen the value of a theory-based approach to career development. This book is based on the widely accepted and well-researched theory of career choice developed by Dr. John Holland, which we have found to be the most practical, most easily understood, and most relevant career development theory in this field.

How is this book different from all other books on careers? No other book provides interviews with real people working in real jobs, who talk about the processes they used to make satisfying career choices. And the interviews are organized around Dr. Holland's theory of career choice, which will give you insight into how your unique interests and values can find outlets in work. Our experience has been that people—students as well as those already working—need help in understanding the relationship between who they are and what they do vocationally. Too many people make career decisions for the wrong reasons, whether it be the result of parental or peer pressure, a mistaken impression of what is "practical," or otherwise. We believe that this book will help you to make sound, well-informed, career decisions.

The interviews in this book are from people who enjoy their work. Some of the people interviewed for this book were brought to our attention by career counseling professionals who had helped them find satisfying and rewarding career fields. Others were people who had completed an interest test and were working in career fields compatible with the test results. But unlike career information found in other books, which attempts to summarize a particular career field, in this book you are listening to real people talk about their work. You have in your hands informational interviews with people carefully chosen to represent a broad spectrum of available career opportunities. You will also find career advice from highly successful and well-known people, including Senators Bill Bradley and Dianne Feinstein, George F. Will, Jane Pauley, and Ralph Nader, who share with you their thoughts on how to make successful career decisions.

This book begins by introducing a four-stage model of career decision making. Subsequent chapters introduce each of the six Holland interest types and include interviews with people working in each of those broad career areas. While you may want to focus your reading on those particular themes and interviews that most interest you, we believe you will enjoy and learn from all of the information and interviews in this book. Reading them all will reassure you that you are headed in the right direction. The concluding chapter, What's Next?, will help you to map out your next steps and provide an array of resources that are available to you.

So find a quiet corner, and sit back and learn more about yourself and about real jobs—from the words of real people!

ACKNOWLEDGMENTS

Many others assisted with the preparation of this book. We first and foremost must recognize the influence of Dr. John Holland, on whose theory this book is based. Richard Bolles, the author of *What Color is Your Parachute?*, provided invaluable feedback. Cindy Boinis and Wende Fazio were major contributors. We are also grateful to Ellen Berger, Lauren Shaham, Helene Fitch, James Hunt, Ann Koebel, Hayden Roberts, and Charlotte Don Vito.

Postscript

To our great sorrow, Zandy Leibowitz, who was a driving force behind this book from conception to completion of galley proofs, passed away as we entered the final stages of making this book a reality. Her contribution to the field of career development will be greatly missed.

CHAPTER ONE

Where to Begin? Targeting Your Career Options

O BE A TEACHER, or a market researcher, or a lawyer, or any other of the myriad choices…or not to be? That is the question that many people ponder, whether they are just starting out in the job market or are looking for a career change. There is an enormous array of career choices out there due to factors such as technological growth, new market demands, and a global marketplace, and choosing among them is not easy.

The fortunate few know what they want to do right from the start. Meanwhile, the vast majority of people may flounder and have a hard time deciding just what it is they want to do. Or worse yet, they end up choosing the wrong career and are unhappy. Most people will not only change jobs a number of times, but will also pursue several different careers throughout their working lives. Deciding what those careers might be can often be the biggest obstacle to moving forward. Career decision making is no longer a onetime event. It's a process that most people will go through at least two to three times in their lifetime.

The best way to ensure that your career decisions are on target is to take a good look at yourself, your interests, your values, and your skills as well as to explore potential work environments. Getting some real or hands-on work experience in your areas of interest will greatly enhance your self-assessment and search for a good career match. The decision should be yours and yours alone, and ideally you will be truly interested in what you do.

～～～ How to Decide

Career decision making can be organized into four distinct phases that can make the process a lot more manageable. Figure 1 depicts these phases in a career decision-making model that will be referred to throughout this book. The model is shown as a cyclical process rather than a onetime event. The phases of career decision making should be revisited, at least on some level, each time you encounter a career transition.

The first phase in the career decision-making process is *assessment* of your interests, values, and skills. The second phase is *identifying and exploring your options* by gathering information through research, direct experience, and information interviewing. The third phase is *goal setting and planning* to identify and set career goals, pinpoint specific actions to reach those goals, and create a plan to achieve the goals. The final phase involves *taking action*—actually implementing your plan and putting it to work.

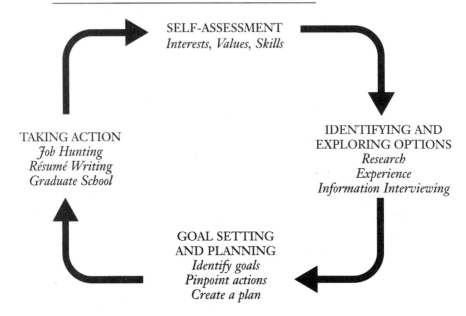

FIGURE 1
CAREER DECISION-MAKING MODEL

SELF-ASSESSMENT
Interests, Values, Skills

IDENTIFYING AND
EXPLORING OPTIONS
Research
Experience
Information Interviewing

GOAL SETTING
AND PLANNING
Identify goals
Pinpoint actions
Create a plan

TAKING ACTION
Job Hunting
Résumé Writing
Graduate School

Although assessment is identified as the first phase of the career decision-making model, it really should be a continuous process that occurs through all the phases. The initial assessment provides a baseline from which to begin the process and helps point you in the right direction. Over time, a person generally grows and learns and experiences new and different things. To keep current and headed in the right direction, assessment needs to occur on an ongoing basis. As mentioned before, most people change jobs and careers a number of times in their lifetime. So constant assessment of yourself and your work environment should prepare you to make the best possible current and future career decisions.

~ ~ ~ How This Book Is Organized

This book focuses on the first two phases of the career decision-making process—*assessment* and *identifying and exploring options*. It is designed to help you better understand yourself and your interests, narrow your choices, and get a realistic picture of what it's really like to work in specific careers. The book presents chapters based on career development theorist John Holland's typology of people and work environments. According to Holland, there are six types, or themes, of people and work environments, within which all jobs in the world of work can fit: Realistic, Investigative, Artistic, Social, Enterprising, and Conventional. Each of these six themes is introduced and described in its own chapter, which includes a partial listing of jobs that fit that category and is then followed by first-person accounts of people working in various corresponding jobs. The first-person accounts are given by people who are successful, satisfied, and happy with their work, providing you with a bird's-eye view of each career and valuable insight into career decision making. So you'll hear from such people as an actor, who describes what it's like finding work in the theater and in movies, and a wetlands ecologist, who describes her experience doing fieldwork and investigating ecosystems. The chapters devoted to careers in the Holland themes are followed by a final chapter outlining the next steps in the career exploration process, including details on further self-assessment, information interviewing, and career planning tools and resources.

Now let's take a look at what this all means for you.

~~~ Beginning the Process

As mentioned earlier, the first phase of career decision making involves assessing your interests, values, and skills. But what exactly do we mean by interests, values, and skills? Figure 2 provides an overview of how we have defined them.

FIGURE 2
DEFINING YOUR INTERESTS, VALUES, AND SKILLS

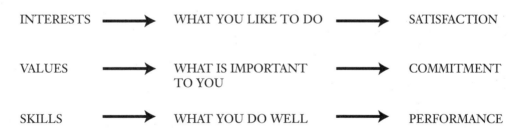

INTERESTS	⟶	WHAT YOU LIKE TO DO	⟶	SATISFACTION
VALUES	⟶	WHAT IS IMPORTANT TO YOU	⟶	COMMITMENT
SKILLS	⟶	WHAT YOU DO WELL	⟶	PERFORMANCE

Interests are the things that you like to do—what fascinates, excites, and inspires you. If you are interested in what you do, you'll derive satisfaction from your work. The main focus of this book is to look at your interests, using Holland's framework, as they relate to possible career options.

Values are the things that are most important to you—what motivates you and contributes to your sense of well-being. If your values are satisfied in your work, you will most likely feel committed to your job, career, and/or organization.

Skills are the things that you do well—your strengths and talents. When your skills match the requirements of your career, your performance on the job will be positively affected.

Self-assessment is the first phase of the career decision-making model for a reason: You must be able to understand and know yourself before you can begin to understand which careers might be right for you. But remember, self-assessment is ongoing throughout the entire career decision-making process. After exploring and experiencing various options, you need to continue to assess yourself and your situation to ensure that you have a good career match. For example, Allen Goldstein, an accountant who is profiled in chapter 7, believes that the changes in his interests—from numbers to dealing with people—have been shaped by his work in public accounting. The final chapter in this book, What's Next?, provides more details and specific resources for assessing your interests, values, and skills.

~ ~ ~ Isn't Holland a Country?

Before we take a close-up look at the various careers that are profiled in this book, we need to first understand a little more about the six career themes identified by John Holland and how this relates to the idea known as *person-work environment fit*. With some background on this theory, you'll be better able to understand your own theme and apply the information in this book to your own career and career options.

According to Holland, people search for work environments in which they can use their skills and abilities and comfortably express their attitudes and values. Career satisfaction, stability, and achievement depend on the compatibility between one's personality and one's work environment—a psychological "fit" occurs as a result of a match between a person and his or her work environment. Career interests flow from life history and are an important aspect of personality. The choice of a career is an expression of one's personality, and career behavior is determined by an interaction between personality and work environment.

Holland's typology creates a structure for this idea of a person-work environment fit. His theory attempts to organize the vast amount of information that exists about people and jobs. It assumes that all people look for enjoyment and seek work situations that make use of their talents, skills, and interests. Development over the life span is seen as a series of person-work environment interactions in which people select, pass through, or avoid situations that encourage particular behaviors or personalities.

The *Strong Interest Inventory*™ (*Strong*) and Holland's *Self-Directed Search* (SDS) are formal interest assessment tools organized around Holland's theory. They are used most often by career counselors helping people target their career direction. The *Strong* compares your interests with the interests of other people who are employed in specific occupations and report that they are satisfied with their work. It also provides suggestions for career directions based on those interests.

* If you've taken the *Strong* or the SDS, you're probably familiar with Holland's theory and the six interest themes and probably have an idea of what your own theme may be. Take a look at the "Snapshot: Summary of Results," which may have been provided by your counselor. Your Holland theme code will be listed under the General Occupational Themes section. Your code is comprised of the one to three Holland themes that you scored highest on—the ones in which you have the highest levels of interest. Record your Holland theme code on page 8 of this book. We'll go into more detail about how you can use your code in your career exploration process later.

* If you haven't taken the *Strong* or the SDS yet, the next section provides a brief exercise that will help you get an initial idea of what your Holland theme code may be.

If you are interested in taking the *Strong* or the SDS, contact the career planning and placement office at a local school or a career center or career counselor. The *Strong* must be administered and interpreted by a qualified professional. Most career planning and placement centers or career counselors have the *Strong* and the SDS available to administer and interpret to their clients.

～～～ Let's Make a Deal

On what dimensions do Holland's themes of people and work environments differ from each other? Each type of person has a unique set of values, characteristics, skills, and attributes, while each corresponding work environment has its own unique conditions and requirements.

To help you identify what your Holland theme code may be, let's play a slightly altered version of the TV game show *Let's Make a Deal*.* This will give you a quick initial look at your Holland theme code. In our game, there are six doors, and behind each is a group of people with distinguishing characteristics:

* Door # 1: People who have athletic or mechanical interests and prefer to work with machines, tools, plants, or animals (R)

* Door # 2: People who like to observe, learn, investigate, analyze, evaluate, or solve problems, particularly in activities that involve math and science (I)

_____

* This is based on "The Party Exercise," from Richard N. Bolles' *What Color is Your Parachute?* (revised annually). Adapted with permission.

* Door # 3: People who have artistic interests, are innovative, and like using their imagination or creativity in unstructured situations through activities such as art, writing, and music (A)

* Door # 4: People who like to work with others by informing, enlightening, helping, training, developing, or curing (S)

* Door # 5: People who like to work with others by influencing, persuading, leading, or managing for organizational goals or economic gain (E)

* Door # 6: People who like to work with data, have clerical or numerical ability, are detail oriented, and follow through (C)

Since you are the lucky contestant, Monty Hall offers you the chance to spend time behind the door of your choice with the group of people you'd most prefer to be around. You make your choice, then, after a few minutes, Monty informs you that your top choice group has a prior engagement across town and all those people must leave immediately. He instructs you to make another selection from the remaining doors. Again, after several minutes, Monty lets you know that your second choice group of people has to rush off as well and that you'll need to choose a third door.

The letter in parentheses at the end of each description corresponds directly to each of the Holland themes—R for Realistic, I for Investigative, A for Artistic, S for Social, E for Enterprising, and C for Conventional. These codes are commonly referred to as RIASEC to reflect the first letter in each of the themes. Your Holland theme code will contain the three letters that correspond to your first, second, and third door choices. If your interest areas (or door choices) are Social, Artistic, and Enterprising, then your three-letter code would be SAE.

▶MY HOLLAND THEME CODE

Record here the Holland theme code that you derived from either your Strong Interest Inventory *or* SDS *results or the* Let's Make a Deal *exercise:*

———————   ———————   ———————

Your code indicates, in order, your top three preferences from the Holland themes. As you'll see later, your three-letter theme code can be instrumental in helping to guide your career exploration.

The descriptions of work settings according to Holland themes sound very similar to the way the types of people working in those areas are described. Table 1 describes people and work environments by Holland theme, highlighting their typical characteristics and qualities.

TABLE 1
PEOPLE AND THEIR WORK ENVIRONMENTS
BY HOLLAND THEME

	PEOPLE	WORK ENVIRONMENTS
REALISTIC	Strong mechanical, psychomotor, and athletic abilities; honest; loyal; like the outdoors; prefer working with machines, tools, plants, and animals	Structured; clear goals and lines of authority; work with hands, machines, or tools; casual dress; focus on tangible results; engineering, military, skilled trades
INVESTIGATIVE	Strong problem solving and analytical skills; mathematically inclined; like to observe, learn, and evaluate; prefer working alone; reserved; idea generators	Nonstructured; research oriented; intellectual; discover, collect, and analyze ideas/data; science, math, medicine, and computer related; labs, universities, high tech, hospitals
ARTISTIC	Creative; complex; emotional; intuitive; idealistic; flair for communicating ideas; prefer working independently; like to sing, write, act, paint, think creatively	Nonstructured; creative; flexible; rewards unconventional and aesthetic values; creation of products and ideas; arts organizations, film/TV, publishing, advertising, museums, theater, galleries
SOCIAL	Friendly; outgoing; find fulfillment in helping others; strong verbal and personal skills; teaching abilities; impulsive	Harmonious; congenial; work on people-related problems/issues; inform train, develop, cure, or enlighten others; team oriented; human resources; training, education, social service, hospitality, health care, nonprofit
ENTERPRISING	Confident; assertive; sociable; speaking and leadership abilities; like to use influence; strong interpersonal skills; status conscious	True business environment; results oriented; driven; high-quality service and product orientation; entrepreneurial; high prestige; power focused; sales, management, politics, finance, retail, leadership
CONVENTIONAL	Dependable; disciplined; precise; persistent; orderly; efficient; practical; detail oriented; clerical and numerical abilities	Ordered; clear rules and policies; systematized manipulation and organization of data; control and handling of money; high income potential; accounting, business, finance, administration

Work environments are often dominated by people of the corresponding themes. People tend to congregate in and create work environments that reflect their interests and characteristics. Realistic work environments are oriented toward working with *things*, using machines, tools, or your hands. Investigative work environments often afford the opportunity to discover, collect, analyze, and/or interpret ideas and data. Artistic work environments focus on creative self-expression through performance or the creation of products or ideas. Social work environments center on helping people with their mental, spiritual, social, physical, or career concerns. Enterprising work environments also involve working with people but focus on selling, influencing, or leading others for organizational or economic gain. Conventional work environments are typically oriented toward the manipulation and computation of numbers and data.

~~~ A Synthesis of Themes

It is unlikely that any person or work environment is purely one Holland theme. Most people are a combination of two or three themes. As we saw in the *Let's Make a Deal* exercise, it's likely that we are interested in being around two, if not three, types of people. Generally, interest inventories and other Holland-based supportive materials include a three-letter Holland summary "code" or "profile." The first letter in the code is usually the dominant theme and tends to determine the direction of career choice. The second and third themes tend to help narrow and identify career choices in a more specific manner.

Architect Page Goolrick recounts in her interview in chapter 4 that she had an aptitude for math and an interest in art when she first began her college education. Her career as an architect has allowed her to combine those interests. The Holland code for an architect is ARI—Artistic, Realistic, and Investigative.

The Dictionary of Holland Occupational Codes, a career resource commonly found in career centers and libraries, lists over twelve thousand occupations indexed by Holland codes. You can also refer to the appendix in the back of this book for additional occupations categorized by Holland theme codes. By looking up your Holland theme code, you'll find a list of occupations that employ people who share your interests. When you're exploring career options, it's important to consider your top three themes and *all combinations* of them, since most people have multiple interests. For example, if your theme code is AES—for Artistic, Enterprising, Social—you should also check for occupations listed under the code combinations of ASE, EAS, ESA, SAE, and SEA.

▶MY CODE COMBINATIONS

Record all combinations of your Holland theme code below:

My Holland theme code:

_____ _____ _____

Combinations of my code:

_____ _____ _____ _____ _____

~ ~ ~ How the Theory Shapes Up

To organize his theory and make it practical and usable, Holland arranged the themes in a hexagonal model, as figure 3 illustrates.

FIGURE 3
THE HOLLAND HEXAGON

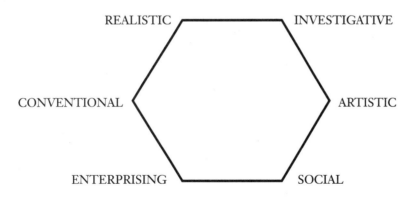

The themes most similar to each other fall next to each other on the hexagon. Those most dissimilar are situated directly across the hexagon from each other. For example, Realistic and Investigative, or Social and Enterprising themes have more in common with each other than those opposite each other, such as Social and Realistic or Artistic and Conventional.

The hexagon serves to define the degree of *consistency* of a person's theme code and the degree of *congruence* of a person's theme code and work environment.

The concept of consistency is based on the themes' positions on the hexagon. Adjacent themes, such as Enterprising and Conventional, are considered consistent because they tend to attract people with compatible interests and personalities. Those opposite on the hexagon, such as Realistic and Social, are inconsistent and generally attract people with incompatible interests. The degree of congruence or fit between a person and a work environment is measured by the distance on the hexagon between them. The closer they are on the hexagon, the more congruent they are. For example, an Enterprising person in a Conventional job is somewhat congruent, while an Enterprising person in a Investigative job is highly incongruent.

A third concept, *differentiation*, helps determine how clearly defined a person's interests are. The degree of differentiation is defined as the difference between the highest and lowest scores on the interest types—called the General Occupational Themes (GOTs) on the *Strong* or the SDS. The greater the difference between the scores, the greater the differentiation. For example, if a person expresses high interest on one or two themes and average to little on the other themes, then his or her interests appear to be differentiated and clearly defined. On the other hand, if a person's interest scores are all about the *same* level (expressing high, average, or little interest), his or her interests are considered undifferentiated or poorly defined.

The next section further discusses the effects of consistency/inconsistency, congruence/incongruence, and differentiation/undifferentiation on career exploration and satisfaction.

~ ~ ~ How Does This Apply to Me?

In this section, we'll take a closer look at your Holland theme code and what it may indicate about your possible career options. We'll also consider how your code relates to your career aspirations and your potential satisfaction with the choices you may make.

Looking at Your Holland Code

There are three questions to consider when looking at your Holland code:

1. What is the degree of consistency within my Holland theme code? Are the letters in your theme code adjacent or spread apart?

Fill in the Holland, or RIASEC hexagon, below and draw lines connecting the themes in your code.

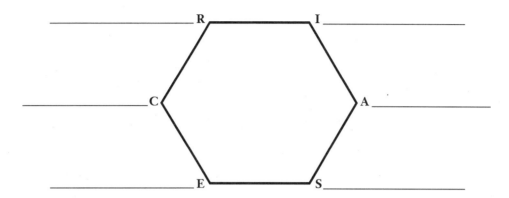

If the letters in your theme code are next to or in close proximity to each other on the hexagon shape, then your code is considered *consistent.* The more consistent your code, the more similar your interests tend to be, and the more likely you'll be able to find a work environment that will enable you to satisfy most of your interests.

If the letters in your theme code are spread apart or opposite each other on the hexagon shape, then your code is considered *inconsistent.* The more inconsistent your code, the more diverse your interests tend to be, and the less likely you'll be able to find a work environment that's compatible with all of your interests. But don't despair if your code is inconsistent. Having an inconsistent code simply means that your interests are very different from each other and probably won't all be satisfied by the same career. It's likely that you'll have to pursue some of your interests outside of a work environment through such things as hobbies, volunteer work, recreation, or other leisure activities.

2. How congruent is my Holland theme code with the work environment theme codes of my career aspirations? Use the *Dictionary of Holland Occupational Codes* or the appendix contained in the back of this book and the subsequent chapters in this book to help you determine the Holland themes of the work environments/careers that you are aspiring to and then compare them to your own Holland theme code.

List your Holland theme code and the theme code and titles of careers that interest you below:

My Holland theme code:

_____

Theme codes and titles of careers I'm aspiring to:

_____   _____

_____   _____

_____   _____

Career satisfaction is a direct result of congruence between people and their work environments. If the letters in your code match or are close on the hexagon to the letters in the codes of the work environments you've chosen, there is congruence between you and your career aspirations. So the more congruent your code and your work environment, the more likely you'll be satisfied in your career.

If the letters in your code do not match or are not close on the hexagon to the letters in the codes of the work environments you've chosen, there is incongruence between you and your career aspirations. The more incongruent your code and your work environment, the more likely you'll feel like a fish out of water. It is not inconceivable that you might be happy in a career that is incongruent with your code, but it is not the norm. If your career aspirations are incongruent with your code, you'll probably need to do some further investigating. Are you sure you're being honest with yourself about your interests, or are there other factors influencing your choices? Have you thoroughly investigated the careers you are aspiring to or do they just sound interesting? If you are having trouble working through some of these issues on your own, you may want to seek the advice of a career counselor or visit a career planning and placement center. See the final chapter in this book for more details.

3. What is the degree of differentiation in my Holland theme code? If you've taken the *Strong* or the SDS, you received a score on each Holland theme—Realistic, Investigative, Artistic, Social, Enterprising, and Conventional. Scores should range from 27 to 80 for the *Strong* and from 4 and 28 for the SDS.

Plot your scores on the graph below to get a picture of the degree of differentiation between your interest themes:

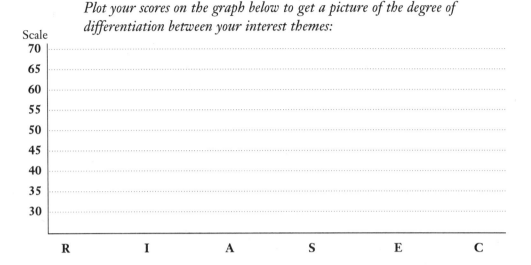

Scale

| 70 |
| 65 |
| 60 |
| 55 |
| 50 |
| 45 |
| 40 |
| 35 |
| 30 |

R   I   A   S   E   C

Looking at Your Profile Pattern

Next, we'll examine your *Strong* Profile or SDS results in some detail. If you are planning to take the *Strong* or the SDS at a later time, you may want to refer to this section after you receive your results.

Now look at the pattern made by the scores you have plotted on the graph above. A pattern with high peaks and low valleys illustrates a differentiated SDS or *Strong* Profile; a flat pattern illustrates an undifferentiated profile. But what does that really mean in terms of career exploration and decision making? The implications of each possible pattern are discussed next.

Single high peak with valleys: Your profile is clearly defined and you are ready to explore career options in your top area of interest. Generally, if your profile is differentiated, you'll probably have little trouble with career decision making, but you should not hesitate to seek assistance from a career counselor —perhaps the one who interpreted your *Strong* or SDS Profile—if you run into some stumbling blocks.

Two or three high peaks with low valleys: Your profile is clearly defined but you may face some decisions between your top interest areas. Perhaps you'll be able to creatively combine your top interests into one career. A person scoring high on the Artistic and Social themes could combine his or her interests into a career as an art teacher or art therapist. Or, he or she may need to pursue some interests in activities outside of work. The same person with high scores on

Artistic and Social may decide to become a social worker and take sculpture or painting classes in the evenings. Some career exploration and research and/or discussion with a career counselor should help steer you in the right direction.

Flat with all high scores: Your profile is not clearly defined but does show a high level of energy and a wide range of interests and talents. You have given relatively high ratings to many activities and were perhaps reluctant to mark "dislike" on the items. Since you have such diverse interests, making your career decisions based on those interests may prove somewhat confusing or difficult. It may be possible to combine several of your interests into one career. Alternatively, your career choices may need to be based more on your values and underlying needs—what really motivates you and satisfies you (see the last chapter in this book, What's Next?, for more on this).

Flat with all mid-range scores: Your profile is not clearly defined and shows a possible tendency to rate everything average. Or you may genuinely have uncertainty about your abilities and interests. One option is to consider retaking the *Strong* or the SDS and attempt to avoid overuse of average ratings and then reevaluate your interests. Another option is do some prioritization of your interests and values, preferably with the assistance of a career counselor (again, refer to the last chapter in this book, What's Next?).

Flat with all low scores: Your profile is not clearly defined and shows a lack of interest in all areas. It's possible that inexperience and lack of exposure to the world of work may have influenced your responses. A low, flat profile may also indicate the inability to make a change or a commitment. Whatever the case may be, there is more work ahead for you. You'll need to engage in further self-assessment, exploration, and career counseling before you can be ready to successfully choose a career.

◤◢◢ Several More Points to Consider

* It is more common to find Investigative, Enterprising, and Social positions held by college-educated people, while there are relatively fewer Realistic, Artistic, and Conventional positions available for the same group. But don't let that discourage you if you happen to be a Realistic, Artistic, or Conventional type. Using Holland's theory for career exploration can help open up some careers to you that you might not have considered or been exposed to before. Plenty of college graduates have chosen careers in the Realistic, Artistic, and Conventional realms. For some examples, check out the interviews in this book with an actuary, a forest manager, a writer/journalist, a banker, an actor, an architect, an accountant, an advertising executive, and a mechanical engineer.

✳ In the following chapters on the Holland themes, we discuss the growth and outlook of various careers. Obviously, when making a career choice, it is more desirable to be pursuing a field with a positive outlook for growth and the future. There's nothing wrong with pursuing your dreams and aspirations, even if they are not in a high growth field, but it's important to know what you're up against. The definitions of growth we've used are based on the job outlook projections through 2005 found in the *1994–1995 Occupational Outlook Handbook*. Growth "much faster than average" means that employment will increase 41 percent or more; "growth faster than average" means a 27 to 40 percent increase; "average growth" means a 14 to 26 percent increase; "little change or slower than average growth" means a 0 to 13 percent increase; and "decline" means a decrease of 1 percent or more. "Excellent," "very good," or "good" opportunities in a particular field mean that job seekers are much more numerous, more numerous, or about the same, respectively, as compared to the number of job openings. People may face "competition" or "keen competition" when there are fewer or much fewer job openings than job seekers. Keep these definitions in mind and refer to them when reading the sections on What's It Like Out There? in the subsequent chapters on the Holland themes.

✳ If you do get discouraged or stuck in the process of career exploration, the best advice is to seek the support of a friend, career counselor, or career center. The final chapter in this book provides more details on exploring career options and refers you to numerous publications and organizations that will provide additional information on career options.

~ ~ ~ In Summary

Holland's theory consists of six personality types, six corresponding work environments, and a hexagonal model that explains their relationships and interactions. The theory can be used as a tool for helping understand work histories, job satisfaction, and career achievement, and as a structure to organize and interpret personal and occupational information.

Holland says that personality types are not passive victims of their environments but actively seek and avoid potentially compatible and incompatible situations. For example, when advertising executive Glenn Miller (see chapter 4) discovered he disliked being a lawyer and wanted to be in a more creative environment, he pursued a career in advertising. Lawyers and advertising executives are both considered Artistic occupations, according to Holland's theory, and may tap some similar interests and skills, but their work environments greatly differ. This book will help you explore your Holland theme code and then actively pursue the careers *and* work environments that support it. You may also find it helpful to use Holland's *Self-Directed Search* (SDS) to gain additional information about yourself.

In the next six chapters, we'll explore each of the six different Holland theme areas in detail and meet people working in those areas who will tell you the stories of their work experiences.

CHAPTER TWO

Put Your Hands on a Realistic Career

RE *HOME IMPROVEMENT*, ESPN fishing shows, and Arnold Schwarzenegger films on your list of favorite TV shows and movies? Do you like to spend Sunday afternoons tinkering in your basement workshop or hiking up a mountain? Are you all action and no talk? Is it important for you to see your results or to have a check in the win/loss column?

If the answer is yes to any of these questions, then read on—you may be cut out for a career in the Realistic fields. Even if you answered no to the questions, you should still read on—you might be surprised and you might get interested.

~ ~ ~ What Are These Careers and Where Can I Find Them?

Realistic work environments generally provide structure with well-established goals and clear lines of authority. The opportunity to work with one's hands with only minimal interpersonal interaction reflects the Realistic occupations. Typically, Realistic occupations are those related to engineering, agriculture, the military, the skilled trades, and technical vocations. Whether you like to work indoors or outdoors, the Realistic fields offer a wide variety of work environments, ranging from business organizations, factories, and laboratories to farms, parks, and forests. It's often important for Realistic people to feel unencumbered at work, dressing in casual clothes and being with similar and familiar people. Job titles considered Realistic include those listed in table 2 below. For a more complete listing of Realistic careers, consult *The Dictionary of Holland Occupational Codes* or the appendix.

TABLE 2
EXAMPLES OF REALISTIC CAREERS

Aircraft sales representative	Forester	Optical engineer
Horticultural worker	Police officer	Software technician
Appraiser	Environmental project manager	Building contractor
Small business owner	Military officer	Fire fighter
Secret service agent	Industrial arts teacher	Electrician
Athletic trainer	Radiologic technologist	Production planner
Emergency medical technician	Vocational agriculture teacher	Pilot
Engineer	Wine maker	
Jeweler	Professional athlete	

Some Realistic people are employed by organizations or institutions (engineers and geologists), while others might be self-employed (architects and opticians). Realistic work goes hand in hand with the practical nature of Realistic people and their orientation for the present and preference for the tangible. Outcomes in Realistic occupations are often specific and/or clear-cut, such as a win or loss, a bumper crop, a pair of eyeglasses, or a new aerodynamic automobile design. Realistic activities often offer a sense of closure and satisfaction for a job well done.

~ ~ ~ Who Are These People and Am I One of Them?

What types of people are attracted to and do well in Realistic occupations? What are their characteristics, values, and interests?

The image of a Mr. or Ms. Fix-it dressed in a flannel shirt and wearing a tool belt may come to mind when picturing a Realistic person. Generally thought of as rugged individualists of few words who like to work with their hands, Realistic people tend to perceive themselves as having strong mechanical, psychomotor, and athletic abilities and as lacking in interpersonal skills. This stereotype is somewhat simplistic and, on further examination, it becomes apparent that there is a lot more to a Realistic person than first meets the eye.

Realistic people are sometimes characterized as unsociable, but the truth is that they may often be shy and reserved so they tend not to show much outward emotion. Although not always the most talkative, Realistic people tend to be quite frank in their opinions and are often the most mature and emotionally stable in a group. They can be extremely loyal to people, organizations, and ideas that have traditional appeal. On the one hand, Realistic people are commonly oriented in the present, conservative, and quite grounded. On the other hand, they are often willing to take risks by doing such things as skydiving, mountain climbing, or auto racing.

The creation of useful, well-made products is frequently central to the Realistic person's work. Realistic people enjoy building and creating with their hands and, because of their practical nature, prefer a tangible outcome from their labor. Tangible results are possible for occupations such as oceanographer, horticulturist, and engineer. Results for athletes, police officers, and emergency medical technicians may not be tangible, but they are often clear-cut, such as a win or loss, guilt or innocence, and life or death.

On the interpersonal side, Realistic people often admit that they need to work on their verbal, listening, and assertiveness skills. Admittedly, many of the

Realistic occupations only call for a minimal amount of interaction with others. However, if a Realistic individual is working directly with customers or aspires to a supervisory or management role, she or he will need to develop his or her social skills. Realistic individuals are often not inclined to take on supervisory or leadership roles and usually play a passive role in interactions and conversations. They find it difficult to reveal personal things about themselves, can be very private people, are often uncomfortable in social settings, and avoid being the center of attention. Realistic people usually maintain a small group of very close friends, and their leisure activities generally revolve around things other than people, such as gardening, camping, boating, or fishing.

Outwardly, Realistic people may appear somewhat casual and laid-back since they avoid formal clothes and prefer wearing comfortable clothes and shoes. However, they can sometimes be inflexible, dislike change, and may be wary of people and situations that are unfamiliar to them. Because of their practical side, Realistic people tend to value tangible personal characteristics such as money, power, and status. They may be conservative in their attitudes, politically conventional, and slow to accept change or radical ideas. As mentioned before, Realistic people are often quite frank in their opinions and may not be sensitive to the effect of their opinions on others.

It may sound as though Realistic people tend to be rigid and quite judgmental. While that may be true for some, Realistic people can be among the most honest, loyal, and genuine individuals, and they work hard to get the job done.

★★★ *"Timing has been very important for me, literally and figuratively. I always had the talent, but I also happened to be in the right place at the right time for the right person to see me. Self-discipline is very important for a professional athlete, especially in a nonteam sport, one with no time-outs, no substitutions, and no coaching allowed. You first of all figure out what's important to you. Second, I think it's important to allow enough time for the things that you want to do or that are important to you. Three, you must learn how to say no. And four, if you feel that things aren't really going the way you want them to go, then you've got to stand up and change them."*

ARTHUR ASHE
ACTIVIST AND PROFESSIONAL TENNIS PLAYER

～～～ Can't Hammer a Nail Straight... Or, Should You Avoid This Field?

If you love open, unstructured environments and crave interpersonal interaction, it's probably best if you stay away from the Realistic careers. Realistic work environments are usually quite structured and don't always provide much opportunity to work with other people. It's true that engineers, military officers, and athletes often work on teams, but they still remain largely independent contributors to those teams.

Other red flags that might suggest that a Realistic career is probably *not* the choice for you include:

* *You are liberal, often bored with conventionality, and seek constant variety.* Realistic careers tend to offer stable, predictable work and co-workers who are often traditional and conservative in their views.

* *You prefer not to get your hands dirty unless you're having a meatball sub for lunch.* Some Realistic careers entail working with machines or tools that may literally result in getting dirt under your fingernails.

* *You picture yourself in a business suit and carrying a briefcase to work each day.* The norm for most Realistic occupations is to dress casually and comfortably. In some cases, uniforms are required.

* *You enjoy deep thought and abstract conceptualizing as part of your daily routine.* Realistic jobs generally require a present orientation and are grounded in achieving concrete, tangible results.

～～～ How Do I Get Started?

While a college degree isn't always necessary, postsecondary or vocational training of some kind is usually needed to become successful in a Realistic career. Applied coursework that is practical, factual, and related to the occupation is more helpful than theoretical coursework. Realistic people tend to be the least scholarly of the Holland types—there aren't many "heads in the clouds" types in this group.

The college degrees sought by Realistic individuals tend to be in the applied areas of engineering, forestry, geology, geophysics, oceanography, or meteorology. A bachelor's degree is generally the minimum required for becoming an engineer, lab technologist, athletic trainer, or physical education teacher. Graduate or postgraduate education is required for a career as a marine surveyor, FBI agent, or research assistant.

Many of the Realistic careers, especially the skilled trades, require vocational-technical training or an apprenticeship to break into the field. Electricians, for instance, must pass through a four- to five-year formal apprenticeship to become certified. Automotive and aircraft mechanics often attend trade schools for formal training. Licensed practical nurses, emergency medical technicians, and dental hygienists generally get their training through community colleges. Some other jobs require the passing of written and physical examinations before a person is put through formal or on-the-job training.

Aside from the requisite training, many Realistic careers demand high physical endurance, manual dexterity, and strong motor skills. Veterinarians, foresters, and athletes are among the most obvious examples of people who need exceptional physical abilities. Often such physical talents are innate but frequently can be developed through a training and workout regimen. Precision and fine motor skills such as those needed for jewelry repair usually come naturally to a person and are not necessarily things one can pick up through training. It's important to consider your physical traits and see if you have what it takes to succeed in a Realistic career.

Hobbies and interests can be telltale signs of whether you have the inclination for a Realistic career. Enjoyment and skill in repairing electronic appliances, plumbing, or automobiles might indicate some areas for career exploration. Proficiency in sketching mechanical drawings or building cabinets and furniture may also hint at potential success in a Realistic career. A preference for the outdoors and an interest in sports, camping, or hiking might point to the pursuit of a Realistic occupation.

Of course, in today's competitive job market, any prior work experience you can bring to the table will increase your chances of getting hired. Serving as a volunteer for the fire department or rescue squad, coaching a team or refereeing sporting events, participating in cooperative or internship programs through school, and completing an apprenticeship are all ways to gain work experience that can help get your foot in the Realistic door.

∿∿∿ What's It Like Out There?

It's no surprise to hear that it can be tough out there, but those who are well prepared, educated, and motivated will have the best chance of finding employment. The outlook for the Realistic field varies, depending on the occupation. According to the *1994–1995 Occupational Outlook Handbook*, Realistic occupations that will have average growth through 2005 include civil engineers, cartographer, optical engineer, facilities planner, mechanical engineers, lab technologists/technicians, and electricians. Those occupations with faster than average growth include construction and building inspectors, safety engineers, emergency medical technicians, and pilots. Occupations that will grow much faster than average include radiologic technologists, nuclear medicine technologists, medical record technicians, dental hygienists, occupational therapists, and metallurgical engineers. Among occupations that will have little change or slower that average growth are aerospace engineers, aircraft mechanics, police officers/detectives/agents, athletes/coaches, mining engineers, and foresters. Employment of petroleum engineers and electronic equipment repairers is likely to decline through 2005.

Geographically, Realistic opportunities are spread all over the map. Most engineering jobs are found in medium to large cities, where most larger engineering firms and businesses are located. People interested in Realistic occupations specializing in areas such as manufacturing, forestry, marine/oceanography, or mining will be geographically bound by their desires to work in those fields. A forest ranger, for example, most likely won't be able to find employment in New York City. Other Realistic occupations have no geographic implications; nearly every neighborhood, town, or city needs athletes, small business owners, and engineers.

~~~ Where Do I Find Out More About Realistic Careers?

Although Realistic people tend to prefer action over words, the best way to find out more about these careers is to talk to people working in them. Most people like to talk about themselves and what they do. Conducting informational interviews with people whose careers interest you can give you the best picture of what the career is like, what's required to work in that career, how to prepare for the career, and whether you'll enjoy the work.

We've done some of the legwork for you by interviewing people in Realistic occupations. The texts of informational interviews with people in Realistic careers comprise the remainder of this chapter. As insightful as these interviews are, they are still no substitute to getting out there and doing the interviews yourself. Refer to the final chapter in this book, What's Next?, for specific steps on doing informational interviewing.

Researching and reading about Realistic occupations is another indispensable way to explore the fields. Information on how to do career research and other tips on career exploration can be found in the final chapter as well. Following is a list of books and professional organizations specifically related to Realistic occupations to help you begin exploring.

Books for Realistic Careers

Allied Health Professions by ARCO Editorial Board, published by Prentice-Hall, 1993

America's Top Technical and Trade Jobs by J. M. Farr, published by JIST, 1994

Careers for Animal Lovers by R. Shorto, published by Millbrook Press, 1992

Careers for Computer Buffs and Other Technological Types by M. Eberts and M. Gisler, published by VGM Career Horizons, 1993

Careers for Crafty People and Other Dexterous Types by M. Rowh, published by VGM Career Horizons, 1993

Careers for Environmental Types by J. Kinney and M. Fasulo, published by VGM Career Horizons, 1993

Careers for Nature Lovers and Other Outdoor Types by L. Miller, published by VGM Career Horizons, 1992

Careers for Sports Nuts and Other Athletic Types by W. R. Heitman, published by VGM Career Horizons, 1991

Careers in Computers by L. Stair, published by VGM Career Horizons, 1991

Careers in Engineering by G. O. Garner, published by VGM Career Horizons, 1993

Careers in High Tech by N. Basta, published by VGM Career Horizons, 1992

Career Opportunities in the Sports Industry by S. Field, published by Facts on File, 1992

Environmental Jobs for Scientists and Engineers by N. Basta, published by Wiley, 1992

Handbook of Health Care Careers by A. Selden, published by VGM Career Horizons, 1993

Health Care Job Explosion: Careers in the 90s by D. V. Damp by D'Amp Publications, 1993

The New Complete Guide to Environmental Careers by J. R. Cook, K. Doyle, and B. Sharp, published by Island Press, 1993

Opportunities in CAD/CAM Careers by J. Bone, published by VGM Career Horizons, 1994

Opportunities in Energy Careers by J. H. Woodburn, published by VGM Career Horizons, 1992

Opportunities in Forestry Careers by C. M. Willie, published by VGM Career Horizons, 1992

Opportunities in Sports Medicine Careers by W. R. Heitzman, published by VGM Career Horizons, 1992

Outdoor Careers: Exploring Occupations in Outdoor Fields by E. Shenk, published by Stackpole Books, 1992

Peterson's Job Opportunities in Engineering, Science, and Computers, published by Peterson's Guides, 1994

Peterson's Job Opportunities in the Environment, published by Peterson's Guides, 1994

VGM's Handbook of Scientific and Technical Careers by C. T. Norback, published by VGM Career Horizons, 1992

Professional Organizations for Realistic Careers

Below are organizations that can provide information about Realistic careers. Consider contacting organizations that interest you. Be sure to include a self-addressed stamped envelope when writing to request information.

Airline Pilots Association
1625 Massachusetts Ave., NW
Washington, DC 20036

American Geological Institute
4220 King St.
Alexandria, VA 22302-1507

American Institute of Aeronautics and Astronautics, Inc.
AIAA Student Programs, The Aerospace Center
370 L'Enfant Promenade, SW
Washington, DC 20024

American Health Care Association
1201 L St., NW
Washington, DC 20005

American Medical Association
Division of Allied Health Education and Accreditation
535 N. Dearborn St.
Chicago, IL 60610

American Meteorological Society
45 Beacon St.
Boston, MA 02108

American Occupational Therapy Association
P.O. Box 1725
1383 Piccard Dr.
Rockville, MD 20849-1725

American Society for Medical Technology
2021 L St., NW, Suite 400
Washington, DC 20036

American Society of Civil Engineers
345 East 47th St.
New York, NY 10017

American Society of Mechanical Engineers
345 East 47th St.
New York, NY 10017

American Society of Radiologic Technologists
15000 Central Ave.
Albuquerque, NM 87123

Automotive Service Industry Association
444 North Michigan Ave.
Chicago, IL 60611

Institute of Electrical and Electronics Engineers
United States Activities Board
1828 L St., NW, Suite 1202
Washington, DC 20036-5104

Institute of Industrial Engineers, Inc.
25 Technology Park
Norcross, GA 30092

International Association of Fire Fighters
1750 New York Ave., NW
Washington, DC 20006

International Society for Clinical Laboratory Technology
818 Olive St., Suite 918
St. Louis, MO 63101

Society of American Foresters
5400 Grosvenor Lane
Bethesda, MD 20814

The International Society of Certified Electronics Technicians
2708 West Berry St.
Fort Worth, TX 76109

The Minerals, Metals, and Materials Foundation
420 Commonwealth Dr.
Warrendale, PA 15086

The Society for Mining, Metallurgy, and Exploration, Inc.
P.O. Box 625002
Littleton, CO 80162-5002

U.S. Department of Agriculture
Office of Higher Education Programs
Room 350A, Administration Bldg.
14th St. and Independence Ave., SW
Washington, DC 20250

~~~~ TED BEAUVAIS

FOREST SERVICE PROGRAM MANAGER

At the time of this interview, Ted was a program manager for a forest conservation program that is sponsored by the U.S. Department of Agriculture's Forest Service. He began his career with the Forest Service at age twenty-eight after completing a bachelor's degree in hydrology and forestry at Colorado State University. After several different positions with the Forest Service, he moved to Washington, D.C., to the program manager position.

I COULD HAVE HAD other opportunities with different agencies or with the private sector, but I kind of wanted to work for the Forest Service. I had worked for them for a summer previously, and I knew this was the type of job I wanted.

I have worked in the field of watershed management and hydrology, where I did stream sampling and stream flow measurements and road location. I also worked in a variety of other assignments just to gain some breadth of experience and familiarity with a lot of the different programs the Forest Service works with, like recreation and minerals management and in what we call special units management, which is the type of permits granted to a person or a company who wants or needs to do something on federal land. I worked on a variety of different projects in my first two years.

The Forest Service does more hiring from the outside now, and, quite literally, off the street, at times. Traditionally, the Forest Service has been very much a promote-from-within organization. There are various understood career ladders within the organization that you find out about by talking to people or having a mentor. You learn that if you want to attain a certain type of job sometime in the future, then it's a real good idea to do several things, including being in different geographic locations so you get a breadth of geographic experience and getting a variety of assignments so you gain familiarity with a lot of different programs. Mainly that's good preparation for the so-called line officer or management-level jobs.

If you want to be a staff specialist and basically focus on one professional area and stay with it, then you don't necessarily want to go into different fields. You probably want to stay with that one field, but you may pursue that field in different geographic locations.

You have to be prepared to move frequently. It doesn't happen automatically. The military pretty much schedules it and orchestrates it, but the Forest Service is a couple of notches down from that. There's a lot of volunteering, applying for jobs, competing for jobs in order to move. Although sometimes people do just get moved laterally, usually it's with their consent. They say, "Hey, how would you like to take this job over somewhere else?" People will take a look at it, consider it, and often go for it.

I started college right out of high school. I went to the University of Massachusetts. The first two years I was a general liberal arts major and then a history major. And at the end of my junior year, I quit. I traveled that summer and I had worked in the travel industry the other summers when I was still in college.

And then when I got back from my travels a year later, I started working at a place called Eastern Mountain Sports, which is a store with recreational equipment. I worked there two years and then I traveled to South America for a year to climb mountains and just kind of trek and journey around.

When I came back, I worked construction in Colorado and ended up getting a job in a mine. I also decided that I wanted to go back to college.

At Colorado State University I decided that I wanted to do something that was related to natural resources because I liked being outdoors and I liked the forest and the mountains.

In some ways, I wish I had a graduate degree. In other ways, I was burned out and had enough academic stuff. I didn't do well in academics when I first went to college because I didn't apply myself. When I went to Colorado State, I did very well academically, but I was twenty-eight years old when I graduated and I was married and had a child and I didn't have a whole lot of stomach to go back and spend several more years in academia.

I appreciated its usefulness, but I learned a lot outside the academic arena, also. I learned a lot from experience. I learned a lot from traveling. I learned a lot when I worked in a mine and when I worked construction. Just life experience that you can't get in the ivory tower, so I just wasn't all that inclined to go for an advanced degree. But I think it is helpful. If you want to be a research scientist or a professor, obviously, you have to have an advanced degree.

What I really love about the job is interacting with people and learning new things and being involved at least around the edges of some of the politics and policy development related to issues that I'm concerned about. Obviously, you don't get your own way because you're not calling all the shots, but you kind of have some influence and help to nudge and move things along in the direction you like, so you feel like you can have something of a beneficial influence on policy as it's developed. Not so much as it's implemented, because it's implemented elsewhere. But it's developed here.

The bureaucracy is worse at this level of the organization than at any other level I have ever worked at. I knew there were a lot more players and people in the national headquarters and all of what that entails, but now it's being cut and streamlined a bit, and it will probably be okay.

Another frustration is that you're very much here and you kind of work as an independent. You have to do a lot of your own support work because there are shared secretaries between six or seven people. It just doesn't work as well as my previous job, where I was in charge of a small ranger district that had thirty people who worked there and I was the boss and you could kind of get things done more. Here, you get a promotion, but you come into an organization where you are several notches down from the top leadership, and that's kind of a psychological adjustment.

I had been at my previous job for six years and I didn't really picture myself retiring there. We really felt that it would be good to move for my career and to get to a better school system for my daughter. It was a family decision. You can't make a job decision in a vacuum—it's connected with other people and you have to balance all those things.

Right now there are literally thousands of Forest Service employees who are away from their families working ungodly hours fighting fire. I did that on occasion, and that's a very difficult, dangerous job. People work twelve, fifteen hours a day, seven days in a row. It's physical labor. They're gone from two to eight weeks from home. There are times when you do that kind of thing.

My job here now is, on paper, forty hours a week. In reality, it's probably forty-five to fifty at the office and another five or ten at home, using a computer and modem. I know people who work a lot more hours and have a lot less flexibility in terms of time off than I do.

Generally, for forestry and natural resource careers in the federal government, the pay scale is not that bad when you compare it to state agencies. Most of the state agencies pay less. Some of those big private companies pay more, and top management at the big companies would make quite a bit more than the top federal executives, but in this particular field, the pay range probably isn't as wide as it might be between government pay scales and the private sector in some other fields.

It's kind of difficult in some ways to change careers and completely go into a new field or a different agency. If I were to make that switch, I would certainly aggressively pursue all kinds of different options. For example, a paper company is decreasing from thirty thousand to twenty thousand employees in a year. It'd be a pretty scary time to be out there. You've got these qualified private sector people in the field of forestry and natural resources laid off, and other companies might value that private sector experience to a larger degree than they would government experience. Basically, making a profit is the goal in all those private-sector forest product industries.

I'm pretty satisfied. I'm doing really well in my career and in my job. Most days I'm pretty enthusiastic about going to work. In terms of forestry and natural resources, I think that there are some opportunities, but they're limited. It's really a fairly tough field to get into, so if people really want to do it, they have to be prepared to persist and take temporary jobs, perhaps do some volunteer work—really kind of hang in there. I think if a person really has some reasonable academic credentials and a good work ethic and is really willing to try hard, he or she can do well.

There are also a lot of workforce diversification efforts going on in government and, to some degree, in the private sector. But there are more opportunities now for women and minorities than there were before. Minority students are being very heavily recruited and can go into what is called cooperative education, which enables them to work summers during college, and, upon graduation, be placed in a permanent full-time job.

~~~ ISABELLE SLIFER

ARMY OFFICER

At the time of this interview, Isabelle was a major in the U.S. Army and was stationed in Fort Dix, New Jersey. She had been with the military for the past twenty years and was the mobilization planning officer, responsible for mobilizing reserve forces in the event of war, natural disasters, or peacekeeping missions.

WHAT FIRST STIMULATED MY INTEREST in the military were the job opportunities. I have a bachelor's and a master's degree in education and had been teaching high school for several years but had been laid off twice. Even in 1969, when I first started to teach, teaching jobs were few and far between. My father, who was in the coast guard, also influenced my decision. He raised me to revere the military and to consider it a tool that could be used to advance oneself; he also instilled in me a strong sense of social consciousness. But I initially enlisted in the army reserves to cushion the blow of any future layoffs. I started in the reserves as a private, while teaching full time, and then made it up to the rank of specialist, which is the equivalent of a corporal.

While in the reserves, I was asked if I had ever considered Officer Candidate School (OCS). It was the mid-seventies, and more and more doors were opening for women, especially in the military, as a result of the civil rights movement, the women's movement, and the feelings surrounding the Vietnam War. Previously, the only real opportunities for women in the military were nursing positions. If someone told me twenty years ago that I would make a career for myself in the military, I would have told them they were nuts!

In my current job, I work with the reserve forces who would mobilize in a time of war, or in nonwar situations such as disaster relief, rioting, or peacekeeping missions. I act as a liaison between the installation staff at Fort Dix and the reserve components that could and would be called upon to mobilize.

Variety is the beauty of a career in the military. It is not a 9-to-5 job, and when you are in active duty, you are considered active twenty-four hours a day. There isn't any overtime, but when you work beyond five or six in the evening or on weekends, your commander will usually give you compensatory time off, so it balances itself out. Being an officer, I manage my own time, which I have learned how to do over the years. My style is to get the mission or the goal done right away and have the extra time for myself. In any military position, if you can prove your credibility, trustworthiness, and ability to get the mission done, your commander and those over you will allow you more flexibility.

Keeping yourself versatile is primary in any function of the military. Principles that are used in the battlefield are carried over into what we call the garrison or nonbattlefield environment. And, of course, there is discipline. Versatility and discipline are key because the more disciplined you are about yourself in basic training, the more able you are to carry that discipline over into your work style.

What I don't like are the early morning wake-ups, when you have to get up at 4:00 A.M. and be ready to perform. Also, being your own boss and delegating your authority to subordinates can be frustrating. I find it very exciting being a part of the military, as it evolves out of gender preference. The military pays women the same salary as men for doing the same job. After so many years at a specific rank, the salary is the same. I like being able to function as a military officer, and not a military officer who is a woman.

When I go from one job to another through job transfers, I don't lose my seniority or my rank structure. The reality of job transfers is exciting because I know I will not be a mobilization planning officer forever, which doesn't lead to stagnation.

When I first joined the military, they had just changed the rules regarding single women with children. Previously, the rules were that if you were married and pregnant, or pregnant and unmarried, you were told to leave the military, because they believed you couldn't do two things at one time. In today's military, a male or female soldier who is a parent, married or not, has to prove that he or she has someone to take care of the children in the event of mobilization and deployment. My husband is retired from the military, and we have a nine-year-old and a five-year-old. When he was in active duty, we participated in what is called the family packet, which is a document about one inch thick that proves to the military that you have caretakers for your children in the event of mobilization, and must be notarized. This is done to enhance the quality of life for soldiers and their families. The reasoning is that if you don't have a happy soldier with a happy family, it hurts the readiness and motivation of the soldier.

Other opportunities that are available to former military personnel with my military experience would include teaching, public relations, management, and a variety of people-oriented careers. One of my job transfers included teaching in an ROTC program. I remember hearing civilians who worked in human resources mention that hirees with former military experience were usually preferred because they get right to a project and get it over with, and get it done right. Military experience is conducive to hiring because discipline is ingrained in soldiers from the time of basic training.

Another positive aspect of a military career is that you must constantly be physically fit. This is the age of physical fitness, which the military has been a forerunner in promoting. So my leisure time is usually spent making sure I'm in good shape. The military's philosophy is that in order to make the mind work, the body has to work. One complements the other. As in any job, the better you manage yourself and your time, the more leisure time you will have. I also find that when I don't keep up with physical fitness, I manage my time poorly and it affects my ability to handle my work. I appreciate that the military has encouraged me to come to a balance in this way, because once you make that balance, the rest of your life becomes balanced as well.

Prospective military personnel should be people oriented and understand and appreciate cultural diversity because the military is probably one of the few institutions that takes people from all around the country and makes them come together as a team. A strong mathematics background is helpful, too, depending on your job focus, as well as a basic knowledge about computer operations and principles. A background in and an understanding of American history are also a plus, as this gives a person an understanding of why we are here, where we have been, and why we want to be where we want to be. A good soldier is a well-rounded person who is open to all kinds of learning. Every soldier must take an oath to defend the Constitution and its freedoms, so tolerance toward others who may not share your opinions is also essential to a successful military career.

Opportunities in the military may not be as plentiful as they were during the cold war, but that should not discourage anyone from options. The military will always need qualified people. The competition is keener, especially in the officer corps, but as long as a person is driven, there will be opportunities.

With every rank or promotion, I receive an increase in my salary. We have an annual cost-of-living allowance, which is determined by Congress, depending on how much it thinks we are worth to the country and what the budget can bear. For example, I am a major, but I reached the plateau of my salary when I was in my sixteenth year. I will get an increase when I become a lieutenant colonel. Again, whether you are male or female, you are going to get the same salary. Salary in the military depends on experience and background, where you are living, and whether you are married and have children.

~ ~ ~ LAWRENCE RUFF

MECHANICAL ENGINEER

Lawrence decided to become a mechanical engineer after working for a year as a machinist. He received his bachelor's degree in mathematics and mechanical engineering and is employed as a design engineer for a small machine tool company in Albany, New York. He attributes the practical experience he gained before college for giving him a competitive edge in the job market after graduation.

I DIDN'T GO DIRECTLY TO COLLEGE when I first got out of high school. I worked first as a bicycle mechanic, and then as a machinist for about one and a half years. While working as a machinist, I decided to take up engineering. I didn't want to spend the rest of my life running equipment; I wanted to do more. So I went to a community college to get an associate degree, and then on to a four-year university to get my bachelor's degree in mathematics and mechanical engineering.

As a senior in college, I applied to seven companies for a job and got offers from three of them. I picked the one that I thought offered the most challenging position. Before entering college, I had a lot of practical experience, and a lot of companies I interviewed with gave me credit for that experience. That is one of the things companies like—practical experience.

At my current job, I work for a fairly small company, so I am also involved in manufacturing engineering, shop work, and machine setup, to name a few. A typical day involves two hours on the board, another two hours in the shop, an hour of paperwork, and the rest of the time in other activities.

Although I am in machine design, my work usually doesn't involve a lot of advanced theoretical design. To be a good design engineer, you really have to know how parts can be made, and if they can be made. The rest of the work is in the design. And there are more and more computer applications to what we do.

In a small company, people really have to work together. Interpersonal skills are key, especially in terms of the ability to get along with the people in the shop. I like the fact that I do a lot of different things and that I get to be involved in all facets of the company. At the same time, a small company means money is tight, and there are often interpersonal problems. Although it may change as business picks up, I currently have some free time by working from 7:30 A.M. to 4:00 P.M.

"Success" in this field means different things to different engineers. I want to stay with the practical end of things, as management doesn't interest me. While I intend to stay where I am and pick up a lot of new skills, I have also thought of getting my Ph.D.

Mechanical engineering is a good field. It may not pay as well as electrical engineering, but it offers the chance to be creative, use your hands, make things work, and see the results of your efforts.

⌁⌁⌁ Some Things to Think About...

Now that you have an understanding of Realistic careers, here are some things to consider:

1. What insights about Realistic occupations have you gained from these interviews?

_____

_____

_____

2. Which characteristics, abilities, and personal qualities discussed in the interviews are similar to your own? Which are different or in contrast to your own?

_____

_____

_____

3. Ask yourself the following:

   * Do you have the ability to work with your hands? How is your manual dexterity? _____

   * Would you mind getting soiled or dirty?_____

   * Do you like structure and clear guidelines in your work?_____

   * Do you have mechanical abilities? Are you athletic? _____

   * Do you prefer casual clothing or a uniform over business attire?_____

   How might your responses to these questions influence your satisfaction with a Realistic career choice?_____

4. Which interviews piqued your interest? Why?_____

   _____

5. Which interviews were not what you expected? Why? _____

   _____

6. Which occupations are you going to investigate further? How?

   _____

   _____

   _____

   _____

CHAPTER THREE

Experiment With an Investigative Career

D O YOU SEE YOURSELF as a future Dr. Spock, Marie Curie, or Margaret Mead? Have you always pictured yourself in a white lab coat, wearing a pocket protector, or in a tweed jacket with elbow patches? Would you like to be the one to come running when someone yells, "Is there a doctor in the house?"

If you're nodding your head in agreement, you may belong in an Investigative career. Read on and *investigate* the possibilities.

~ ~ ~ What Are These Careers and Where Can I Find Them?

Investigative work environments tend to support creative investigation, research, and an inquisitive nature. Investigative occupations are generally found in non-structured settings rather than traditionally bureaucratic organizations and are usually related to science, math, medicine, computers, and other technical areas. The computer industry especially has grown into a large employer of the idea-generating, technical Investigative types and should continue to be so in the future. Typical work settings include laboratories, libraries, universities, high-tech businesses, and hospitals. Some careers that are Investigative include those listed in table 3 below. For a complete listing of Investigative careers, consult *The Dictionary of Holland Occupational Codes* or the appendix.

TABLE 3
EXAMPLES OF INVESTIGATIVE CAREERS

Biologist	Inventor	Physicist
Chemist	Mathematician	Psychologist
Chiropractor	Art appraiser	R & D manager
College professor	Pediatrician	Science teacher
Pharmacist	Computer programmer	Sociologist
Dentist	Respiratory therapist	Systems analyst
Dietitian	Physician	Veterinarian
Geographer	Archeologist	Zoologist
Astronomer	Occupational analyst	Psychiatrist
Geneticist	Chemical engineer	Economist
Medical researcher	Meteorologist	Statistician
Audiologist	Geologist	Medical technologist

You may have noticed that there is some overlap between the Investigative and the Realistic careers. A number of the occupations have characteristics that appeal to both types. However, even within the same discipline, slight variations in how and where the work is done can make a difference in who would be interested in the career. For example, some branches of engineering are considered Realistic (e.g., mechanical), while others are considered Investigative (e.g., chemical). Although the two types may have some similarities, you'll see that the heads-in-the-clouds Investigative types are quite different from the here-and-now Realistic types.

★★★ *"Some areas of astronomy are in need of good people, despite limitations on funding; others are completely saturated. If your skills are in a rapidly developing area of astronomy and you rank high competitively, I think you would not have to worry too much about employment problems. As an undergraduate, get a thorough grounding in higher mathematics and physics, then pursue astronomy at the graduate level. We don't even necessarily recommend taking an introductory astronomy course in the first two or three years of college. Descriptive astronomy is easy; you can always learn that later. There is the danger, in learning it early without the appropriate physics, of acquiring material which is oversimplified to the point of distortion."*

CARL SAGAN
ASTRONOMER

∿ ∿ ∿ Who Are These People and Am I One of Them?

What types of people are drawn to and do well in Investigative occupations? What are their characteristics, values, and interests?

Stereotypic images of the absent-minded professor or the mad scientist may come to mind when picturing an Investigative person, and, actually, they are not too far off the mark. Known as abstract problem solvers and analytical thinkers, Investigative types often appear to be lost in a fog of thought.

Generally, Investigative individuals perceive themselves as scholarly, intellectual, mathematically and scientifically inclined, and lacking in leadership abilities. They tend to prefer working alone, enjoy dealing with unknowns, and are comfortable with abstractions. Investigative people often possess a high degree of originality and tend to analyze many possibilities before they are able to make a decision.

Sometimes described as the idea or "blue-sky" people, Investigative types are usually the free spirits in organizations. Often serving as individual contributors, Investigative people can also be effective team members when properly motivated and given ample time to do individual work. They like to be around achievement-oriented, intelligent, logical-thinking people.

Investigative people can appear to have strong verbal skills and a high degree of self-confidence. They tend to enjoy strong, lively discussions on intellectual topics of interest. Despite this appearance of strong verbal ability, Investigative people can sometimes be lacking in social or persuasive skills. They can sometimes seem withdrawn if they are deeply involved in a project or in a new activity. Generally, they tend to avoid close interpersonal relationships with groups or new individuals. Investigative people are inclined to maintain faithful and long-term relationships with a small, close group of friends and colleagues.

Outwardly, Investigative people often appear aloof and quite reserved. They can be highly introspective and may become lost in thought in their own worlds. Sometimes conservative in their attitudes and values, Investigative types are usually concerned with independence, intellectual status, the latest frontiers of knowledge, and challenging problems. Most of all, they value their time and freedom and can spend hours on end researching, diagnosing, conceptualizing, and analyzing ideas and information.

★ ★ ★ *"We have two types of astronauts: The pilots, who do all the flying, and the mission specialists, who do the experiments. The pilots have extensive high-performance jet training, most of them have been to a test-pilot school, many of them have advanced degrees, and I believe that they're all engineers of some sort. The mission specialists, because the Shuttle is a versatile tool, do different projects each time the Shuttle goes up. We have engineers, scientists, physicians, geologists, biologists, civil engineers, people with all kinds of science and technical backgrounds. There are a lot of very interesting and very dedicated people here. That's not just the astronauts; that's all the people at NASA in general. There are a lot of dedicated people at NASA willing to put their all into what they do. We work hard and long hours, but that doesn't exclude us from having private time. I think it's an atmosphere that's probably fairly unique. I've never run across it anyplace else."*

JUDITH RESNIK
NASA SPACE SHUTTLE MISSION SPECIALIST,
ENGINEER, AND SCIENTIST

~~~ So, Einstein You're Not... Or, Should You Avoid This Field?

If you like to cut to the chase and make snap decisions, a career in the Investigative fields is probably not for you. Investigative occupations often entail thorough research and the weighing of a multitude of possibilities before a decision can be reached. Investigative people usually like to wade through all the details and analyze all their options in each situation.

Other red flags to alert you that an Investigative career is probably *not* the choice for you include:

* *You aren't the scholarly type and don't really enjoy studying or learning new things.* Investigative careers tend to stress intellectual curiosity and the desire to attain new knowledge.

* *You enjoy having people as the focus of your work.* Although some Investigative careers do call for interpersonal interaction, generally the focus is on ideas or things rather than people.

* *You want a regular 9-to-5 weekday schedule.* Some Investigative careers may allow for this, but many, especially those in the medical/health fields, may require irregular schedules including shifts, on-call hours, and weekends.

* *You need definite answers and don't like to be left hanging.* Sometimes definite answers are not attained in Investigative careers, since the search for additional possibilities is often ongoing. The ability to tolerate ambiguity and a lack of closure is needed.

~~~ How Do I Get Started?

Since Investigative people are often considered the most scholarly of the Holland types, it's no surprise that careers in the Investigative fields generally require a high level of education. Those interested in Investigative careers need to be prepared and motivated to spend quite a bit of time in school prior to entering the working world.

A bachelor's degree in the appropriate discipline is the minimum amount of education needed for careers as computer systems analysts, mathematicians, statisticians, economists, medical researchers, respiratory therapists, and dietitians. Many people in these careers do go on to earn master's and doctoral degrees to enhance their skills and knowledge and to increase their chances for advancement.

Nearly all specialties within the Investigative arena demand advanced degrees. Biologists, chemists, geologists, meteorologists, and sociologists require a master's degree as the minimum for entrance into the field. A Ph.D. is a prerequisite for many careers in the pure sciences or academia. Pharmacists, college professors, physicists, and psychologists all need a Ph.D. before they can get their foot in the door. Dentists, physicians, and veterinarians must all be graduates of their respective professional schools to be able to practice in their fields.

Obviously, preparation can be quite lengthy in the pursuit of many Investigative careers. Before beginning such a long journey, you must consider whether you have the stamina, desire, and motivation to become an established professional in the Investigative fields.

Many people know early on that they are interested in the Investigative, scientific fields. Investigative types are often students who enjoy participating in science fairs and working with computers. They are constantly trying to figure things out through abstract thinking and reasoning. Often women and minorities have not been historically encouraged to pursue Investigative careers and sometimes they may find their niche only after taking their first college chemistry course.

In addition to educational preparation, it's important to gain some hands-on experience to validate your aspirations and to bolster your credentials. Those with the right combination of education and experience will always be the most sought after by employers. Volunteering in hospitals, clinics, laboratories, or other settings will give you exposure to your chosen field. Part-time jobs, internships, and co-op programs are other ways to combine school with work. Joining clubs or organizations that support your interests and career goals can broaden your experience and help open career doors. Becoming involved in research studies, participating in science fairs, or taking a course in CPR/first aid can also be ways to enhance your preparation for a career in the Investigative fields.

❧❧❧ What's It Like Out There?

There will always be a need for people trained in some of the Investigative fields, especially health care. In fact, the demand exceeds the supply for nurses, occupational therapists, and physical therapists, creating severe shortages in some areas. The outlook for other Investigative opportunities is determined more by changes in technology and the economy.

According to the *1994–1995 Occupational Outlook Handbook*, Investigative occupations that will have average growth through 2005 include geologists, geophysicists, economists, sociologists, chemists, dietitians, and meteorologists. Those occupations with faster than average growth include biochemists, biologists, pharmacists, physicians, and veterinarians. Occupations that will grow much faster than average include computer systems analysts and psychologists. Several occupations that will have little change or slower than average growth are mathematicians, statisticians, and dentists. The demand for physicists and astronomers is expected to decline through the year 2005.

Geographically, people who go into health and medicine-oriented Investigative fields will probably be able to find employment in any places they might choose—urban or rural. Research-based occupations are somewhat more geographically bound, usually being found in universities, government, and large private organizations.

~~~ Where Do I Find Out More About Investigative Careers?

The best way to find out what people in Investigative careers do is to ask them. Don't worry if you feel a little tentative about your small-talk skills. Most people are flattered and enjoy talking about themselves when they are asked to. Conducting informational interviews with people whose careers interest you can give you the best picture of what a career is like, what's required to work in that career, how to prepare for it, and whether you'll enjoy the work.

Lucky for you, we've done some informational interviewing for you. On the next pages, you'll find the texts of interviews with people in Investigative careers. Reading these interviews will no doubt be invaluable, but you'll still need to get out there and do some interviewing in person. Refer to the final chapter in this book, What's Next, for specific steps on doing informational interviewing.

Researching and reading about possible occupations is the Investigative person's forte. Information on how to do career research and other tips on career exploration can also be found in the final chapter. Following is a list of books and professional organizations specifically focused on Investigative careers to get you started.

Books for Investigative Careers

Allied Health Professions by ARCO Editorial Board, published by Prentice-Hall, 1993

America's Top Medical Jobs by M. J. Farr, published by JIST, 1992

Careers for Computer Buffs and Other Technological Types by M. Eberts and M. Gisler, published by VGM Career Horizons, 1993

Careers in Computers by L. Stair, published by VGM Career Horizons, 1991

Careers in High Tech by N. Basta, published by VGM Career Horizons, 1992

Careers in Medicine by T. Sacks, published by VGM Career Horizons, 1993

Careers in Medicine: Traditional and Alternative Opportunities by D. Rucker and M. Keller, published by Garrett Park Press, 1990

Careers in Psychology by L. Clayton, published by Rosen Publishing, 1992

Careers in Science by T. Easton, published by VGM Career Horizons, 1990

Handbook of Health Care Careers by A. Selden, published by VGM Career Horizons, 1993

Health Care Career Directory—Nurses and Physicians by B. J. Morgan, published by Visible Ink Press, 1993

Health Care Job Explosion: Careers in the 90s by D. Damp, published by D'Amp Publications, 1993

Opportunities in Biotechnology Careers by S. Brown, published by VGM Career Horizons, 1994

Opportunities in Library and Information Science Careers by K. Heim and M. Myers, published by VGM Career Horizons, 1992

Opportunities in Nutrition Careers by C. C. Caldwell, published by VGM Career Horizons, 1992

Opportunities in Technical Writing and Communications Careers by J. R. Gould and W. A. Losano, published by VGM Career Horizons, 1994

Nurses: The Human Touch by W. M. Brown, published by Ivy Books, 1992

1994–1995 Allied Health Education Directory, published by the American Medical Association

1994–1995 Continuing Medical Education Directory, published by the American Medical Association

1994–1995 Graduate Medical Education Directory, published by the American Medical Association

Peterson's Job Opportunities in Engineering, Science, and Computer Jobs, published by Peterson's Guides, 1994

Peterson's Job Opportunities in Health Care, published by Peterson's Guides, 1994

So, You Want to Be a Doctor? by S. Zeman, published by Ten Speed Press, 1992

The Tech Writing Game: A Comprehensive Guide for Aspiring Technical Writers by J. Van Wicklen, published by Facts on File, 1992

VGM's Handbook of Scientific and Technical Careers by C. T. Norback, published by VGM Career Horizons, 1992

Professional Organizations for Investigative Careers

Below are organizations that can provide information about Investigative careers. Consider contacting organizations that interest you. Be sure to include a self-addressed stamped envelope when writing to request information.

American Academy of Actuaries
1720 I St., NW, 7th floor
Washington, DC 20006

American Association of Colleges of Pharmacy
1426 Prince St.
Alexandria, VA 22314

American Chemical Society
Career Services
1155 16th St., NW
Washington, DC 20036

American Dental Association
SELECT Program
211 E. Chicago Ave.
Chicago, IL 60611

American Dietetic Association
216 West Jackson Blvd., Suite 800
Chicago, IL 60606-6995

American Geological Association
4220 King St.
Alexandria, VA 22302-1507

American Institute of Biological Sciences
Office of Career Services
730 11th St., NW
Washington, DC 20001-4521

American Institute of Physics
335 East 45th St.
New York, NY 10017

American Medical Association
515 N. State St.
Chicago, IL 60610

American Meteorological Society
45 Beacon St.
Boston, MA 02108

American Nurses Association
600 Maryland Ave., SW
Washington, DC 20024-2571

American Physical Society
335 East 45th St.
New York, NY 10017

American Physical Therapy Association
1111 North Fairfax St.
Alexandria, VA 22314

American Psychological Association
Educational Programs Office
1200 17th St., NW
Washington, DC 20036

American Sociological Association
1722 N St., NW
Washington, DC 20036

American Statistical Association
1429 Duke St.
Alexandria, VA 22314

American Veterinary Medical Association
1931 N. Meacham Rd., Suite 100
Schaumburg, IL 60173-4360

Association of Systems Management
24587 Bagley Rd.
Cleveland, OH 44138

Mathematical Association of America
1529 18th St., NW
Washington, DC 20036

National Association of Business Economists
28790 Chagrin Blvd., Suite 300
Cleveland, OH 44122

The Operations Research Society of America
428 East Preston St.
Baltimore, MD 21202

~~~ WILLIAM SPENCER

BIOLOGIST

William has been working as a biologist in the chemical industry for the past twenty years. He has held positions in both research and marketing for several American as well as European companies. At the time of this interview, he was manager of field development for Elf Atochem North America.

I HAVE ALWAYS BEEN INTERESTED in the natural world. As a kid, I would collect turtles, snakes, frogs, and everything else I could find in the woods. As I grew older, I never gave those things up. During my sophomore year in high school, I had a biology teacher who was much more natural-history oriented than strict laboratory-biology oriented. She showed interest in my likes and dislikes and, as a result, I knew from the tenth grade on that I wanted to major in biology, but I wasn't sure what I wanted to do with it. Being part of the Boy Scouts also helped shape my career choice. The Scouts helped me get an understanding of the natural world by emphasizing outdoor activities.

In college, I took mostly the general courses and started my biology curriculum with ornithology—the study of birds. I was able to work as a biology lab assistant for the next three years. During summer breaks—from the end of my first year until graduation—I worked for the Mosquito Control Commission of Middlesex County, New Jersey. I worked as a laborer, spraying a fuel-oil mixture on top of standing water to keep mosquitoes from hatching and breeding. During my third summer with the commission, my supervisor realized my background and got me more involved with the identification of mosquitoes and with the home and office end, such as answering residents' questions on mosquito control—typically, how to clean up standing water.

After graduating with a bachelor's degree in biology and four years' experience working with the Mosquito Control Commission, I enlisted in the air force, during the Vietnam War. I had always wanted to travel to the South Pole, so I volunteered for weather duty, figuring that would be one way to get there. But I ended up stationed the entire four years in the desert, running and operating computers—one year in Libya and three years in Las Vegas!

I am currently in the Agricultural Division of Elf Atochem, which deals with insecticides, pesticides, fungicides, and herbicides for use in crop protection. Up until about a year ago, I was also the marketing manager for our division. I have gone back and forth between research and marketing, which has given me a much broader background than I would have if I had stuck with just one.

I got out of the air force in 1974 and moved to New Hampshire, where my wife's family was living, and enrolled in graduate school in the Entomology Department at the University of New Hampshire. At that point, I was leaning very heavily toward forestry. I wanted to be a forest ranger and work on a tower out in the middle of nowhere. I soon found out that my professors were split into two areas of focus. Two of them were agriculture-chemical oriented, and two of them were forestry oriented. The forestry professors were more "green" oriented, while the other two were more pesticide oriented. The two professors on the chemical side were very interested in me, and they took me under their wing. During my first summer break, I worked as an intern with an extension specialist at CROPS, doing testing with chemicals, visiting with the farmers while trying to find out what problems they were having with insects in order to help them develop higher yields. During the spring semester of my second year at grad school, I taught entomology at a local community college.

After receiving my master's degree, I started to work for a small company, where I did research, testing, spraying, and product development. I did that job for about a year and a half, until they had an opening in their home office in New Jersey for a project manager. I then worked as an entomologist doing data analysis. In that position, I got to work closely with the Research Department. I also spent a lot of time in the field, with our field research people, traveling around managing experimental use permits. One of the products we were working on was an insecticide that attacked primarily cotton insects. When this product was getting ready to go to market, I was asked if I would like to try marketing it, since I knew the product so well. It was a great opportunity for me to get to know the people in the cotton market. I got to know the whole part of the market—the research people, the growers, and the distributors. At my current company, I was the market manager for our division up until about a year and a half ago, when I took over field research with seven professionals covering the United States and Canada. For a year, I did both jobs, then took the field research job permanently.

I keep myself active in some of the support groups of the agricultural crop protection area. The biggest one is the Agricultural Container Research Council (ACRC), which looks for new uses for, and ways to recycle, empty plastic chemical containers.

There is no typical day or week. One week I will be at an ACRC meeting at the beginning of the week, then fly somewhere midweek for the National Potato Conference, where I sit in a booth and talk to growers from everywhere, from northern Maine to northern Idaho. Another week I'll be in the office trying to write up a couple of articles and put together some marketing plans. I am out of town an average of two weeks out of every month. The traveling is a plus, in that I get to see a whole lot of places. With my company's headquarters primarily in France, I get to see Europe. However, traveling is not a plus if your kids are young and you have to miss things like Little League games. I've been lucky because I've been able to schedule my travel around my children's activities.

There are a variety of opportunities available in related fields within the chemical industry. With my background and education, which is the agricultural chemical area, a person could go from research to marketing to sales and back and forth. You can't go the other way around unless you have a master's degree. My advice to anyone considering this field is that if you think you want to get your Ph.D., go for it. You can always work down, but you can't always work up. Changing fields from agricultural chemicals into another related industry, such as animal health, is a little harder to do except in the first few years of your career. Most biologists who start off in agricultural chemicals have been there most of their careers. It is the same group of people all the way around. We run into each other at all the meetings, and we all know each other. It's not a closed society, but a very small society, as far as knowledge is concerned.

I have a nice balance between work and leisure. I stay active with my family, taking vacations together every year and occasionally squeezing in camping trips. I take my family on business trips as often as I can.

In the next five years, I would like to take the next step, which would be director of sales and marketing research. I would probably have a limitation on being a director of research for some companies because I don't have a Ph.D. Long-term, I could work myself up to a director and eventually a general manager. If I could pick it, I would probably like to be a professor at a university. I would love to teach, especially in the agricultural-related fields, because I have a real interest in what I do.

The best job-hunting strategy any student could have in this industry is to get an internship over the summer. Our company and all our competitors hire students to work in the summer to help our sales and technical staffs. Interns run errands, examine fields, talk to growers when there is a complaint, and simply lend an extra hand. Interns are hired May through August. Our company usually hires two or three interns, pays them a salary plus expenses, and sometimes rents them a car. Interns get a chance to visit with distributors and dealers, and handle farmers' calls. It pays fairly well, and it gets a person closer to the business. Internships allow you to get to know some of the people working in a field and begin networking.

At this time, the agricultural-chemical business is downsizing, which is both positive and negative. The negative side is that industry people in their forties and fifties are being asked to retire early. The positive side is that companies are hiring people at lower salaries, so if you are a real go-getter, you will have opportunities.

If you are thinking of working in chemical research, you have to have at least a master's degree and, if possible, a Ph.D. If you are thinking of sales, you should have a bachelor's degree and show that you are working toward either a master's degree or an MBA. Even if you can show that you have had only two classes toward your MBA, and even if you intend not to go any further, at least show them that you are pursuing it. A Ph.D. student who graduates with a straight-A average from Princeton is going to get a job, no matter who she knows. But an average student from any other college can still get that job and be competitive with that graduate from Princeton if he knows people and shows that he is a hard worker.

Forestry is the only branch of agriculture right now where there is a glut. I have heard that there is one job for every one thousand applicants! A good choice would be to major in something that is flexible. Entomology is a good example. I can do what I'm doing now and, if I ever wanted to, I could go into forestry. In today's job market, you have to adapt.

In terms of salary, the more technical areas in this field start out higher and pay less later. Salespeople can make the most if they are on a bonus program. Research people with master's degrees or Ph.D.s are going to start off at a higher base rate, but there will be no bonus program. This industry pays the same from region to region, meaning an employee in Mississippi is going to be paid the same amount as an employee living in New Jersey.

The type of person who typically succeeds in this field has to be willing to adapt to the constant changes in the industry. If you are the kind of person who insists on only working with hard chemicals, you're not going to get far. A candidate must be willing to read the regulations and understand what the Environmental Protection Agency is doing today and tomorrow, and learn to work with environmental groups, to a certain extent. The adaptable person, one who is willing to move around for the company and willing to take chances, is the one who will succeed.

～～～ MARGARET L. BON

PHARMACIST

At the time of this interview, Margaret was a pharmacist, working in clinical research for a pharmaceutical company. She was coordinating the different kinds of testing that are part of marketing a new drug. She began her career as a retail pharmacist, switching to the research side of the field when a divorce forced her to seek full-time work that offered benefits. She was also teaching chemistry at the community-college level.

I GOT INTO PHARMACY essentially when I was fifteen working in the corner drugstore. I was in retail for years and into teaching, teaching some chemistry. And I just kind of fell into industry. It was appealing, it had regular hours, and things like that. Getting into the clinical research turned out to be very interesting.

I work on a set group of drugs, but they're always changing—some are dropped, some are added. There's always something different going on, something

I have to read about, something I have to learn, background to fill in, new things happening. It's just different every day.

My day consists of a lot of paperwork and a lot of meetings. Sometimes the meetings are with many people, which help get things rolling. When one particular group needs information, I will be able to get it from another group. I'm a go-between in a lot of areas as far as scientific information.

I have an administrative position. If a study with a certain drug is being done and the study is written up, then I figure out how much of a drug the person needs, how it needs to be packaged or blinded, how many patients are needed for the study, and when it is needed, where, and I do the ordering from the actual manufacturing facility that makes it and tell them all the specifics of how to put it together. It's an in-between type of administrative position, not a laboratory position.

Retail came to be very routine, very boring. The public is hard to deal with, and the older I got, the less tolerant it was. I enjoy parts of the retail, dealing with sick people and explaining their medication and helping with things like that, but you can only deal with potentially crabby, sick people for so long. They're buying something they don't want to buy. They're not happy about it and it's seen as my fault.

In retail, you work every other weekend, every other holiday. It's real tough working over the holidays when your children are home; whereas what I'm doing now is 8:30 to 4:30, five days a week. There are times when I put in more hours, but it's because I need to get something done, not because I'm required to. But if somebody says, "Can you do something on the fourth Tuesday of November?" I can say yes because I know what my schedule is going to be and it's a definite advantage to have a regular schedule. Once you start having a family and kids going to school and homework and things, then you need regular hours.

There are several paths to get into clinical research, but some are easier than others. If you have the background and the years of pharmacy practice— either retail or hospital—it's easier. If you come right out of pharmacy school and have your degree and then get your license and go right into industry, the positions available to you are more limited. And then you have to work your way into these positions.

You need a pharmacy degree—a bachelor of science in pharmacy now takes six years to complete. When you get out of pharmacy school, you've got to take the licensure exam of the state you're in and then you can become a pharmacist. You can either work in retail or hospital or industry. Some industry positions don't require the pharmacy license, but ours does. We are all pharmacists working in a standard-type pharmacy position.

Internships are limited to six or nine weeks and you spend some time in retail and some in hospital and some in a clinical setting. It's more of an education position than a co-op program.

Schools are always helpful, and recruiters are out there about January of a person's senior year. The major pharmaceutical chains are always looking for new pharmacists. There are always ads in the paper: local hospitals, things like that. The pharmaceutical companies often have ads in the paper looking for people with a bachelor of science in pharmacy or related science. It's kind of an entry-level position, but you've got to start somewhere.

In retail you are counting out pills, but they better be the right pills and you better know what else that patient is taking and what possible interactions there are. This is not stuff you can look up. The computerization available today helps, but this is really where your six years of schooling comes in.

If something happened to my job tomorrow—and the pharmaceutical industry is on real shaky ground at the moment—I have my license, I could go back to retail, I could go back to the hospital. It wouldn't be easy, I wouldn't want to do it, but I could still support myself and my children. This country needs more pharmacists than it has. There's always a position somewhere and if you don't like the one you have, there's always another one.

This job has its frustrations. I've been with this company over six years, and not one of my products has been marketed yet. Only one has been filed for approval, and we're waiting on that. There are twice as many drugs that have been dropped from testing as I'm working on because of either toxicities or lack of efficacy. There are millions of chemicals or products tested to a certain point and then dropped because they're not going to make it.

It's frustrating sometimes when you put two or three years into a project and you do your first real study that will show you how it's going to work and it shows you that it doesn't work at all; yes, it's frustrating.

I wish my job were a little more scientific, but without a Ph.D., that doesn't happen. But I do work with so many different drugs and so many different groups of people that it's always stimulating.

I have two bachelor's degrees and a master's degree; however, I don't have the Ph.D. I can become manager of our department, maybe move up to a couple of other positions within our company, sort of regulatory affairs positions, still in drug development. But other than that, there's not a lot of places that I can go up.

What would have been something to think about would have been the M.D. Those are the people who make money in the company and have what I would consider a better position. I wish I had gone to medical school, but when I started college, women just didn't do that.

Pharmacy is family-friendly, though. I supported my two children and myself working three days a week. There are always part-time jobs available. If you want to work a couple nights a week for four or five hours and be home with your children all day or have some free time, the part-time opportunities are phenomenal. And full-time positions are always there.

Coming out of school and going into retail would probably be the most lucrative. The problem with pharmacy is you don't go anywhere. Pharmacists start high, but then go up so slowly over the next twenty or thirty years. But it's still a good salary—I'm not saying it's not.

My advice to those considering pharmacy is go as far as you can educationally. If you can possibly go for that Pharm.D. or Ph.D., do it. It makes a difference in the end. I have a master's in organic chemistry and that makes a difference for me, compared to the other people in my group, who don't have that. Education is very important in this field.

 ROBERT W. STONE

SYSTEMS ANALYST

At the time of this interview, Robert was a systems analyst, doing computer programming for a company whose primary clients are financial institutions. He had been involved in the designing, coding, and debugging of program systems, specifically with programs that process income taxes for banks. He is a graduate of Rensselaer Polytechnic Institute and has had a variety of hands-on technical experience in computer programming.

MY INTEREST IN COMPUTERS began when I was in the fourth grade. I was always good in math, and, as a result, I was offered a special computer program course for kids with above-average mathematics abilities. I continued with computer classes in high school and took an independent study program in my senior year. That program allowed me to leave school early and work on a volunteer basis at Honeywell Information Systems. I didn't receive any pay, but I learned several computer languages and gained hands-on experience in the computer field. My father also inspired me. Being an engineer, he taught me a lot about engineering and mechanics and gave me a strong technical background.

I now work as a computer programmer. Since banks are my company's primary clients, we design a series of programs that actually generate computerized tax forms.

While in college, I worked at Honeywell during summer vacations. After completing my first year at Rensselaer Polytechnic Institute, I went back to Honeywell and applied for a job and did primarily the same thing as before, which was programming reports and information systems. It was very simple stuff compared to what I'm doing now, but it gave me a strong background in the field. After I completed my projects at Honeywell, I worked the remainder of that summer for a construction company in Boston, where I was involved in a more in-depth project and learned even more about computers and programming. In my senior year, I worked as a teaching assistant for a computer class and was a member of a professional leadership program, which helped me develop management and interpersonal skills. Essentially, I took advantage of any opportunity that came along that furthered my experience and knowledge in computers.

While in school, I constantly updated my résumé as I gained academic as well as technical experience in computers. By my senior year, I was able to be interviewed by twenty-four companies, all of them technical. I now know that the work experience and professional leadership programs I was involved in while at school definitely helped me gain an edge on the competition in the job market. Also, hands-on experience is essential, no matter how elementary it may seem. Working at Radio Shack in programming, for instance, or even in one of their retail stores, can be very valuable.

Computer programming is filled with many different challenges, which I find exciting. My current official title is systems analyst. I am the number-two person on a project, with a project team of about seven people. There is a lot more pressure with my kind of job than with a regular computer job. I work with my team at our client's site, so we have to constantly watch what we do and what we say. We must always impress the clients with professionalism, since they're paying us by the hour. We have to deal with a different type of management, namely, upper-level management, who know nothing about computers. We must always meet our deadlines, regardless of whether we have to work late in the evening or on weekends.

The field is constantly changing, and although there is a lot of pressure in my line of computer programming, there are also a lot of rewards. I am never stuck on one project for any great length of time, which means I am involved in many different aspects of computers. The pay and the benefits are good, and each project is usually in a very nice location.

My day-to-day responsibilities involve designing and coding programs requested by a client. If our client wants tax returns or reports, we have to figure out what their specific needs are, design the reports, and write and test the programs. Time management is very important in my position. At any given time, I'm usually working on three or four different things, which forces me to budget my time between each project. Client interaction and interpersonal skills are essential in my position. We have to be able to deal with all kinds of different clients on all kinds of different levels—from middle managers to bank presidents. For example, every so often I prepare presentations for my clients. This means I have to be able to talk in banking terms because most clients do not understand computer terminology. This is probably one of the most difficult aspects of my work: The client can't talk "computers," but we have to talk "banks."

There are many opportunities that exist in computer programming, depending on one's background and past experience. I could move into another type of programming field relatively easy, whether it be technical programming or business programming. My current background and experience can take me basically into any type of programming or computer environment I want. If I wanted to switch to a related field, I could consider a junior-management-type position involving people, planning, scheduling, and/or planning other people's schedules.

Anyone thinking of a career in computer programming must keep in mind that the field is constantly changing. Finding work has not been a problem for me because I've been willing to keep on top of the competition through continually upgrading my computer and professional skills. A person must be able and willing to keep up with the new technology, its new languages and new programs. Keeping versatile and being able to deal with all different types of new computer technologies is a must.

The computer programming field can be as challenging as you make it. If you want, you can get a 9-to-5 job where you go home and forget about your job at the end of the day, or you can go after a very fast-tracked and fast-paced job that will give you as much as you want to get out of it. Those just starting out should keep in mind that it is important to change companies every year or two, unless they feel they have opportunities at their present company, in order to make different contacts in the different types of computer work available to them.

~~~ JOHN TABOR

DENTIST

At the time of this interview, John, a DDS, had been practicing general dentistry for thirty-one years. He spent the first four years after graduating from dental school in the navy and has been with a dental group in private practice for twenty-seven years in the San Francisco Bay area.

MY SON'S COLLEGE PRESIDENT once said that high school and college students today are probably going to have at least three or four careers in their lifetime. His point was that a strong liberal arts education is even more important than ever, in order to cultivate a well-rounded set of values and interests, and to be able to communicate well, both in speech and in writing. And I think this is especially true for anyone considering dentistry. I have been practicing dentistry for thirty-one years, and I still feel the most important part of my education was my strong liberal arts background. An undergraduate liberal arts background gives you exposure to a variety of subjects, and if you are going into dental school, you are going to have one narrow, highly specialized area of expertise that narrows you down academically. In a way, an undergraduate liberal arts education is a future dentist's last chance to develop well-rounded interests in other things before becoming highly specialized.

When I was growing up in Minneapolis, we had a family friend who was a dentist, and he piqued my interest in dentistry. He would often show me around his office, letting me touch the instruments and watch what was going on in his office. I started seriously discussing dentistry with a friend of mine while doing my undergraduate work. During my sophomore year, I had pretty much decided that I wanted to be a dentist. So in my junior year, I toured the University of Minnesota's dental school. I spoke with a lot of the students and spent time with an admissions counselor to be certain that I understood the many prerequisite courses I needed to enter dentistry school.

I finished my undergraduate studies with a major in chemistry and a minor in history and another minor in English. I entered dental school in 1959 and graduated in 1963. At that time, I believe there was a higher academic requirement for admission. Most dental schools would not admit anyone who had a GPA lower than 3.5. Academically, you had to be in pretty good shape.

After graduating from dental school, I was drafted into the navy as a dentist for four years. This experience was a very positive part of my education. When you first leave dental school, you think you know everything. In the navy, you are hooking up with other dentists from other schools all over the country, and you quickly learn that there are a variety of different ways to do things. The exchange of ideas and techniques and procedures was an invaluable part of my education. You begin to compare yourself with your peers and senior officers and you soon find out that there are many different ways to do things.

I have been with my current dental group, which now consists of eight dentists, for twenty-seven years. When I first joined the group, I was very fortunate to have had one of the older members of the group take me under his wing. He became my mentor, and I am trying, in turn, to do the same with some of the younger dentists coming into our group. Having someone you respect and admire in your profession and someone who has the time and will take the time and spend it on you is tremendously important.

What I like most about my practice is the people—not only the patients I care for but the people I work with. We all work together as a team. Dentistry is a nice profession in that respect. I consider dentistry a low-pressure situation and it allows me to work with people I really like being with, and that's very important in dentistry. It is also important for dentists to enjoy being with people. Stanford University is here, so I am very lucky in that we have a lot of business and professional people as our patients. We are in an affluent area, so people can afford to pay their bills! It's a real benefit to be around people who are your patients and who have the same level of education and interests that you have. Again, I attribute my liberal arts background to my ability to find the common ground within a diverse patient population. Also, my experience in a lot of different high school and college clubs taught me how to get along with people I disagree with without a confrontation.

It is also a tremendous feeling to know that you have not only helped but also inspired a patient to turn his or her dental health around. We have even been able to encourage a lot of our patients to quit smoking. Prevention has been a big part of the practice of dentistry, and I think it will continue to become ever more important. With fluoride in the water, we are not seeing as much decay as we once did. The American Dental Association (ADA) has played a very active role in introducing fluoride in drinking water all over the country, which has had a very positive impact on dental health, and I am very proud of my profession for that. In my opinion, health-care professionals who are not essentially trying to put themselves out of business—metaphorically speaking, of course—aren't doing their jobs!

Dentistry is usually a negative experience for most people. No one likes going to the dentist. Most patients feel you are invading a part of their private space. I try to make my patients feel in control, because I think the feeling of being out of control is what frightens most people about dentists. It's a challenge for me to get patients to relax and talk them through their anxieties. It's very gratifying when these once-frightened patients come back and want to sit down in the chair and chat with you.

I currently work a four-day workweek. I see approximately ten patients a day and spend approximately forty-five minutes to an hour on each patient. As a dentist, you are your own boss in terms of how much you want to work and when you want to work, but that usually depends on how much money you want and need to make. I am with a group practice, which means all eight of us share overhead expenses, including receptionists, business managers, and hygienists.

When I first started with the group, I worked a five-and-a-half-day week, and I did that for five years or so. As my family grew, I started working a five-day week in order to be able to spend more time at home. Dentistry, especially in group practice, offers this kind of flexibility. It can be groomed to meet your needs. It is different from many other businesses in that you are not accountable to someone else. We can cover for one another in the event we want to take a long weekend, or even an extended vacation of a month or so. These options are not possible in a single office setting.

Unfortunately, I see dentistry being invaded by many outsiders, which is apparent with such things as state and federal regulations. We are also seeing a lot of third-party interference—insurance carriers dictating how you are to practice dentistry, similar to what managed care is doing to the medical health-care profession. I do see a lot of changes coming.

Related fields are pretty narrow. You enter a narrower and narrower section of your profession the more you specialize. Teaching is an option, or further specializing, such as orthodontics, periodontics, oral surgery, or pediatric dentistry. But these specialties require another two years of school, on top of four years of dental school.

The field of dentistry is tougher to get into because there are not that many jobs available, particularly in this area. I live in an area where a lot of people want to live, so the competition is tough, but I am sure there are areas in other parts of the country that are not as populated where jobs are more available. I stayed in this area after getting out of the navy. I took a part-time job in a dental clinic, getting paid by the hour, making just enough to get by while I looked for something else. I went to the professional dental fraternities and the dental supply houses—they were good to talk to because they are going in and out of dentists' offices all day and they know who is looking for help and who is good. Also, the *ADA Journal* and other professional journals advertise positions available all over the country. Professors at dental schools have friends in practice who may need help, so I would recommend keeping in touch with professors from school.

Another recent difficulty in getting work in dentistry is that it takes an enormous amount of collateral to get a practice going. It has become more difficult to borrow the capital needed. Unfortunately, dentistry is still very much a "good old boys" club, and women have an especially difficult time setting up a practice. As a result, more and more female dentists will be working for the HMOs. But I see this changing. Dentistry is a great profession for women because you can slow down and stop practicing for a few years to have a family while keeping up with the field through things like seminars and clinics.

More than anything else, a successful dentist must care about other people, enjoy being around other people, and possess an ability to establish a trusting relationship with patients. A certain amount of mechanical as well as scientific ability is also essential.

The pay scale for dentists depends on how much a person wants to work. A very important consideration in dentistry is the cost of the education. Today, the total cost is approximately $100,000 to $120,000. To go into private practice costs another $150,000. There is a tremendous amount of money needed up front, plus, most graduates are in their late twenties to early thirties and are looking to get married, buy a home, and start a family—it's very tight financially at first. Unless you have had financial support from your parents or spouse, there is an enormous financial burden to contend with.

~~~ JILLIAN DAVIES

WETLANDS ECOLOGIST

Jillian has worked as an environmental wetlands ecologist since receiving her master's degree from the Yale School of Forestry and Environmental Studies. She has done extensive wetlands research throughout the entire East Coast and at the time of this interview was about to receive certification as a soil scientist.

I HAVE ALWAYS BEEN INTERESTED in science and the natural world. My husband and I have a real passion for the outdoors and the mountains, so I wanted to have a career that contributed in some way to solving some of the problems facing modern society. The environmental field, specifically wetlands ecology, combined my intellectual interest in science and the natural world and my personal interest in the outdoors, as well as my desire to contribute to making the world a better place.

I am a wetlands ecologist for Jason M. Cortell & Associates, which is a private-sector, full-service environmental consulting company. Wetlands consulting includes the component of fieldwork, which means I'm not in the office all the time—I get out in the woods—which is my favorite part of my job. The work is intellectually challenging in that it is going to take a long time to develop a really thorough knowledge of wetland science, which in itself is always changing. Ecologists and other scientists are always coming up with new ways to evaluate wetlands and new understandings of wetlands ecosystems. I never worry about being bored. My boss, who has worked in this field for twenty years, is still learning new things.

I attended an unusual elementary school, in that it had a science program coordinated with the Academy of Natural Sciences in Philadelphia. Field trips were an integral component of that program, and we studied science in terms of ecosystems. Each year, we studied a different ecosystem. As a result of this program, I developed a strong intellectual interest in the whole ecosystem approach to understanding the natural world.

I went to Williams College, which was an excellent experience, but the biology department was oriented toward premed students and students heading for laboratory research. The program was not oriented toward students who wanted to get out in the woods and deal with whole organisms and ecosystems. As a result, I ended up not majoring in biology, although I took basic sciences, such as chemistry and biology. I majored in psychology and minored in studio art.

After graduation, I had the opportunity to teach English in a refugee camp in Thailand. While I was in Asia, I was profoundly struck by the deterioration of its environment. I was aware of environmental deterioration in this country, too, but I was more struck by it out of the context of the world in which I had grown up. I came back to this country and decided that I wanted to get back into the environmental world. I applied to and was accepted at the Yale School of Forestry and Environmental Studies Graduate Program, with concentration in ecosystem ecology. My degree is in environmental studies. Upon graduation, I started working for Cortell & Associates, and have been in my current position for three and a half years.

I enjoy working for the private sector, as opposed to the government or nonprofit organizations. Citizens and their representatives have made up laws to protect the environment, and scientists and ecologists who work for private consulting companies are often the first people to have to deal with those regulations. If I do a good job, then, hopefully, regulators and the nonprofit groups aren't going to have much to complain about. Another positive aspect about working for a private company is that you earn a reasonable salary. Government salaries tend to be a little less than they are in the private sector, and the nonprofit groups are traditionally lower than that, unless you are in the upper echelon of the organization. I have had experience working for a few nonprofit groups when I was first out of school, which was fine for that stage of my life, but there comes a time when you would like to do a little better than meet your minimal rent requirements!

My minor in studio art has been very helpful to me in my current work. Learning to able to put artwork up on the wall and have the class critique it taught me to separate my sense of self from my work. It also taught me how to think as a method of investigative problem solving. I learned to use constructive criticism to improve myself, which has proven to be a very useful tool. All of the outdoor activities I've been involved in—hiking, mountaineering, camping— have given me a good comfort level with being out in the woods by myself.

I have recently starting taking classes at the University of Massachusetts to become a certified soil scientist. My field is constantly changing, and soils have become more important in the analysis of wetlands in the last few years. In order to do wetlands delineations in Connecticut, ecologists are required by the state to be certified soil scientists, so our company, wanting to increase its soil capabilities and its market, offered me this opportunity.

I love being paid to be outdoors, in the woods, on the first days of spring, on beautiful fall New England days, and on winter days when the sun's shining on freshly fallen snow and the sky is cobalt blue. The flip side of that same coin is that I really hate the heat, and, of course, I am also out in extremely hot weather, with poison ivy, ticks, mosquitoes, briars, and cold, rainy weather. Both aspects come with the job, but for me, the positives far outweigh the negatives.

I think my work has the potential to keep me interested for at least another twenty to thirty years. There are continuous opportunities to learn, and one of the nicest things about dealing with natural systems is that each one is unique. Every time I go out and evaluate a new wetland area, there is a new problem to solve. I am always seeing unusual habitats and wildlife, which never cease to excite me.

As a result of my love of fieldwork, I often have a hard time staying indoors in the office for eight hours at a time, wrapped up in the office routine and the lack of flexibility in an office schedule. And because I travel occasionally, I will some-times miss something going on at home, but, again, this negative is balanced by the fun of traveling and seeing new places. I spend approximately 20 to 25 per-cent of the time involved in fieldwork, and the rest of the time in the office writing documents and doing office work

I am motivated by a desire to increase my knowledge of the natural resources and the federal, state, and local environmental regulations and, as a result, be a better ecologist. I also know that if I don't do my best on a wetlands delineation, it's the environment that will ultimately pay. I also enjoy developing my ability to interpret the landscape, which is an art as much as a science. I sometimes feel like I am a "natural archaeologist"—especially with soils—because I am trying to find out the natural history of a particular ecosystem, which can go back ten thousand years in this part of the country.

A typical field day includes preparing and organizing whatever background you have on the site. One of the first things we do is a reconnaissance walk through the site, and then we begin to develop a theory as to what drives the creation of the wetlands at that site and, therefore, where its boundaries are. At the beginning of the day, you'll spend most of your time identifying plants and digging soil pits. As the day goes on, you get more familiar with the site and you can choose your wetlands boundary based on what you developed in the earlier part of the day. Your field day ends by sketching and tying flags onto the vegetation and sketching where your boundary is on the map, as well as taking notes and recording data on the vegetation and the hydrology flow of the site. We always collect data on the functions and values of the wetlands, and on the wildlife.

A typical office day might include a few hours of writing text based on the results of fieldwork, for an environmental impact statement or a wetland delineation report, as well as reviewing various documents that address regulatory requirements pertaining to wetlands. The rest of the day is usually spent discussing projects with other people in the office, and with the engineering company you are working with, as well as your client or the regulatory people. The report writing is challenging, and talking to people about projects is interesting. But there is a definite component, particularly working at a small company, that everybody has to do a little bit of everything.

There are three, possibly four career path components in the environmental field to think about: One is the private side, where I am now; the second would be working for the government; and the third would be working for a nonprofit organization. A fourth component might possibly be education. It would probably be easy for me to go from what I am doing now to a regulatory kind of job, meaning government work—a lot of people with my background do that. I've heard that it is more difficult to go from the regulatory side to the private sector, and in terms of getting work with the nonprofit sector—I don't know how they would look at my skills. I could teach, but I think that would be more difficult for me because I would probably have to go back to school and get some kind of teaching certificate.

If I could live two or three lifestyles simultaneously, I would! My life would be completely busy. I never feel like I have enough time, and I think that would be true no matter what job I had. I basically work a forty-hour week, although there are crunch times when we need to put in longer hours, and there are times I am traveling and I am away from whatever I want to be doing at home. But overall, for an interesting, challenging career that's serious, I think what I have is a good balance—but I know not every workplace in this field is like this. I have friends who put in really long hours, but that's more apt to happen in the private sector than in government work. I also have a friend who has worked a number of years in the government sector. He's an avid rock climber and is able to work a longer day four days a week and have more time to go climbing. It really depends on what you are looking for—in the field as a whole, the flexibility is there.

I look forward to increased responsibility. I am moving into management and I see the next five years as a time to develop that skill and move into ever-more complex projects. And I am about to have my first baby. I am looking at the next one to two years as a time to juggle work and family, because I definitely want to do both.

I graduated from graduate school in 1991 when all the newspapers were saying that year was the worst in living history for graduates. I was fortunate to get my job very quickly, after answering an ad in the *Boston Globe*. I was hired about six weeks after I graduated. Friends of mine who were just as qualified as me took six months, others nine months, to get a job—so I think there is the element of luck about being the right person at the right time.

If you want to get a job in a certain kind of fieldwork, it's a good idea to go to graduate school in the region of the country where you want to get a job, because then you are going to know the plants, the soils, and the geology specific to that area of the country. Get to know your professors in graduate school, even undergraduate school, since they have connections to the professional world and they can be very helpful in getting you an internship or a summer job. This can plug you into the local job market—you'll have some connections of your own to help you find a full-time job. They may know somebody in the region. A biology, botany, soils, or wildlife major is helpful at the undergraduate level, although having a solid academic grounding, such as liberal arts, is more important. My psychology major was not at all a deterrent for me getting my job, and, besides, the time to really focus on the more technical side is in graduate school. Part of why I went on to get my soil certification is because I wanted to develop my technical strengths, even more than the master's degree. It's good to have both a liberal arts, general academic background and later add on to it with really solid, technical knowledge on a graduate level and beyond.

Success in this field comes to those who are self-motivated, willing and interested in learning, possess a love for the outdoors, and are not too bothered by the physical discomforts that go along with it. You have to be willing to deal with regulations without having gone through law school, which can be frustrating. Environmental regulations—which is the context in which we do our work—at the federal and state level provide the framework that directs our work in the field, and you have to develop a facility with those regulations as you work.

The pay scale, in the private sector, coming out of graduate school without experience, is roughly in the upper $20K's to low $30K's. With a few years' experience, a salary increase to the mid- to upper $30K's can be expected, and then after ten years' experience, an increase to the mid-$40K's to mid-$50K's, depending on your responsibilities and what part of the business you have specialized in. Top management probably does very well and is comparable to the upper management in other businesses. Government work starts out traditionally lower but usually offers better benefits than a small company. Mid-level government work probably comes a little closer to the private-sector pay scale, but upper-level government management probably makes significantly less than upper-level management at private companies. Nonprofit organizations offer subsistence salaries at the entry level, if that. People in the upper level of nonprofit organizations probably earn salaries in the mid-$30K's to mid-$40K's. The nonprofit sector is more apt to be involved in the political side of things, such as passing legislation and protecting, maintaining, and caring for specific tracts of land.

My advice to anyone making a career decision is to try to pursue an area that has at least one component that ties into your personal and/or your intellectual interests. My work and my recreational interests complement one another. Having this component makes it so much easier to stay motivated and to be good at something you have a genuine interest in. Every job is going to have some component that is not enjoyable, but once you get through that part, you need the interesting parts.

Get some job experience prior to graduate school, because that experience will influence your choice of school and area of study. You will inevitably be in an entry-level job, and you are going to have to do a lot of the tedious tasks that need getting done. The key is to look at people who are a few years ahead of you. If they are involved in interesting tasks, then you can assume that things for you are going to get better. As you become more familiar with the whole picture, you will get to do the fun stuff, too.

My field is perfect for people who love the outdoors. People who do not enjoy the outdoors shouldn't go after this kind of job.

~ ~ ~ CHARLES E. RAUCH

COMPUTER CONSULTANT

At the time of this interview, Charles was a self-employed computer consultant. After working several years as assistant to the director of Sperry and Hutchison's Information Services Department, he took an early retirement option and began his own business. He was still working for himself at age sixty-nine, offering consulting in system design, application feasibility studies, programming, mainframe computers, and personal computers.

IN THE LATE 1950s, I got into computers and I've been working with them ever since. That's when computers were first getting started.

At one time, I studied mechanical engineering, but I never finished that. I eventually got a bachelor's degree in business administration and a master's degree in a very specialized field called operations research.

I was in evening school for four years at Drexel Technical Institute and, after the war was over, I went to the day school for two years. That was all engineering. Then I got married and finished my undergraduate work at LaSalle College with a degree in business administration and a major in production management. I had visions of being a vice president in charge of manufacturing.

After I got my college degree, I went to work in low-level management at the Curtis Publishing Company in their subscription fulfillment department. They had ten thousand names on addressograph plates and a staff of maybe two thousand clerks, supervisors, assistant managers, and section managers to administer all of this. I got into computers when they computerized.

One of the reasons for putting the information on the computer was to reduce the number of clerical staff. I went to the library and read about computers and I said, "That's it." I let it be known that I wanted to work on the project, and I did.

I left Curtis Publishing and Philadelphia in 1960 and came up to the New York area and went to work for Sperry and Hutchison. I worked for them for twenty-one years and decided that was enough. The company was changing management, there was an opportunity to elect early retirement, which I did. I had no intention of not working just because I was technically retired. I started consulting and I've been doing it ever since.

In the beginning, the consulting was a case of scrambling to try to find a client. The kind of consulting I do or did then was kind of long-term, in a sense—a project that might take six months to a year and involved me being there for the whole project. And when it was over, then I had to find another client. That was always the least enjoyable part of it, though it was never really a problem.

What I liked about being a consultant and still do like about it is that you are expected to offer advice. Not that you can't be a salaried employee and be expected to advise your manager or your superior. This is just a little bit different. You're independent, presumably you have no ax to grind. You're there to offer technical judgments, and that's fun. Even if your ideas don't sell. And then when they do sell, you implement them. Okay, you sold it, now do it. Yesterday, preferably.

I guess about 50 percent of the projects I have had over the years have been ones where I have been a subcontractor to a primary contractor. There's a considerable amount of that that goes on. A consulting outfit that needs a specialty and doesn't have it on their staff or doesn't have their specialist in that area available will look for someone who has the expertise and subcontract to them.

Normally, my workday is 9 to 5, but, for many reasons, I try not to keep regular hours along with my clients' employees. There's a very practical reason for that: It reduces the possibility that the IRS will look at you as an employee as opposed to a consultant. There are a lot of things a consultant does to make it quite clear that he or she is consulting and not a long-term temporary employee. I don't really try to keep rigid hours.

I do not work at home. For the kind of work I do, the clients want you on site. There are occasions when I have done some programming on my own computer simply because I had an idea on a Saturday afternoon and I wanted to implement and test it, but then I import it to the client site and it is integrated into what I am doing there. In general, I do not bill clients for things like that. Clients are unhappy with billings for things they can't see. If you're on site and you work until 7:30, they know it, and if they get billed for it, there are no questions asked. If it's a Saturday afternoon in your own home and you say you spent three and a half hours on the project, the client wants evidence of it. I've never been challenged, and one of the reasons is that I've very seldom had occasion to bill for work done on my own computer.

I enjoy low-level programming and I am as comfortable and get just as much satisfaction out of high-level design work. I say low-level only because that's the last thing that gets done—not because it's trivial or doesn't require expertise and experience.

There's not a great difference for me between consulting and being salaried, except for one thing. During the twenty-one years I was at Sperry and Hutchison and the six years I was at Curtis Publishing, I would guess about half of those years it was necessary, for instance, to work on Christmas Day. The program was overdue, we were behind schedule, work needed to be done. Or the program had failed on Christmas Eve and it needed fixing. In the work I do, if you look at the job as a 9-to-5 job, then that is what it is and you probably find your satisfaction somewhere else. I don't mean to imply that I'm a workaholic, but I do enjoy my work and I'm not a 9-to-5 type of person.

For me, consulting has offered about 100 percent more in take-home income. It's very rewarding, financially. If you want to do other things in computer science, hardware maintenance would be one option, and that's a real wide-open field. There are a lot of computers out there and they break down like any machine.

I've known systems analysts who were successful but didn't know how to program and considered it beneath them somehow. They didn't want to know how to program. And I think they might have been successful analysts and application designers, but they weren't in my mind the best, simply because of the fact that they really didn't understand. It's like designing a power plant without really understanding what kind of machinery you're going to have inside it. There's something missing there.

If a person wants to continue to program, one can earn a very good living doing just that. To my mind, it's not absolutely essential; it's only a beginning or a stepping-stone to other things. Crackerjack programmers can earn a very nice living. So you don't have to go on to be a systems analyst or a systems designer or whatever.

The computer field is like anything else: it goes up and down. When the economy is weak and things are running slow, new projects don't get implemented because they cost money and that means there aren't as many programming and analyst jobs around.

Philosophically, my work is a very creative thing. It's a very satisfying function for me because it means I am in control of something. I do not control people well. I've been in management jobs, I've been in supervisory jobs, and I know that it's just not my strength. But being in control of something is very rewarding, and with a computer, the programmer is in complete control. Computers are not capricious machines; they do precisely what you tell them to do, unerringly and without fault they do precisely what you tell them to do. There's a real sense of power behind that. That's very satisfying for me.

It's creative because you're making the computer do something that presumably no one else has ever tried to make it do before. Perhaps because no one saw the need; it doesn't matter why. The point is that you're doing something, which in the environment you're working in, has not been done before, and that's very creative and I enjoy that.

As a consultant, don't overextend yourself, don't sell yourself into areas where you really don't have any expertise or don't have sufficient expertise. When you're advising your client on a feasibility study that a new application that you're proposing is feasible and can be done for this amount of dollars and this amount of time and this amount of resources, that's very satisfying to be able to say that, to know that you're right, and to have a client accept your advice on the basis of your established integrity.

I don't find it frustrating if clients don't take my advice. I guess I get a little philosophical. I say, "Okay, you're the boss, it's your money, and your resources, and you paid me for my advice and this is my advice. Now, what do you want and let's figure out how we're going to do that instead." Turn it around and do what the client says. The client's the boss, the client's paying. Do what the client wants even if it's against your best judgment. And then, of course, you have to avoid saying, "I told you so." That can be tough.

But working with people in the sense of trying to understand their job, if you're trying to automate something that's already being used; or talking to a client and trying to get a feel for how she sees her business and what she expects to help her run her business—that's great.

I get a great deal of satisfaction out of my work. Sometimes I really wonder what I'd be doing today if computers hadn't come along. I don't know the answer to that. More than once, I've spent some time thinking about it, and I think I'm the luckiest guy that they came along. And I happen to have the innate skills and talent to master them.

~~~ Some Things to Think About...

Now that you have an understanding of Investigative careers, here are some things to consider:

1. What insights about Investigative occupations have you gained from these interviews?

   _____

   _____

   _____

2. Which characteristics, abilities, and personal qualities discussed in the interviews are similar to your own? How might the similarities or differences affect your satisfaction with your possible career choices?

   _____

   _____

   _____

3. Ask yourself the following:

* Do you enjoy science, math, medicine, and computers? _____

* Do you like analyzing and solving problems? _____

* Do you prefer working alone? _____

* Are you future focused? Do you enjoy learning and facing new challenges?

  _____

* Are you flexible about your work schedule? _____

* Are you willing and motivated to stay in school beyond an undergraduate degree? _____

How might your responses to these questions suggest satisfaction with an Investigative career choice? _____

4. Which interviews held your interest? Why? _____

_____

5. Which interviews were not what you expected? Why? _____

_____

6. Which occupations are you going to investigate further? How?

_____

_____

_____

_____

CHAPTER FOUR

Imagine Yourself in an Artistic Career

ARE YOU AN ASPIRING Meryl Streep, Pablo Picasso, or Danielle Steele? Even if you're not, you might be suited to a career in the Artistic field. Traditionally, people have considered Artistic occupations to be only those relating to music, literature, fine arts, and performing arts, such as dancers, actors, artists, or writers. This notion has expanded to include other creative and self-expressive careers that call for creative thinking, imagination, and design skills.

～～～ What Are These Careers and Where Can I Find Them?

In general, Artistic work environments stimulate creativity and self-expression, provide flexibility, lack structure, and reward unconventional and artistic values. Artistic opportunities can be found in a wide range of settings: business organizations, schools, museums and other arts organizations, film/TV studios, theaters, publishing companies (newspaper, book, magazine), and home-based businesses. A sampling of the many careers that fall into the Artistic realm include those listed in table 4 below. For a complete listing of Artistic careers, consult *The Dictionary of Holland Occupational Codes* or the appendix.

TABLE 4
EXAMPLES OF ARTISTIC CAREERS

Poet	Music teacher	Composer
Artist	Interior decorator	Fashion model
Art teacher	Costume designer	Author
Technical writer	Motion pictures set designer	Entertainer
English teacher	Architect	Art museum director
Reporter	Photographer	Broadcaster
Public relations director	Screen writer	Painting restorer
Advertising executive	Makeup artist	Commercial artist
Sculptor	Social scientist	Creative director
Illustrator	Orchestra conductor	Medical illustrator
Playwright	Police artist	Public administrator
Copy writer	Lawyer	Translator
Corporate trainer	Arranger	Librarian

Artistic careers can be intellectually and/or physically demanding and often become the lifestyle of the person involved in them. Work tends to encompass or influence most aspects of a person's life because of the dedication involved in Artistic careers. The creation of products or ideas, which may be tangible or intangible, becomes the central focus of the Artistic person.

~~~ Who Are These People and Am I One of Them?

What kinds of people gravitate toward and do well in the Artistic fields? What are their characteristics, values, and interests?

A stereotypical description of an Artistic person often includes the words "temperamental," "emotional," and "flaky." While sometimes these adjectives may ring true, describing the Artistic personality is much more complex. In fact, *complex* is an excellent word to characterize the Artistic person.

Generally, the Artistic person has a passion to create fueled by his or her emotions, feelings, and imagination. Ambiguity does not tend to bother Artistic people, and, in fact, they relish change and seek constant variety in their lives. At one end of the spectrum, Artistic people can be introspective, intuitive, and sensitive. On the other end, they can be flamboyant, impulsive, and idealistic. Most are dedicated individualists who are more interested in doing the actual work and creating a product than belonging to a particular profession or achieving a specific status.

Talent and endurance in a creative field of interest are usually prerequisites for entering the Artistic arena. This doesn't necessarily mean that you must be able to draw, sing, act, or write in the traditional sense. But you must be able and willing to commit the time and creative energy necessary to become accomplished in your chosen field. Advertising executives and copywriters use creative thinking skills to come up with new and exciting ad campaigns. Commercial artists now use computers for their layouts rather than drawing by hand. Artistic people communicate through the expression of their creative abilities—whatever they may be.

On the interpersonal side, Artistic people like to work independently but not necessarily to the exclusion of others. It's true that often much of their work is done quietly, without interaction with others. However, Artistic people frequently like to be around other creative types and tend to have a flair for communicating their ideas with great style and emotion.

Artistic people often have lofty goals of becoming famous in their fields of endeavor. This is not to say that they are overly concerned with status, stability, or wealth. Such concerns are often the complete antithesis of their value systems. Rather, they are concerned with being recognized for the quality of their work—public notice that they are a true artist in their chosen field. Artistic people often need to gain a sense of meaning from their work. Choosing an Artistic career can be like choosing a lifestyle; the decision can be very personal. The Artistic person's sense of self-worth is often derived from how others judge his or her work. More than for any other Holland type, professional rejection for the Artistic individual may be taken the most personally.

★ ★ ★ *"Basically I was a talented kid. Creativity was never taught to me; I think that kids should be taught to think creatively. While it is seldom taught, it is a good way to get through school, and, ultimately, it will get you further ahead. I have never been able to plan my career. Instead, I found that one thing always led to another. I have engaged in things that interest me. I have always encouraged others to do that, too. When you stop enjoying what you're doing, look for something else. If you're good, you'll know it. You'll be recognized. I think talent does get recognized. If creative people get into the machinery, they will be spotted. These people rise to the top. Writers are tremendously in demand. Producing and directing television and working in comedy are also areas that require creativity and are in demand. The entertainment world is always looking for talented people who are creative and willing to work hard to deliver. It is hard to balance personal and professional life when you work in the entertainment field. The work is your entire life. It had better be something you really like to do a lot of the time. Your professional life becomes your whole life."*

JIM HENSON
DIRECTOR AND CREATOR OF THE MUPPETS

So, Michelangelo You're Not... Or, Should You Avoid This Field?

If you're looking for a 9-to-5 job with stability, an Artistic career is probably not for you. The hours can be irregular: evenings, weekends, on and off. Film and modeling work is often done on location and is usually on a project-to-project basis. Stage work is usually in the evenings and may involve moving from city to city. Often the hours are set by the individual according to when she or he works best. A writer may do his or her best writing after midnight or an artist may like to get up at dawn to paint.

Other red flags to alert you that an Artistic career is probably *not* the choice for you include:

* *You want a high degree of interpersonal interaction on a regular basis.* Creative careers usually entail a great deal of independent work, often without a lot of people contact.

* *You like highly structured environments with well-defined schedules and tasks.* Creative work environments are more informal, less structured, and relaxed.

* *You're looking for high status, stability, and big bucks.* It's possible to attain these in an Artistic career, but only after years of hard work and/or lots of luck. Usually those aren't the top career goals for an Artistic person, anyway.

* *You can't tolerate ambiguity or change.* Artistic jobs are often on a project basis without much security or stability. People in these fields are frequently self-employed or are freelancers and don't necessarily receive a regular paycheck.

～～～ How Do I Get Started?

While many Artistic careers share common characteristics and attributes, the actual tasks, working conditions, requirements, and preparation vary widely from occupation to occupation. Of all the Holland types, the Artistic cluster probably has the most diverse set of occupations under its umbrella. So it's difficult to summarize what is needed to prepare for an Artistic career in an overall statement.

It's no doubt extreme to say that to pursue an Artistic career, you need to have been born with a paintbrush (pen, flute, tutu) in hand. But many people in the Artistic fields began focusing on their work at a young age: Classical dancers and musicians often start intensive training before the age of ten. Developing a talent—whether innate or not—to the level needed to be a professional "artist" sometimes requires starting at a young age. But not always. A person with creative talents/abilities/ambitions can frequently learn the skills necessary to succeed within a more reasonable time frame—such as the skills needed to become a photographer, a model, an advertising executive, or an interior decorator.

Having an interest in the arts is not enough to be successful in the field. Those aspiring to Artistic careers must learn whether they have the talent and the endurance to pursue a career in their specific area of interest. Due to the product orientation of many of the Artistic careers, a high premium is placed on the quality of the person's ability to do the work. Most of the Artistic fields are very competitive and require experience and evidence of competence via portfolios, credits, or auditions to land a job. Entrance to the reputable training programs and schools usually requires some experience and evidence of talent, skill, and/or potential. An aspiring commercial artist must show his or her design skills; an aspiring dancer must show his or her ability to dance. So starting young or at least prior to formal training is often necessary in the Artistic fields.

Although a formal education is not always required, the more education and experience you can bring to the table, the better, because of the stiff competition for Artistic jobs. College degrees in journalism, English, fine arts, performing arts, and the like can enhance a person's résumé, while the time spent in school can allow for the person's talent to grow and mature. Additionally, a college education can provide a cushion to fall back on in case things get tough. For example, a struggling actor with a college education may have a better chance of finding something more enjoyable and/or lucrative than waiting tables to pay the bills.

Even more importantly, previous experience in the field can give a person the edge in a competitive job market. Extracurricular activities or part-time jobs might include working on school publications as writers, editors, photographers, or layout artists; performing, directing, or designing sets for school plays and community theater; designing flyers and brochures for school/community events; and belonging to a literary or book club. Prior experience allows people to show their competence through auditions, portfolios, or lists of credits, which, in turn, can make or break an Artistic career.

Realistically, a person who wishes to pursue a career in the Artistic field more than likely has hobbies and interests that support his or her desire. Involvement in clubs, classes, and organizations that revolve around those interests can also help the person gain experience and might open up career avenues to pursue. Interests such as painting, playing an instrument, reading, visiting art galleries, making jewelry, and writing short stories or poetry might point to some opportunities for career exploration in the Artistic field.

～～～ What's It Like Out There?

As mentioned before, the Artistic field is quite competitive, but the need for artistically talented individuals will exist as long as the public continues to support the arts, demands entertainment and new products, and appreciates beauty in the world. According to the *1994–1995 Occupational Outlook Handbook*,

Artistic occupations that will have average growth through 2005 include architects, landscape architects, dancers/choreographers, graphic artists, fine artists, writers/editors, musicians, public relations specialists, radio/TV announcers, reporters, photographers, and jewelers. Those occupations with faster than average growth include industrial designers, interior designers, set designers, fashion designers, floral designers, lawyers, advertising managers, corporate trainers, and chefs. Occupations that will grow much faster than average include technical writers, actors, directors, and producers. Two occupations that will have slower than average growth are photojournalists and librarians.

An important point to remember is that no matter what the expected growth of the occupation, the competition for all occupations in the Artistic field is extremely high. Not only is entering the field competitive, but often a person will also face stiff competition throughout his or her career. Freelancers or self-employed people are usually in competition for the next client and project. Despite the projected growth in much of the Artistic field, the supply of those wishing to enter the occupations will exceed the demand. Only those with the most talent and perseverance will be likely to find regular employment.

Many Artistic jobs are geographically clustered in metropolitan areas where film/TV studios, large publishing and advertising firms, and art centers are located. Other artistically inclined people are self-employed or are freelancers and don't necessarily need to be geographically tied to an area.

~~~ Where Can I Find Out More About Artistic Careers?

Talking to people who work in the field is the absolute best way to find out more about Artistic careers. Conducting informational interviews with people whose careers interest you can give you the best picture of what a career is like, what's required to work in that career, how to prepare for it, and whether you'll enjoy the work.

Insightful informational interviews with people in Artistic careers comprise the remainder of this chapter. We still encourage you to get out there and do some informational interviewing on your own. Refer to the final chapter in this book, What's Next?, for specific steps on doing informational interviewing.

Another must is researching and reading about Artistic careers. The final chapter in this book also includes information on how to do career research and tips on career exploration. Following is a list of books and professional organizations geared to Artistic careers to help you get started.

Books for Artistic Careers

Book Publishing Career Directory, 4th Edition, by R. W. Fry, published by Career Press, 1990

Careers for Bookworms and Other Literary Types by M. Eberts and M. Gisler, published by VGM Career Horizons, 1991

Careers for Crafty People and Other Dexterous Types by M. Rowh, published by VGM Career Horizons, 1993

Careers for Culture Lovers and Other Artsy Types by M. Eberts and M. Gisler, published by VGM Career Horizons, 1991

Careers for Film Buffs and Other Hollywood Types by J. Greenspon, published by VGM Career Horizons, 1993

Careers for Gourmets and Others Who Relish Food by M. Donovan, published by VGM Career Horizons, 1993

Careers in Advertising by S. W. Pattis, published by VGM Career Horizons, 1990

Careers in Communications by S. F. R. Noronha, published by VGM Career Horizons, 1994

Careers in the Graphic Arts by V. L. Roberson, published by Rosen Publishing Group, 1993

Careers in Journalism by J. Goldberg, published by VGM Career Horizons. 1994

Careers in Law by G. Munneker, published by VGM Career Horizons, 1992

Careers in Photography by A. Evans, published by Photo Data Research, 1992

Careers in the Visual Arts: A Guide to Jobs, Money, Opportunities, and An Artistic Life by D. Ito, published by Watson-Guptill Publications, 1993

Career Opportunities in the Music Industry by S. Field, published by Facts on File, 1990

Career Opportunities in Television and Video by M. K. Reed, published by Facts on File, 1991

Career Opportunities in the Theater and the Performing Arts. by S. Field, published by Facts on File, 1992

Directory of Theatre Training Programs, 3rd Edition, by J. Charles, published by Theatre Directories, 1991

Career Opportunities for Writers by R. Guiley, published by Facts on File, 1991

Getting Started in Film: The Official AFI Guide to Exciting Film Careers, published by The American Film Institute, 1991

How to Make It in Hollywood: All the Right Moves by L. Buzzell, published by Harper Collins, 1992

How To Put Your Book Together and Get a Job in Advertising by M. Paetro, published by The Copy Workshop, 1990

How to Survive and Prosper as an Artist: Selling Yourself Without Selling Your Soul by C. Michels, published by Holt, 1992

Museum Jobs From A–Z: What They Are, How to Prepare, & Where to Find Them by G. W. Bates, published by Batav Museum Publishing, 1994

1992 Guide to Cooking Schools, published by Shaw Guides, 1991

Opportunities in Broadcasting Careers by E. I. Ellis, published by VGM Career Horizons, 1992

Opportunities in Magazine Publishing by S. W. Pattis, published by VGM Career Horizons, 1992

Opportunities in Music Careers by R. Gerardi, published by VGM Career Horizons, 1991

Opportunities in Technical Writing and Communications Careers by J. R. Gould and W. A. Losano, published by VGM Career Horizons, 1994

The Music Business: Career Opportunities and Self-Defense by D. Weissman, published by Crown Publishing Group, 1990

The Tech Writing Game: A Comprehensive Guide for Aspiring Technical Writers by J. Van Wicklen, published by Facts on File, 1992

Working in TV News: The Insider's Guide by C. Filoreto and L. Setzer, published by Mustang Publications, 1993

You Can Do It: Careers in Television by H. J. Blumenthal, published by Little, Brown, 1992

Your Film Acting Career by M. K. Lewis and R. R. Lewis, published by Gorham House, 1993

Professional Organizations for Artistic Careers

Below are organizations that can provide information about Artistic careers. Consider contacting organizations that interest you. Be sure to include a self-addressed stamped envelope when writing to request information.

American Bar Association
Information Services

750 North Lake Shore Dr.
Chicago, IL 60611

American Culinary Federation
P.O. Box 3466
St. Augustine, FL 32085

American Dance Guild
33 West 21st St., Third Floor
New York, NY 10010

The American Institute of Architects
Director, Education Programs
1735 New York Ave., NW
Washington, DC 20006

The American Institute of Graphic Designers
1059 3rd Ave.
New York, NY 10021

American Newspaper Publishers Association Foundation
The Newspaper Center
Box 17407, Dulles International Airport
Washington, DC 20041

American Society for Interior Designers
608 Massachusetts Ave., NE
Washington, DC 20002

American Society of Furniture Designers
P.O. Box 2688
High Point, NC 27261

American Society of Landscape Architects
4401 Connecticut Ave., NW
Washington, DC 20008

American Society of Magazine Photographers
419 Park Ave., South
New York, NY 10016

Associated Actors and Artists of America
165 West 46th St.
New York, NY 10036

Industrial Designers Society of America
1142-E Walker Rd.
Great Falls, VA 22066

Jewelers of America
1185 Avenue of the Americas
New York, NY 10036

Manufacturing Jewelers and Silversmiths of America
100 India St.
Providence, RI 02903

National Association of Broadcasters
1771 N St., NW
Washington, DC 20036

National Association of Schools of Dance
11250 Roger Bacon Dr.
Reston, VA 22090

National Association of Schools of Music
11250 Roger Bacon Dr.
Reston, VA 22090

Professional Photographers of America, Inc.
1090 Executive Way
Des Plaines, IL 60018

Public Relations Society of America
33 Irving Place
New York, NY 10003-2376

Society for Technical Communication, Inc.
901 N. Stuart St., Suite 304
Arlington, VA 22203

Society of American Florists
1601 Duke St.
Alexandria, VA 22314

The Society of Illustrators
128 East 63rd St.
New York, NY 10021

The Society of Publication Designers
60 East 42nd St., Suite 1416
New York, NY 10165

Theatre Communications Group, Inc.
355 Lexington Ave.
New York, NY 10017

★★★

★★★ JANE PAULEY

TELEVISION BROADCASTER

Q What career advice would you have for high school students who are planning to go on to college, and college students as they start to consider different career fields?

A I would urge a student to take a very serious interest in their education generically. The stronger your base, the more flexibility you have. I have a mental image of my high school phys-ed teacher trying to teach us badminton or tennis, I forget which one, explaining how you had to stand feet apart with your knees bent; that will position you to go forward, backward, or lateral either way, depending on where the ball comes from. I see this image as very strongly applying to one's education. It's got to prepare you to go any direction that life and opportunities afford you. I know very few people in life who, when they were in the ninth or tenth year of high school or for that matter a junior or senior in college, really knew what their ultimate career would be. And those few who did know have been almost exclusively the ones who were going to be doctors. The rest of us have been freelancing and ad-libbing and responding to opportunities that came our way.

Q In addition to the purely academic work, do you feel students should become involved in extracurricular activities and other things for which there may not be any immediate or short-term gain but would just give them that flexibility?

A Yes! In my case, the fact that I had been very active on a speech and debate team in high school could not have been better preparation, but it certainly wasn't a calculated strategy. Speech and debate is always high on my list in so many ways.

This subject brings up in particular my personal peeve, the college mass communications degree, and it is filtering down to the high school level as well. The problem is that there is an enormous imbalance in the number of students preparing for a career in broadcasting and the number of jobs that will ever be available in the industry. And many of the jobs will go to people who studied English or economics or languages or political science, like me. So I worry that kids are preparing too narrowly for careers. My advice is to prepare broadly to give you that flexibility. Extracurricular activities and elective courses offer sampling opportunities which are invaluable in terms of finding undiscovered talents and interests. For instance, aspiring journalists might spend entire weekends and three nights a week at the college newspaper or the radio station. But I think it should be an extracurricular passion. As an aside, I've often thought how my life would have been changed had I made cheerleader in the tenth grade. Thank heavens I didn't or I never would have discovered my talent at speaking and my passion for current events.

Q So I assume that some of the things that you are describing have contributed to your own particular success, that is, having a broad base of experiences and having a general education?

A Yes, and I can also pinpoint with some regret, under education, some of the things I missed; the things I had opportunities to learn and didn't, in my case, mastery of a foreign language. I could have, and I have no one to blame but myself. I was grateful that I had a number of very competent high school English teachers who were well educated themselves, very demanding, and wouldn't let me get by with much. I remember being near tears once when my favorite, beloved English teacher berated me in front of the whole class for writing in pencil and not pen. I will never forget it! She had exacting standards! And I never repeated the mistake. But, I learned how to write. Schools aren't very exacting anymore. I see a lot of sloppy writing, but I can't emphasize enough how much good writing counts. If you have a résumé or a letter of introduction with a couple of stupid mistakes, it says you're a careless person. Those things count, and they should.

Q Any advice specific to young women starting out—you've balanced your career and life well. Is there anything unique to women in the workplace that you want to comment on?

A This is true for both men and women. "How will a family fit my ambition?" Marry well! That's one of the smartest things I did. After you have fallen in love, but before you marry, make sure you've picked someone who expects to be a partner, because not everyone does.

Q Any advice for people thinking of switching careers? For instance, someone who might have started out down one path and then decided to move on to something else—maybe they realize they've made a bad initial decision. What advice do you have for them? Some people feel trapped. They may be making good money, but they get caught up in their lives and find it difficult to switch—what advice do you have for people who feel they have gotten off to a bad start, for whatever reasons?

A The best advice I ever gave anybody is that if you are looking for another job or career, it is best to explore those options and opportunities from the safety of your current job. If you are making a career change and you have to reeducate, well, that's why they invented night school. Keep the job you have while preparing for phase two. It's a measure of your commitment.

Q Do you have any other advice?

A Play to your strengths. Find out where your strengths are and enhance them with liberal doses of hard work and discipline. An awful lot of what your parents said is true. Having an interest in something or a passion for something in and of itself may not be enough.

★★★

★★★ GEORGE F. WILL

SYNDICATED COLUMNIST

M Y CAREER HAS BEEN the result of accident and serendipity. I went through graduate school intending to become, and did in fact become, a professor of political philosophy, first at Michigan State and then at the University of Toronto. When Everett Dirksen died and the Republican Senate leadership changed, Gordon Allott of Colorado became Chairman of the Policy Committee (the third ranking position) and he was looking around for an academic type to help with his writing and his politics. Allott asked some people in Colorado if they knew a Republican academic, and one of the people he contacted had been at Princeton when I was there. That was how I got to Washington.

I thought it would be nice to write, and I had written a few things for *National Review*. I asked Bill Buckley if he needed a Washington editor. As it turned out, at about that time, Frank Meyer, who had been with the magazine from day one, was dying of cancer. His death was a great loss. Therefore, Bill Buckley knew that he needed someone to edit the back of a book for him and said if I could do both the book and the magazine, then he would take me on. So that's how I started. In 1973, I sort of wandered into syndicating a column. At the invitation of Meg Greenfield, I had begun submitting columns to the *Washington Post*, and soon after that, the *Post* decided to launch a syndicate, principally, I think, for David Broder. It was an interesting set of circumstances and coincidences.

I think it's very wise, if you're going into journalism, not to be tempted to study with practicality in mind. I double majored in government and religion at Trinity College. After my undergraduate years, I spent three years at Oxford getting a PPE degree (Politics, Philosophy, and Economics) and then went to Princeton and got a Ph.D. in Political Science.

In terms of how my time is spent, I file columns on Tuesdays and Thursdays for the newspapers and every other Friday morning for *Newsweek*. I used to tape the *Martin Agronsky Show* on Fridays. Now I appear live on Sunday on *This Week with David Brinkley*.

Today that means seven deadlines, counting television, every 14 days. That certainly gives structure to my week. The pressure is never off, so I don't really seem to notice it.… I don't think a fish notices water. I do stop the column for two weeks in the summer in an effort to get some vacation.

I don't feel that getting feedback from peers and colleagues is very important. I used to work at home; today my office downtown is in a small ramshackle townhouse apart from the crush of Washington.

With regard to balancing my private life and my professional life, as I said before, I used to work at home. Now I work in a small office outside the home. Working at home helps in one way and hinders in another. When I worked at home, I did get to spend time around the children as they were growing up. The trouble was that in a way, I never left the office. Having an office outside of my home provides necessary privacy at home and beneficial detachment from work. I drive home from my office downtown earlier than I walked out of my study at home.

You asked how I spend my free time? A good many of the friends with whom I socialize also happen to be in the political system. I read a lot and go to Orioles games.

In order to be successful in my field, I try to look at it as baseball people look at their craft. Earl Weaver, who managed the Orioles, said, "This ain't a football game. We do this every day." And I do my job, in effect, every day. Willie Stargell said baseball's not a game you can play with your teeth clenched. It's long and constant, and you have to have a combination of intensity and relaxation. You have to be calm about it, but you have to have great concentration. Anyone can write a "Grade B" 750 words. But to keep it consistently "Grade A" is very difficult.

I'd like to think I'm getting better as I go along—I think I'm a better columnist today than I was a year ago. I derive my greatest satisfaction from just writing.

I frequently talk to people who want to do the kind of work I do. My advice to them begins with a remark uttered by Mark Twain, who said there are three pieces of advice for someone who wants to be a writer. The first is "Write," the second is "Write," and the third is "Write." It's like everything else in life—like hitting a tennis ball—if you're going to do it well, you have to do it 10,000 times, until you begin to get the hang of it.

It would be impossible for me to say that there is a clear career path leading to my particular line of work. If someone were to say, as they got out of college, "I want to be a syndicated columnist," you'd have to tell them, "Well, that's good and give it a try." But there are a lot more Congressmen than there are syndicated columnists, there are even a lot more Senators, a lot more of almost everything. It's a very, very small profession. I'd suggest having a fallback position. Approach this career by saying to yourself, "I want to be a syndicated columnist, but if that doesn't work out, I'll run a bait and tackle store in Minnesota"…something like that.

★★

~~~ ANNA CHEN

COPYWRITER

Anna graduated from college with a bachelor's degree in communications, where she was involved in extensive television and radio production. Upon graduation, she wrote publicity, commercials, and print ads for a politician campaigning for Congress. She later moved to New York City to pursue a writing career. She has written comedy, worked in clubs, and authored several short stories. At the time of this interview, she worked for a New York-based advertising agency as a copywriter.

I SAW MYSELF AS BEING some sort of writer or performer in high school. I wrote a lot of stories and was in a lot of school plays.

I wanted to be a serious writer. After about a year and a half as an English major in college, I found I was becoming a reader and not a writer. So I switched to a journalism major. I was only a journalism major for one semester. Journalism was a little too straight for me. I really didn't enjoy it. I took some production courses for one semester. Then I became a general communications major.

I was influenced by a professor I had for a copywriting class. I talked to him extensively about it, and he really influenced me. We talked about my background, which was, broadly, communications. I thought this would be a good way to use all of my interests and my background.

During the summer, I worked at a local radio station in my hometown of Danville, Illinois. They let me write all of their commercials. They also let me produce and be in them. I did a lot of dialects and accents. I even cowrote a comedy show with a disc jockey, which lasted for about a month.

After that summer, I concentrated on television and radio production. I took some advertising courses and journalism courses. But my specialization was television and radio production. I did a couple of short films, a few videotapes, a comedy show, and some more radio work. I was even in some local musicals. You can see that I really wanted to be a performer, too. I eventually completed a bachelor's in communications.

After graduation, I worked for a guy who was running for Congress. I wrote all his publicity and created all his commercials and print ads. I was his all-around campaign writer, so to speak. After he lost the election, I moved to New York.

I knew for some time that I wanted to live in New York. That's one of the reasons I moved to Syracuse. To live in New York was a dream I had for several years. I had a relative there whom I could stay with for a while. I was always kind of scared of New York—from a writer-actor point of view. I heard starving artists stories, and I really wasn't interested in going hungry. Upon arrival, I looked for a job as a copywriter. I was in for a surprise. I really didn't have what it took to make it here in the big city. Everyone else was going around with solid portfolios. Mine was simply a collection of various writings. I really needed a focus. But most of all, I needed a job. I took a media planning job at NW Ayer. It gave me money to live on while adjusting to New York. I forgot about copywriting for about a year. I tried my hand at comedy and worked in some clubs around the city. I did some writing of my own, including some short stories.

Media planning was less than exciting. So after a year, I went back to the copywriting. My entire job search took about nine months. I threw away everything I had from the first time I had looked for a copy job. I put together a bunch of products that I liked and showed them to my friends at NW Ayer. They helped me lay it out in a professional manner, and about three months later, I went out with my first book. I wanted to get in anywhere. During the next four months, I beat the streets. I had some good contacts now. I was constantly revising, cutting, and adding. But I learned not to change my book every time someone suggested their personal point of view. I would generally change it when I heard the same thing two or three times. After another three months, I realized very little was changing in my book. I thought I was there. And I was.

Companies who didn't have jobs would pass me on to their friends. But even with my book as good as it was, it took another four months before I was actually hired. I had nibbles during these four months, and I had people tell me they loved the book and that they'd love to hire me. After hearing that three or four times I tended not to believe anyone, but I kept going around. These were the worst four months of my life. During this time, I had met a creative director. He hired me three months later.

If you have a great portfolio, or book—and that's what it takes to get a job—you get one right away. It takes at least four months to get a great book together. If you know people, you may not have to have so great a book. But unless you know a creative director or someone with clout, it's difficult even with a great book.

Also, it takes time to meet someone with the right chemistry. When you are creating advertising, it is very much a personality thing, because it's such a personal business. You're dealing with people all the time—from your art director to your creative director—and it's important to have good chemistry.

I was hired as a junior copywriter. I am expected to solve print problems. For television assignments, the senior writers get the recommended commercial, but I am expected to provide alternative television ideas that can be presented to the client.

On a typical day or week, we're usually given a strategy statement for a print ad or a television campaign. It will say something like: "This deodorant dries faster than any other deodorant." After I set this strategy statement, I work with my art director. We'll sit down and go over lines and visual ideas that can satisfy that strategy. I've solved these problems in five minutes. Sometimes it will take two weeks to solve it. Essentially, what we come up with is some concepts in the form of a main headline and a main visual. We try to make it look as much like a real ad as possible. Then I'll present it to my supervisor. If he approves it, it goes to the associate creative director. Then it goes to another creative director. Once it goes through our department, that same idea will go through the account executive department. The account executive is a liaison between the creative department and the client. There may be three or four people in the account department who have to approve it, then it goes to the client and another three people have to approve it. On a print ad, we select some talent for it—an actor/actress or model. We select a photographer. You get to pick from your suppliers what would best satisfy the ad. It always varies and that's what makes it so interesting. If it's a television campaign, we'll work up something called a television storyboard, and that goes through the same process.

I'm very new to this business. The pressures haven't been so intense for me yet. One reason is that I'm a junior member of a group and I don't usually go to the client. My supervisor will usually show material to the client. That's a lot of pressure in itself, which is something that I haven't been exposed to.

TV is much more complicated. I've only been involved in a few TV commercials. After the storyboard has been sold, it is up to the writer, art director, and the agency producer. The producer brings us examples of directors' work. We pick one. Then we go into casting. We will work with the casting people and the producer and sometimes the director to pick the right people for the role. We will select a location if it's an outside location; if not, the producer or director will suggest which studio it should be shot at. At that point, we will also select music, if it's necessary. We'll have some of the music houses come in and talk to us, tell them what we have in mind, and they'll bring back piano demos. The piano demo is usually just a piano and single vocal, which lets us know the general melody.

At this point, everybody gets involved—the client, the creative people, the account people. We all sit down and go over our choice for director, talent, music, location, and other particulars. This is all preproduction.

Then we go to the shoot. If preproduction was thorough, all should go smoothly. Now we're ready for an edit and rough cut. We sit down at the editing house, select the shots we had on the storyboard, and come up with a rough cut that we'll show to our creative director, client, and down through the ranks.

The music calls for a recording session. You get all the musicians and singers together and mix the music in with the rough cut. If you need an announcer, you add that as well. We show this to the creative director, the client, and the account people. If everyone agrees on what you have, you do a final cut. Most commercials are tested for effectiveness. After all this, if there are no problems, it will go on the air.

This work has been a little bit different than what I expected. After my first year, I expected to have a major TV campaign. Although I've been able to fill out the presentations, I expected to sell something by now. I'm not expected to have a TV campaign, but I wanted one. I am happy with the print work I've done.

In the last few months, I have received some good training. Prior to that, I was working for my associate creative director. He didn't really have the time to walk me through things, and he shouldn't have had to. Recently, the group has been reorganized, and I'm working for three different supervisors on three different parts of the business. I really think now that I am getting the training I need to develop a TV campaign.

The best of this first year was lots of print work that I got through. Also, another good part has been getting to know the people I work with and the people at the agency. Going on shoots and recordings were both fun, and it was good experience.

The worst part is that you could do this job with a lot fewer people than are usually involved. Once you've solved the problem strategically, acceptance becomes a matter of judgment and subjectivity. An excess of subjectivity can be more hurt than help. It waters down the creative product. It is very frustrating for me, as it probably is for everyone in this business.

Another worst: At the beginning of this year, I had a creative partner who was tough to work with. We got the work done, but the chemistry was bad. Chemistry is so vital in this business because you work all the time with a partner. It's a very personal process. You share everything, and if the personal chemistry isn't there, it can be a nightmare.

If you are a philosophy major or a law student, with a warped edge, you'll do very well in this business. Most successful people have a keen sense of logic. Another quality is being smart politically, since much of this business is talk and selling abstract ideas. People who sell and read people well make out very well in this business. Successful people know when to fight and when to be cool. Most successful people in this business are warped enough to let their minds wander in as many directions as possible.

Other successful traits in this field include: above-average intelligence, aggressiveness, political savvy, and the right breaks. The most successful people are not necessarily the most creative, but a combination of these traits. There's a lot of compromise, and you have to have the ability to do this; an egomaniacal artist cannot survive—you have to let things go.

I was hired for my ability to translate strategies into a language that sells and says something that no one has ever said before. That's a skill—being able to reword the word; to think abstractly about a strategy you're given that's very straightforward; to be able to see the same thing in a number of different ways.

My production background has made me familiar with some of the techniques of film, music, videotape, and print. Another skill is knowing what directors, actors, musicians, and locations are right for an advertisement. The writer comes up with a script. But it's just paper. Unless you have the skill to make this abstract piece of paper come to life, via all these individuals involved, you'll have a pretty ordinary product.

Selling is an invaluable skill. It also helps to have good taste and an artistic touch. If you have an individual way of seeing things, you're golden.

I happen to respect my current boss tremendously. He is a great advertising person. He never loses sight of the fact that we are not here to create clever advertising, but rather to sell. He is a very solid thinker and his expectations are high. He is truly a professional. Personally we get along well. He's cynical, almost caustic. So am I at times. One thing that could make it better here for me is he could be better with his staff. His responsibility is to criticize and encourage work, which he does very well. But he should also be the first to reward his people. He should play his people up to the client, to agency management, and to guide their growth. He does not give the same thoroughness to this area as he does to supervising advertising. This is a common problem in dealing with supervisors in this business. One learns to always put one's work first. If you don't, you're out. It's difficult to change roles, to lay back, when you become a manager, and to put your people first.

I like this business so far. I would like to get a television campaign this year, maybe two. And I would like to see how far I can go in this business. It's worked out well for me. I really don't know enough to know if I'll be here for five more years. I've been fairly insulated from client contact and from upper-level agency management, so it could change dramatically. But it's been satisfying so far.

My original plans for the future changed when I left college. I really thought I'd be a copywriter two or three years ago, and that has set me back some. I also thought I'd be doing more comedy writing and performing, but this is a fairly grueling job. It shrinks your brain. And when you've been thinking of how to sell antiperspirants all day, it's pretty tough to wash it out of your mind and start writing something totally different.

Creative advertising can be a cheap thrill. It satisfies my need to create something, to see something of mine in print, to get recognition, and to be a show-off. In that respect, it's taken the place of any immediate need to be a comedian or a writer.

At first it was difficult to have a social life. I was put to work immediately. I was given six ads in about two months, which is a lot, and it was my first job. So I took a lot of it home because I wanted to do very well. I really gave myself to the job. It took four months to get into the rhythm of the work.

This job is rarely an after-five or weekend kind of job. So now it's generally pretty easy to balance personal and work life. The attitude concerning professionalism in this field is as high in the creative department as in any other business. But creative people are given a license. Their idiosyncrasies are allowed. It's a liberal atmosphere. It's actually part of the client show for creative people to be "creative" and eccentric. That's one of the reasons that I got into this. When I was in media, I had to keep myself under wraps during the day; here I don't have to. But you can only be weird here to a point. You have to relate to clients and make them feel comfortable.

Most of my friends are either artists, photographers, actors, writers, or models. We talk a lot about our jobs and we share a lot of the same acquaintances. It's very good in that way for me. I'm not alien to my friends at all, or they to me. We're all in creative environments.

A point of difference between advertising and other creative industries in town, like fashion, is that people in advertising are fairly unpretentious in the creative department. Many people here want to be artists or writers. You see a lot of double lives in this business, mostly from people who are not satisfied by creating advertising. Also, advertising is not as eccentric as the fashion community, or as decadent. You find a lot of married folks in this group with fairly mainstream American values not really too close to the edge.

Many people come into advertising expecting to create a work of art. However, there are a number of factors that do not allow one to write with the intelligence that one possesses. One is the American audience, which is pretty conservative. When you try something new, they're not always ready for it.

They're not able to understand that collection of images that you wish to put into their head. That in itself is a limit on how much you can do.

You also have clients who may not want to take risks. You are playing with other people's money here. And it is a lot of money to gamble with. That's frustrating at times. You are not here to be too eccentric, you are here to sell. The sooner you face that, the sooner you learn to love or hate this business.

Something to look forward to is a tremendous amount of compromise. This is a very subjective business. There are a number of ways to solve your marketing/advertising problem, and everyone has his or her own opinion—from your supervisor to your client—and an excellent idea could be squashed by about nine different people on its way. It can be very frustrating. You must be prepared to change some of your ideas.

Politics is something one should be aware of in this business. Politics are unavoidable anywhere, but I'm talking about dealing with people. There are some very large egos in this business. Competition is stiff. So if you want to succeed politically, you may have to take some pretty selfish measures. I've seen people fired from this business for not going along when they should have. Which is not to say that some did not get the job done. Probably that person had a problem politically. But, for the most part, people are pretty nice.

It really helps to have interpersonal skills. They are as important as creative skills, because you have to convince these egos that your idea is better than theirs. In a way, any job that involves selling is like copywriting. You have a product, and you have to sell it to people, which takes personal salesmanship. The more unique you can make your sales pitch to the people you're trying to sell your idea to, the better chance it will survive. This applies internally and to the writing of ads.

As for the creative end, copywriting is in a way very much like newswriting. Your aim is to find a unique point of view, an informational point of view. You're informing people of your product and that's somewhat like news. It's more persuasive, of course, but you are being informational.

Copywriting is also like filmwriting. The bulk of what we do at this agency is television commercials. You're visualizing a sales message. You want to make it dramatic. You want to make it humorous. You want to make it beautiful and persuasive. The language of commercial film is usually less sophisticated than motion picture film. I think that perhaps some television commercial experience is good for you if you feel like moving into film directing/writing.

Generally speaking, copywriting is a creative endeavor. This is a good place to flex your creative muscles. Working in advertising is not a hindrance to moving anywhere else, although I think advertising is looked down on by people in the arts.

If you are considering this type of work, talk to someone who really knows the business. Talk to someone who's been in it for a while. Ask them about the people involved, ask about the amount of work involved. See if it fits you. There's one thing to keep in mind. I haven't seen many older people in this business. Most of the writers are young. Unless you are a creative director or above, you usually don't stay past thirty-five. Where people go after that, I don't know.

Copywriting is opening up to new forms, because people are being educated through TV and film, but it's coming slowly. So if you're a great breakthrough artist with a great individual style, I would not recommend you pursue it. You can do great work in advertising, but advertising is rarely in the forefront of art. Your point of view must appeal across the board—to everyone in America—and it must be simple. That puts a strain on how creative and how satisfying this job can be.

My advice, if you really want to get into this business, is to get a good book together. Take a class in copywriting that is oriented toward making a book. Get three campaigns with three ads each and get about five more ads that are very good, solid, simple ideas. Get contacts—it is tough getting a job in this business if you don't know anyone. People have to take a chance on you. In tight economic times, people aren't always ready to do that.

In getting your book together, be wild. There's a lack of new ideas in this business. I did some wild new stuff in my book, and it came off well. It was conceptually solid. I think it gave me this job. It's much easier to be wild and have them pull you back than not to be wild and have to stretch yourself once you get into this business. And that's probably as wild as you'll get until you can flex your political muscles enough to push something fun through.

I like the people in this business; they're fairly interesting and fun. I've made some good contacts that could be useful if I decide to pursue other creative endeavors like writing for TV or film, or directing.

The money isn't bad. If you handle your career well and get a few breaks, you can make a good living. I like the challenge of trying to condense an endless stream of information into a headline or a television commercial. And I like coming up with ideas and ways of saying things that no one has ever said before. The general atmosphere of this business is liberal, fun, and weirded out. I like the fact that I can apply everything I've learned about music, film, acting, and writing at something. And I like the recognition I get for my work. It's satisfying to see what you've done in print or on television.

~~~ WILLIAM YOUMANS

ACTOR

At the time of this interview, William had had ten jobs in three years, which is not unusual for full-time actors and actresses. His experience has ranged from regional theater productions to Broadway and film. His acting jobs depend on his agent arranging auditions, and his skill and ability in auditioning well. When not working, he has spent most of his time working on new audition material, contacting theaters, and attending acting classes.

HERE ARE THREE TYPICAL DAYS in the life of an actor. The first typical day is the day of unemployment, a day that you spend looking for jobs. This is done in a variety of ways. If you have an agent, you see if there are any interviews or auditions that day; you work on new audition material; you buy the trade newspapers and go around auditioning for jobs listed; you call people you know; you make the rounds to the theaters you know; you write letters reminding people of yourself; you have your picture taken. You can also go to acting classes and meet people there, or singing lessons and other things.

When you have a job, it is another typical day. This is one of rehearsals, which starts usually anywhere from 10:00 A.M. to noon and goes until 7:00 to 8:00 P.M., at which time you are rehearsing the play that you are doing with your directors. You utilize whatever skills are necessary for the play. In the play I am doing now, I am mainly using my acting skills. In another play, I may utilize dance, gymnastics, singing—all kinds of things. Some of the pressures in a typical day of rehearsing are coming into rehearsal with a certain level of worth. That is to say that you have to come into rehearsal and be good, and you have to have a certain degree of proficiency at your craft and have done your homework on the play. Every day you are under this pressure to make progress, and this is a heavy pressure.

Every time you are up in front of the director, he or she is thinking, all the time, "Is this person going to be able to achieve this role by the time we have to open the curtain on opening night?", which makes for a tremendously pressure-filled job from start to finish. From the auditioning phase and rehearsal phase, and all the way to performance, the pressure only lets up well after you are into the performance.

Work setting can be anything from a basement to a garage to a studio or someone's living room. When you go into performing, it is usually in a theater, but not always. Sometimes you work on the street or in private homes.

Hours per week vary from two hours to ten hours a day. The colleagues you work with in rehearsal are your fellow actors. Usually everyone gets along pretty well, and everyone feels good in the cast. There is usually a lot of competition and a lot of judging of other people's work and your own work—trying to measure up. You do the things you have to do in acting. These are also part of the pressures of the job.

The day of the performance is the third typical day. You really don't do much during the day; you tend to sleep late and then go in around 6:00 P.M. and do the play, and you usually retire to some bar afterward and try to relax because you need to unwind after the pressure.

I would say that you really need to be personable. You need to be able to walk into an office and make an impression on people, and you need to have ambition. If you have any doubts about acting, then you have to get out of the business. You must want this more than anything in the world and have a burning desire to get in front of the camera, and you must know that you can do it. When you walk in for an audition, you should know that you can do this part better than anyone else. That is not really an ego thing because it does not come across that you are stuck-up, but rather that you are confident and assertive. These are the qualities you need when you are on stage. You have to command the attention of an entire house of potentially bored people, and they're going to be looking for someone who can do that. If you walk into an audition apologizing for yourself and acting kind of wimpy, they are not going to be interested. If you are not sure if you want to be an actor, then don't be an actor.

There are a lot of skills involved. The main skill—and the better you are at this the more jobs you will get—is just to be able to simply talk the lines of a script. It is surprising how few actors can really do this. This is the main skill—all others are secondary. Other skills range from tap-dancing and singing to speech and movement training. This depends on the types of roles you wish to play. For example, you may need to use driving for some roles. The ability to act believably is something you have to keep working on all your life as an actor.

The best part about acting is that you grow as a person. Hopefully, you keep working and trying to grow. Sometimes it can be painful if you are not as good as you would like to be or not satisfied with your work, but the show must go on. Another bad part is that you are sort of at the mercy of the director: This again depends on personal skill as an actor. Many times, personality conflicts happen; they can be very detrimental to your work and your sense of yourself. You are very vulnerable on stage, and it is very easy to tear an actor down.

Another skill to possess is the ability to grow from criticism. The wisdom to know the people to listen to and not to listen to. That is a personal quality that you must have as you begin working. Another personal quality is to be able to make anything work. That is to say, if you are working with someone who is a real pain, you have to be able to adapt, without editing yourself. You have to be assertive and not let people trample over you but, in turn, not override the other person. You have to adjust. The job of an actor is unpredictable.

I would say that more and more you get a sense of how difficult it is to act—the more you act, the more you realize that you don't know anything—and that motivates you to do more ambitious material. There are always new fields to explore. I have not done much film work and would like to do more.

What motivates me is the constant desire to do better, to be able to do more things, to be able to expand my range, to be able to portray more colors and present more emotions, and bring more of myself into the work, and to develop more and more of an ease and reality. Those are the things you constantly work on as an actor. You can never get to the point of saying that you have achieved everything.

There is always new input, new angles. For example, you can be working on one play for more than a year and find that there are new approaches to a scene and different approaches to a character.

In the last three years, I have had ten jobs. I have had jobs in three basic categories: regional theater, Broadway, and film. The regional theater jobs are when you go out of town and do plays that have been done already and stay for ten weeks or so and then return unemployed again. I did a Mark Twain film for PBS that failed. This you do bit by bit for the camera. That was seven weeks of work in Pennsylvania. Then it was on to *A Bunch of Boys*. That was more highly paid and was done in New York. The Broadway play I did was

The Little Foxes with Elizabeth Taylor. We toured it for a week on Broadway and then brought it to New Orleans, Los Angeles, and London. That was very fascinating. Again, I think it should be said that the moment-to-moment relating on stage, the quality of acting, is the same in all three types of roles.

I chose a larger agency when I first came to New York. I had another offer from a very small agent who offered to work with me. That is really the only decision I've made. I think it should be said that until you get established as an actor, you really don't have any decisions to make at all—you take what comes along. On average, most actors work one-tenth of their time; the rest is spent out of work. I have been very lucky that I am not a typical case. I have had the opportunity to work a great deal of time. I was out of work for four months at one time and two months at another. Other than that, I have been quite lucky—not only lucky, it has to do with a desire and ability to audition well. Usually, I can audition quite well.

The main thing that has helped my career is my agent. They send me out on a lot of good auditions. The things that have hindered it have been my own failures as an actor. If you don't measure up all the time—which you can't always do—it hinders your career. People are hesitant to work with you again. On the other hand, I have also been good, and people remember.

All the training you can get is beneficial. If you want to do just television work, you really don't need too much training. If you want to expand yourself, then you need a good deal of advanced training. You may need things like speech and advanced acting classes. Most actors are constantly going back to acting class workshops. There they can do things that they might not be able to do in the professional theater. All the great British actors have had advanced training, which is just beginning to catch on in America. There is always a certain amount of training for an actor, no matter how good you are. Most people think acting does not take much skill, but that is beginning to change. More and more in this country, actors are beginning to be trained in the basic skill of acting. Casting directors and others look at your résumé for formal training. You can get by, but it is better to have advanced training. There are exceptions, but they are very rare. Most actors will always benefit from training. Fortunately, I have had good training. I had a brilliant acting teacher. There have been times when I failed to come across. These are the only things that help or hinder an actor that I can see, from the point of view of a young actor.

It is very difficult for a young actor to make career plans. You are at the mercy of what comes your way. I would say that I would like to do more regional plays and could say to my agent that I want to be set up for these particular roles. They, in turn, might say, "Let's try for soap operas because we make more money that way off of you." Then I would have to make a decision about whether to go along with that or change agents. It is very fortunate to have any agent at all. Many young actors do not. As you become more known in the business, then you have more and more options at your disposal.

I would like to do more movies, and regional theater, but I really would not want to do anything differently. I am really quite happy. I would like to work at different theaters. I would not want to move. One decision you could make as an actor is whether to move to Los Angeles and try to be in the television world or movie world or decide to be in New York. For me, the right choice has been to stay in New York.

Personally, I do not see any real plans in my life. I do not plan to get married for quite some time. The compromises that you have to make in your career with family and marriage can change your career quickly.

What has personally hindered me is my absentmindedness. If you forget to call your agent for auditions, then you miss auditions. I personally missed a role in a major film. That mistake has hindered my career. I am constantly doing that sort of thing, because I can be an absentminded fool!

~~~ CHRISTIAN WILLIAMS

WRITER/JOURNALIST

Christian's first assignment as a journalist was writing the daily obituaries for a New Jersey newspaper. At the time of this interview, he was working for the Washington Post as a staff writer for the Style section, and was an assignment editor at the Post during Watergate. He has been nominated by the Post for a Pulitzer Prize and has written and published several independent projects. He has also been the East Coast movie critic for a twenty-four-hour-a-day cable television news network.

MY FIRST JOB AS A REPORTER was at the *Elizabeth Daily Journal*, out of Elizabeth, New Jersey. I was hired without any experience, with a bachelor's degree in English, on the basis of a sheaf of poems, which I innocently presented to the editor. A lucky accident! I spent one year learning to write obituaries. It took me the entire year before I could understand what was required in an obituary. Each week, I despaired of ever learning how to write a simple obituary, which is a very brief and seemingly innocent and easy assignment. But, indeed, it was a year before I could do it to the city editor's satisfaction. I was made to start off writing obituaries because the need for accuracy is so high. To make a mistake in the time or place of the funeral is to cause two hundred people, all of whom are upset by the death, to go to the wrong place at the wrong time. One such mistake drives home forever the importance of getting the minor facts right.

I worked in that job for about eighteen months, saved up some money, and quit and went off for a year in North Africa and Spain. While abroad, I took notes and wrote short stories, and filed articles for the *Journal* and for a few magazines. After exhausting all my savings, I returned to the paper, where I was made a political writer and, two years later, chief political writer, covering Union County and the city government. I later got in a disagreement with the manager of the paper over some stories I was writing and quit. I spent the next year writing a novel and working in a welding job. The novel has not been published because, frankly, it isn't any good. However, writing the novel taught me to write well enough to be worth some money to newspapers.

While waiting to be hired for a teaching job in the Virgin Islands, I accepted a job in Camden, New Jersey, as an early morning rewrite man for the Camden *Courier Post*. I actually turned down the Virgin Islands job to go to Camden and work for $85 a week! After I had been in Camden as a reporter for about six months, they made me the editor of the magazine, and within a year I became the metropolitan editor. Among other things, I organized an investigative team and founded a consumer page for the paper. I then decided I should work for a larger paper and went to the *Washington Post* as an editor in the Style section. At the *Post*, I was an assignment editor during Watergate. I was later named arts editor, and then deputy editor of the Style section. After that, I took a year's leave of absence to write a biography of Ted Turner under the title *Lead, Follow or Get Out of the Way*. I returned to the *Post* as a staff writer in Style, and I am expecting to go off on another leave of absence, eventually, to complete a novel now under contract.

I am also the East Coast movie critic for a twenty-four-hour-a-day cable television news network.

I have an area of specialization at the *Post*, which is called "general assignment" in the Style section. The idea of the Style section is to cover the way people live, and that means a wide variety of assignments, half of which come from my editors and half of which are made up by me. Recently, I did a very long series on a man who was imprisoned wrongly for twenty-five years for a crime he didn't commit. For this revelation about the way the American courts and prison systems work, I was nominated for a Pulitzer Prize by the paper. Some of the other things I have been doing are quite different—a long essay on overeating, for example, and interviews with movie stars like Karen Allen when she was in *Raiders of the Lost Ark*, and Kathleen Turner of *Body Heat*. I try to do a piece or two a week to fulfill my obligation to write readable interviews and profiles and entertainment pieces for the Sunday paper and the daily paper.

Most of the responsibility I feel is individual responsibility: Get it right, don't twist things too much out of proportion, and try to reflect the way things are—perhaps the strange way they are, but, nevertheless, the way they are. My duties are merely to research and write well.

There is no typical day. For the most part, it's something along the lines of 10:00 A.M. to 10:00 P.M. The *Washington Post* is probably not unlike any big-city organization, filled with talented people, all of them trying to do well. There is a sense of togetherness on a newspaper because everyone has to work to put out a product every day; but there is also inevitably a feeling of protecting oneself, one's hope, one's space. And certainly there is the necessity not to get too much sleep—otherwise, the others will get ahead of you. It's often said that the *Post* is like an aircraft carrier staffed entirely with lieutenant commanders. This is a condition that you put up with as a matter of course. Ben Bradlee's phrase "creative tension," used to describe the atmosphere that is appropriate in order to get everybody working at his or her best, is pretty accurate.

The best thing about my current position is that it allows me to do what I do in a way that will be noticed by a lot of people. I think anybody who wants to be a newspaper writer will have a hard time finding anything wrong with being a newspaper writer for the *Washington Post* or the *New York Times*.

The kind of person who tends to do well in journalism is a person who is extremely interested in being noticed and has the skills to make him or her worthy of notice. All the reporters I know are very smart; they have gone to the best colleges; they have high IQs; and they have the ability to survive in a multitude of environments. They go from lunch with fighter pilots one day to dinner with the vegetarian caucus the next, and come away from both experiences fascinated and with strong opinions. Reporters ask questions. They are naturally inquisitive people, and I dare say that one of the most appalling qualities of *the Washington Post* or any other newspaper is that the level of gossip is extraordinarily high. Gossip and inquisitive personalities go together.

I think journalistic skills don't come from schools. The educational background of successful people is very varied. Some of the best reporters were mathematics majors or political science majors. We don't have that many journalism majors. A reporter has to be able to think very quickly, and he or she has to be able to type and to get answers to good questions. The motivation for all this is probably some personal interest in having issues noticed and knowing the motivation of the people who get things done in this society. Most newspaper stories are about things that happen. They're not particularly intellectual, but rather a study of the behavior of society.

Journalism is a great springboard. Particularly for somebody unsure of a career, journalism should be a first consideration. Just out of college, perhaps somewhat at sea about what to do next, you can get a job for a weekly, and you really don't need any prior experience to start working for the paper. There is nothing bad about it; it's just that it's very competitive, and I think individuals will quickly find out from experience whether or not they are going to be any good at it. It's not complicated. If you are good at it, it shows right away. The chances of getting to a good paper eventually are good if you are good. But, again, if you can't do it, you will be able to find that out very quickly. Opportunities are probably better than most people think.

Most changes in my career were based on a feeling that the more you do, the more fun you have. The writer's world is essentially bordered by his or her own perceptions of it; a writer is hindered only by self-doubt.

If you want to be the editor of the newspaper, there is a clear-cut career path. You must get three to five years of reporting experience, then immediately become some type of editor, the top person, in some very small paper. It could be a weekly. It could be a small daily in the Midwest or at some resort community. You must try to move in increments every year to a slightly larger paper. You try to make the paper you are running win prizes and try to be noticed, and you travel around and flex your intellectual muscles. Pretty soon, the Gannett chain says they are going to buy a chain in South Succotash and they would like you to run it. That's the track for people who want to run their own newspaper. There are a lot of newspapers in this country needing a lot of editors.

For writers, the career path is to pick an area of specialization, such as politics or the arts or interviews, and to start off on a newspaper that will at least allow you to pay your rent while you develop skills, make contacts, and figure out what life is all about. You then write for as large a paper as you can find so that your work will be noticed by agents in New York City. At the same time, you try to get some books and magazine articles written between the hours of midnight and 6:00 A.M., or on Saturday and Sunday evenings. It's very clear that if you are going to be successful in terms of making money, you are going to have to spend a lot of time writing. You are going to have to write for a variety of publications. In this way, you will be noticed and people will buy your books.

Moving out of journalism to a closely related career field is always easy. The easiest thing in the world to be is a former journalist. I think that journalists and journalism students can always look sideways to public relations or management or small business operations.

Writers don't necessarily plan their careers, but what they must confront is the necessity to be in the place where something of interest is going to happen. I will always try to be in a place where I can observe the raw material that might make useful books, articles, and stories. In other words, if you are a political reporter, you had better get yourself to the Middle East, Northern Ireland, or Central America to find out what it looks like and what it smells like, and to be there when something happens so that you'll be able to help interpret it.

While the demands on one's time are either overwhelming or nonexistent, you somehow figure it out. I suppose that one's life is at the same time all work and at the same time no work. It has to be fun if you are going to be engaged in the business of writing. The world has to appeal to you in all of its forms: personal, social, family, and community. You don't see these forms as demands but as things to be observed. That doesn't mean you know how they work; it just means that they always need to be observed and written about. I generally wake up at 5:45 A.M., work three hours on my novel, then work for the *Washington Post* all day. In the evenings, I go to the movies; and somewhere along the line, I find time to write a script so that I can tape my weekly television programs in advance. On the weekends, I like to race sailboats in Annapolis. There isn't much time to complain about not having much time.

If you are working in Washington, D.C., salary is a problem. I have two children in private school, and I find it very difficult to support myself in the style to which I would like to become accustomed. But, of course, it's not the money, it's the life. It's a very stimulating, exciting, challenging, somewhat crazy, but altogether entertaining way to go through your years, and all you need to start is a pencil and a piece of paper.

▰▰▰ CUYLER M. OVERHOLT

ATTORNEY

At the time of this interview, Cuyler was a third-year associate in a small-city law firm, with full responsibility for all phases of the litigation process. Her notions of a career upon graduation from law school were vague. In this position, she encountered new clients each week from all walks of life with new, thought-provoking legal issues. She had soon decided to retire from the practice of law to pursue a writing career.

COLLEGE GRADUATES HAVE FLOCKED to law schools in record numbers in recent years, despite pessimistic employment predictions and the public's palpable distrust of lawyers. I rode the crest of the law-school wave into a job with a private law firm, and after working for brief stints in the corporate and probate departments, decided to specialize in litigation.

Unlike colleagues in other departments who put together businesses, advise on tax matters, or offer other constructive advice, litigators take over when something has gone wrong. They handle all cases that go to court for resolution and are versed in the special procedural rules that govern the presentation of facts and legal argument to a judge or jury.

As a third-year associate in a small-city law firm, I now have full responsibility for all phases of the litigation process. I meet with clients to solicit crucial facts about a case; prepare written "pleadings" that articulate the client's claims or defenses; research and prepare written memoranda and present oral arguments addressing the legal sufficiency of my client's claims or the insufficiency of his opponent's; gather witnesses and tangible evidence to support each factual allegation; and finally, present the evidence to a judge or jury in court. My cases cover areas of contract, personal injury, bankruptcy, note collections, mortgage and mechanic's lien foreclosures, municipal zoning and tax appeals, landlord-tenant disputes, and criminal matters.

Since the cost of going to trial can be high, and since the outcome is never certain, part of a litigator's job is to constantly assess the possibility of working out a voluntary settlement between the parties to the lawsuit. The litigator evaluates the strength of the client's case and attempts to persuade the adversary, and sometimes the client, to reach a satisfactory compromise.

The qualities that make a good litigator are as diverse as the litigator's tasks. An ability to distill essential information from the client's effusive and often emotional outpourings is key, as is a talent for controlling the client without alienating him or her. Since litigation is an adversarial business, a faculty for engaging in and even enjoying confrontation is a tremendous asset, as long as it is tempered by a willingness to listen and compromise. Some of the most effective attorneys also possess large measures of warmth and wit that, once outside their adversarial role, they bestow generously upon their colleagues. Also, a healthy respect for authority figures comes in handy in judge-attorney interactions, although controlled aggression is not necessarily out of place in the courtroom.

But the ability to conceptualize, confront, and compromise alone do not make a good advocate. The cornerstone of effective lawyering is exhaustive research. Most of an associate's early years are spent in the library, finding, reading, and updating court decisions and legal treatises that bear on various cases. Attention to factual detail is essential and often means the difference between winning or losing a case. Of course, writing and speaking skills are also critical, and conciseness is prized.

Blessed with these personal traits and skills, a lawyer can expect to encounter success. Enjoying the process is an individual matter, although certain aspects of the job seem to have universal appeal. Unlike many occupations, litigation offers tremendous diversity. Every week, I encounter new clients from all walks of life and new, thought-provoking legal issues. As I familiarize myself with the problems of clients ranging from auto mechanics to architects, my expertise expands accordingly. I derive tremendous satisfaction from successfully representing people who have reposed their trust in me. I enjoy being my own boss, developing my own case strategies, and arranging my own time schedule; and I find the adrenaline rush of court appearances exhilarating.

On the flip side, the influx of new and unexpected problems occasionally reaches crisis proportions, and I am forced to handle some matters within very limited time and with little information at hand. For someone trained in thoroughness, this can be both frustrating and anxiety provoking. So can a judge's ill-reasoned refusal to accept a sound legal argument; although appeal is always a theoretical possibility, the expense is often prohibitive, and the decision of the all-too-human and fallible trial judge is usually final. Client dissatisfaction with flaws in the legal system is often vented on the attorney, and the public perception of attorneys' fees as exorbitant can create tension in the attorney-client relationship.

A young associate faces a particular set of problems. Long hours of hard work under high pressure may produce reams of material yet very little feedback from the members of the firm. Too much responsibility may be given too soon, or too little too late, depending on the size, sophistication, and client base of the firm. Because the work is so demanding, it requires a concerted effort to "leave it at the office" and to enjoy personal time. The prospect of working for five to ten years as a salaried associate in the hope of being made a partner, without any promise or commitment from the firm, can also have a chilling effect. To be sure, the salary will be handsome and life's luxuries affordable, even if the attorney has little time to enjoy them.

In my three years in the work world, I have overcome some fairly large internal obstacles and achieved a degree of success. My notions of a career were vague upon graduation from college. My concept of the world of work was based largely, and mistakenly, on the world of academia, where expectations are understood and work is always rewarded. My decision to become a lawyer was based on a desire to be self-sufficient rather than simply on ambition.

As a trial attorney, I had to overcome fear of failure in all its forms; fear of not knowing, fear of not comprehending, fear of not caring. I had to work through clients' skepticism toward novice attorneys and judges' preconceptions about women. I learned to play a role—to suppress my own personality and convictions and be, first and foremost, my client's champion. My success in these endeavors has secured both my position in the firm and a great deal of self-respect. I now know that I can do it. Finally, I am asking myself, Do I want to do it?, and the answer is no. Sensing an urge to create, and unwilling to give up the dream of self-actualization, I am retiring from the practice of law at the ripe old age of twenty-eight to embark on a writing career.

My idea is to write magazine articles and nonfiction books. I don't regret my legal experience for a minute—it has given me a broad base of general knowledge useful in living and writing. I enjoyed my visit to the world of law and order but simply do not choose to live there. I confess to a feeling of being reborn—of finally finding where my true interest lies. I look forward to injecting my writing with the idiosyncratic perceptions and reactions so out of place in attorneys' work.

I see tremendous challenges ahead and new inner fears to conquer. Overall, I couldn't be more delighted.

▨▨▨ PAGE GOOLRICK

ARCHITECT

At the time of this interview, Page was a partner at a small architectural firm in New York that has specialized in residential work. After working for architectural firms in San Francisco and New York, she formed her own company in 1988 and formed a partnership in 1992.

OST ARCHITECTS I WOULD SAY, or a great number of them, are exposed to it at a very early age—either from having a family in architecture or an acquaintance in the business. I was actually a math major. I had an aptitude for math and an interest in art when I first went to college. Everyone in my family besides myself is a writer and wanted me to be a journalist or a freelance writer or editor. I switched over from math to English because math wasn't just fun for me and I really enjoy writing.

In my second year of school, I took an architectural appreciation course, and, frankly, I took it on a whim and to fill out my curriculum. And I loved it; we saw lots of slides and talked a lot about buildings all around the world and the sort of cultural and social political aspects that shape them. It was the first thing that I'd ever thought of that I wouldn't mind doing forty or fifty hours a week for the rest of my life.

I ended up finishing my English degree, but doing a number of independent studies. I was at the University of Connecticut and there's no architectural course there, but I had put together preparation for a master's in architecture. I took courses in calculus and advanced geometry, along with a number of art courses. There was one architect there who was teaching a few courses, and I did several independent studies with him so that when I finished school, I would be able to get into an architectural program. Graduate school for me was a three-year program because my undergraduate degree was not in architecture.

After graduation, I went to a seminar in San Francisco on multifamily housing, which I was very interested in. I left résumés in San Francisco, then came to New York and left résumés here. I was very fortunate that at the time, things were bustling, so I had offers on both coasts. I decided to go to San Francisco because it was so idyllic. I was there for four years.

I worked for a large firm for one year and then about two and a half years for a smaller firm. I left the large firm because I was sort of pigeonholed as a designer. I had a wonderful time, but I didn't learn enough about the whole process of putting buildings together. It was sort of an elitist approach to architecture because we weren't working in certain studios.

I wanted to design and to be involved in the construction of the buildings. The firm I went to after that was a medium-sized firm, but they were still working on very large projects. I was able to take them for the most part all the way through. And then I spent six months working on a freelance project, a house that I renovated, before moving to New York to work for an even smaller firm. After two and a half years, I was ready to really run things on my own.

There are a couple of different routes you can take in this business. If you do intend to have your own practice, it is a good idea to get into a small firm fairly quickly. The corporate experience is valuable because it is very good to know how to run a larger job and then bring some of the knowledge to a smaller project.

Some people take a different route and want to take part in bigger projects and travel and work with bigger budgets and bigger square footage, more prestigious projects. So they might take a corporate route and work in a large firm for a long time, with no intention of opening their own firm.

It was a little intimidating, at first, to be on my own. When I got out, there were very few women in the field. It was probably 20 percent. Now, it's more like 40 percent. It is also interesting that I find women on every new construction site. You have to prove yourself in terms of knowledge a little more than a man would; I don't think you are as easily accepted. The trades by and large are waiting to see if you know what you are talking about. Once you prove yourself it's okay, but I do feel that, unfortunately, there is a testing period on every single job.

There was an article in the *Wall Street Journal* a number of years ago saying that architects make more decisions in an average day than people in any other profession. The combination of decisions about budget, construction, and people needs, materials, detailing—you have to have agreement like a matrix so that every decision you make keeps all those things in line, and that's part of what makes it fun.

We're getting involved in product development because we would like to have something in addition to a service fee. We don't do much selling of furniture to our clients; we use interior designers or decorators for that, but we're really involved in construction and design.

You begin to think how everything functions—whether it's a building or a coffee cup or a salt shaker. Everything we use is made by a series of decisions by someone. People don't see that, and take it for granted, but there are a lot of things out there that could be a little simpler, better, or a little more beautiful without necessarily costing more.

I love what I do and feel very spoiled being able to support myself doing something that is delightful for me, being able to think about how things are put together and how people will use them—behavioral aspects, aesthetic aspects—and being able to sit around and make those decisions and educate people about the potential of architecture to make their lives better. I really love what I do.

It is not as lucrative as it might be. Architects go to school for the same length of time as lawyers and doctors. We go though an internship program before we are able to take exams to be licensed. It is a very rigorous examination process—three eight-hour days and a twelve-hour day exam. We pay large fees to be registered in various states and to other organizations in order to show that we are accredited, and then we also carry liability insurance.

Yet we do not make the kind of money that lawyers and doctors make. In part, it's because we're not seen as essential by the whole community, by all of society, as lawyers and doctors are. We find we spend a fair amount of time as part of the education process with clients, informing them about what we can provide in terms of technical and aesthetic qualities. That's a bit of a problem; I feel as if I work with clients that have a great deal of money and yet I'm not as well off as I'd like to be.

I should mention that to some, architecture is prestigious, sort of an elegant, elitist old-boy's profession. A good number of people who go into it have money of their own and don't need to rely on it as their sole means of support. They can pay to have a speculative house built appropriate for magazine publication and further their career by doing that. But my partner and I and the people who work for us—none of us is independently wealthy. At times, it's marvelous and at times it's very scary.

I don't know how to say all that without turning someone off. That was never a concern for me when I was in school because my family were writers and artists. So the lack of security never deterred me, but I do wish I'd had a better sense of what it would be like. I'm thirty-nine and most of my friends are beginning to own homes now, and that's not a possibility for me.

Because it is a service industry, you will never make the kind of money that someone would, for example, in the stock market or real estate or something where there might be a windfall. Every hour that you fill is an hour you worked. Our fees are typically based on a percentage of the cost of construction, so certainly on a larger job we do get a higher fee, but I think it can be a bit of a struggle. I love it, but particularly with residential work, there is a lot of hand-holding with the client. The great level of detail is such that you often work a number of hours that you are not able to bill.

The marketing is in the development, and even when we have a project, we often work many more hours than we are able to bill because we put a cap on our fees, again related to the percentage of construction. But if we want something to be really beautiful and very well thought out, we will spend a lot of time working on the details. Clients might not even understand until they see how wonderful the pieces came to a corner or a special window in a house.

Anyone who really loves architecture and is really committed ought to go into it. Anyone who is choosing architecture because it might be prestigious or fun or just attractive in sort of a superficial sense ought to think twice about it, and anyone who wants to make a quarter of a million dollars ought not go into it at all.

~~~ GLENN MILLER

ADVERTISING EXECUTIVE

At the time of this interview, Glenn was the senior creative director and senior vice president for a prominent advertising agency in the New York metropolitan area. He was also a law school graduate and worked for one year as an administrative legal assistant.

I graduated from law school and worked for a year as an administrative legal assistant to a New Jersey Superior Court judge. I then worked for about six months for a small law firm and found that I hated being a lawyer. I have always been fascinated by advertising. I thought I had the talent for it and could do it well and enjoy doing it. So I left the law and took a job as a junior copywriter with my present agency. I was promoted shortly thereafter to copywriter, then to creative supervisor, and most recently to associate creative director and senior vice president. I am presently a senior creative director and senior vice president.

I am currently responsible for creating, and supervising the creation of, print, television, and radio advertising for clients that include Gillette, Hellmann's, and Lever Brothers. There are five creative people—writers and art directors—in my group.

We develop, along with the agency account management team and the client, the advertising strategy for each product and service. We then present a range of advertising ideas to communicate that strategy, and follow to production the idea chosen, whether it be television, radio, or print. All this requires a range of skills: creative, of course, but also managerial, diplomatic, marketing, administrative, and a little bit of show business instinct.

A typical day might include meeting with one or more account management people to discuss strategy or go over creative work in progress; a meeting with my boss, the executive creative director, to brief him on creative projects; a discussion with one of the agency's TV producers about an upcoming commercial shooting; and a session with the art director to create an advertising campaign for a new product.

Because of the number of projects in progress and the deadlines we face, the work schedule can get hectic and the hours long. But, as in any business, there are peaks of frenzied activity and valleys of more relaxed work. My hours in the office range from forty to fifty per week, and I spend a lot of time conceptualizing on weekends and on my four-hour daily commute.

The best parts of my job are the salary, the opportunity to do work I am good at and enjoy, the chance to work with some of the most interesting, intelligent, sophisticated, and funny people in the business world, and the chance to move quickly in title, salary, and benefits. One of the worst parts of my job is being forced to assume more administrative and managerial functions, which leaves less time for creating advertising. The creative field is not the most secure—a creative person's professional life span is notoriously short. And the old saying "You're only as good as your last idea" is true to a great extent. Also, some clients can be very difficult. In a large agency and for a large client, there are many layers of management that a piece of creative work must go through. Sometimes it's a frustrating process to see ideas changed or killed by a committee. Finally, there are often great time pressures, which can lessen the quality of work done.

All types of people have done well in advertising. There is really no particular kind of personality, training, or educational background that makes a successful agency creative person. If you want to be an art director or TV producer, there are, of course, certain design and technical skills that are helpful. But writers come from all backgrounds—from high school dropouts to Ph.D.s, from ex-cab drivers to ex-lawyers. People come into advertising with degrees in everything from journalism to zoology. The only thing really necessary is the basic talent to sell a product or service in a unique and memorable way, and the ability to do it over and over again, often on short notice. It helps to be culturally astute, patient, hardworking, and able to keep successes and failures, highs and lows, in perspective.

If you really have the aptitude for it and are willing to suffer through what can be a very difficult time of breaking into the business, it is a career that can be very rewarding, both monetarily and personally. Plus, it's just great fun! For someone who has the talent, creating consistently good advertising is no mysterious or complicated process. It really boils down to "Hey, I can write a better commercial than that!"

Opportunities in the field are limited at all times, but especially in times of economic slump. The advertising business has always been somewhat of a closed fraternity—few agencies actively solicit new creative talent from outside the business. It requires patience, aggressiveness, and perseverance for the inexperienced job seeker to get that first break.

My work requires the ability to compromise when necessary. It takes a sense of humor. I must get along well with all types of people—a process in which my communication skills have helped. High-level creative management positions are relatively few, but there is a fairly clear career path to the top. Job hopping is common—not necessarily for better positions, but for a salary increase or better accounts or an improved creative environment. Movement to other fields is relatively easy, although a number of jobs may not be as interesting or pay as well as advertising, such as product managers, advertising directors, public relations or product promoters, or film directors or producers, or creative consultants for manufacturers.

I will most likely stay in advertising for the next several years, but I will also be exploring other fields that offer new and different creative challenges.

～～～ Some Things to Think About...

Now that have an understanding of Artistic careers, here are some things to consider.

1. What insights about Investigative occupations have you gained from these interviews?

_____

_____

_____

2. Which characteristics, abilities, and personal qualities discussed in the interviews are similar to your own? Which are different or in contrast to your own? How might the similarities or differences affect your satisfaction with your possible career choices?

_____

_____

_____

3. Ask yourself the following:

* Are you imaginative? Are you creative? _____

* Could you handle personal rejection?_____

* Do you need to derive a sense of meaning from your work?_____

* Are you comfortable with a lack of structure and a relaxed environment?

_____

* Do you seek constant change and variety? _____

* Are you flexible about your work hours and schedule?_____

* Do you have some sort of artistic talent—painting, drawing, writing, dancing, designing, thinking creatively? _____

* Do you like working independently? _____

How might your responses to these questions suggest satisfaction with an Artistic career choice? _____

4. Which interviews held your interest? Why? _____

_____

5. Which interviews were not what you expected? Why? _____

_____

6. Which occupations are you going to investigate further? How?

_____

_____

_____

_____

CHAPTER FIVE

Find Fulfillment in a Social Career

DID YOU ONCE HAVE DREAMS of following in the footsteps of Mrs. Applebee, your first-grade teacher? Are you the one your friends always come to for advice and comfort when they are experiencing problems in their lives? Is joining the Peace Corps something you have seriously considered?

If your answer is yes to any of these questions, you may have a future in a Social career. Read on, other people may be counting on you!

~ ~ ~ What Are These Careers and Where Can I Find Them?

Social work environments tend to be congenial and harmonious and are generally devoid of conflict, rigidity, and negativity. The opportunity to inform, train, develop, cure, or enlighten others as well as work on teams to solve people-related issues is central to Social careers. Typically, Social occupations are those related to education, social welfare/service, leisure/hospitality, and health care.

Because they are so adaptable, Social people work well in a wide variety of settings. Many educational and social service opportunities are available in government and nonprofit organizations. At the same time, more Social opportunities are opening up in businesses, as companies assume more responsibility for their employees' needs. Human resources, career development, employee counseling, and employee health and recreation are some areas that might entice Social types to business and industry. Most importantly, Social people need to feel they are making a contribution by serving others or forwarding ideas that support the common good. A sample of many Social job titles include those listed in table 5 below. For a more complete listing of Social careers, consult *The Dictionary of Holland Occupational Codes* or the appendix.

TABLE 5
EXAMPLES OF SOCIAL CAREERS

School administrator	Nurse	Mental health counselor
Guidance counselor	Minister	Social worker
Occupational therapist	Priest	Recreation leader
Physical therapist	Rabbi	Child care provider
Social science teacher	Physical education teacher	Athletic trainer
Employment interviewer	School superintendent	Parks and recreation coordinator
Job development specialist	Political scientist	Dietitian
Elementary school teacher	Speech pathologist	Food & drug inspector
Foreign language teacher	Special education teacher	School psychologist
Psychiatric technician	Guidance counselor	

Often, Social people are attracted to careers such as nursing and physical therapy because of the direct patient contact and care required. A health care career can be a natural fit for a Social individual who has an affinity for the sciences. Social people often find fulfillment in helping others and have a preference for working with those in need.

〜〜〜 Who Are These People and Am I One of Them?

What types of people are attracted to and do well in the Social occupations? What are their characteristics, values, and interests?

Thoughts of Mother Theresa or other more talkative, selfless martyrs may come to mind when envisioning a Social person. Although some Social people are not all sweetness and light, most are well described by the cluster's name and its connotations. They tend to be social and sociable in all respects: friendly, outgoing, eager to extend themselves to others. They are not always the loudest or most gregarious of people, but are usually the most empathetic and tend to be the best listeners. Social people can have a quiet and reflective side. They are usually introspective about their own well-being and needs and often make taking care of themselves a priority as well.

Generally, Social individuals perceive themselves as enjoying helping people, understanding others' needs, and having teaching abilities. They tend to have strong verbal and interpersonal skills and are often able to influence others' behavior in a positive way. On the one hand, Social people can be impulsive—doing or saying things without thinking them through beforehand. On the other hand, they can be very flexible, cooperative, and adaptable, so that if they make an error in judgment, they are quick to amend their behavior. Social types prefer problem solving by discussing the issues with others rather than by logical thinking or authoritarian edicts. For them, feelings and the impact on others take precedence over rules and regulations.

Interpersonal skills are the strong suit of people in this group. Social people are often characterized as warm, open, and communicative. They favor group activities and often have a wide circle of friends and colleagues. Their tact, insight, and sensitivity to others provides them with an empathetic ear that allows them to serve as informal counselors to their friends.

Outwardly, Social people may appear timid in the face of conflict, preferring to back off or avoid unpleasant situations. They adhere to humanism, optimism, and idealism and are concerned with ethical and social problems. Most of all, Social people value harmony, faith, and spirituality, and they usually place personal feelings over logic or scientific reasoning.

~~~ So, Mr. Rogers You're Not...
Or, Should You Avoid This Field?

If you tend to be cynical or pessimistic and are unconcerned with your impact on others, you probably would not do well in a Social career. Social occupations, such as nursing and physical therapy, often call for optimistic and hopeful attitudes in the face of adversity. Additionally, people in Social occupations such as teaching and the ministry frequently serve as role models and have a significant impact on others.

Other red flags to alert you that a Social career is probably *not* the choice for you include:

* *You are not very talkative and are uncomfortable with verbal communication.* Nearly all Social occupations involve a high degree of interpersonal interaction. Conversations usually comprise a high percentage of the daily routine in these fields.

* *You tend to be impatient with other people's problems or concerns and think everyone should just "keep a stiff upper lip."* Most Social jobs require patience with others and a strong interest in helping people solve their problems and recognize their emotions.

* *You are competitive and are concerned with individual achievement and material gain.* Many Social careers support the common good, are team oriented, and de-emphasize self-serving attitudes and actions.

* *You apply logic and objectivity when making decisions and solving problems.* Those in Social careers tend to favor subjective feelings and take individual circumstances into account when making decisions and solving problems.

~~~ How Do I Get Started?

The major prerequisite for entering the Social fields is that you must truly like and care about people. Early on, people inclined toward the Social arena show interest in psychology, ethics, human relations, religion, and education. Social types tend to be scholarly and pursue academic interests that revolve around people and the human condition.

The majority of Social careers require at least a bachelor's degree in a related discipline. Majors typically chosen by Social people include sociology, psychology, social work, counseling, criminology, education, and religion. Supplemental coursework in accounting, business, human resources management, economics, and computers can be invaluable in grounding Social individuals in the realities of the working world and in making them more competitive in the job market. Teachers, nurses, hotel managers, and human resource specialists are among the Social occupations that require a bachelor's degree as the minimum. Master's degrees and sometimes other advanced degrees are needed to become educational administrators, counselors, social workers, and ministers, priests, or rabbis.

In today's competitive job market, it's important to bolster your résumé with extracurricular activities and previous experience. Extracurricular activities are a natural for Social people, who tend to gravitate toward group activities and opportunities for leadership and public speaking. Joining athletic teams, running for student government, coaching a team, organizing an event, and baby-sitting are opportunities to build skills needed in the Social careers. Hands-on experience, whether formal or informal, helps to validate a person's interest in a Social career as well as add to a résumé. Working as a camp counselor, advising friends or family on personal problems, tutoring a student, and volunteering at the Red Cross or local nursing home are ways to gain valuable work experience.

~~~ What's It Like Out There?

As you've heard before, trying to find a job these days is no picnic. Many Social opportunities are found in government and nonprofit organizations, which, unfortunately, in recent years have been hit with some reductions in force due to changes in the economy, public policy, and politics. As previously mentioned, more Social opportunities are opening up in businesses that support the personal and career needs of their employees.

According to the *1994–1995 Occupational Outlook Handbook*, Social occupations that will have average growth through 2005 include educational administrators, employment interviewers, and hotel managers. Those occupations with faster than average growth include kindergarten, elementary, and secondary school teachers; human resource specialists; social workers; adult education teachers; and counselors. Two occupations that will grow much faster than average include human services workers and nurses. The outlook is competitive for ministers, favorable for rabbis, and very favorable for priests.

In general, Social careers are not geographically constraining. For the most part, teachers, nurses, religious workers, and child care providers are found in more populated areas—whether urban or rural. Those who wish to work for the government or larger corporations will most likely have to settle in somewhat urban locations.

~ ~ ~ Where Do I Find Out More About Social Careers?

Talking to people about what they do—what a perfect way for Social individuals to learn more about career possibilities! Conducting informational interviews with people whose careers interest you can give you the best picture of what a career is like, what's required for the career, how to prepare for it, and whether you'll enjoy the work. Get Social people talking about what they do and you'll probably find out more than you ever wanted to know!

We've done some of the chatting for you and have conducted informational interviews with people in Social occupations; these make up the remainder of this chapter. But don't stop here. Get out there and do your own informational interviewing. Refer to the final chapter in this book, What's Next?, for specific steps on doing informational interviewing.

Another key way to find out more is to do some research and reading on Social careers. Information on how to do career research and other tips on career exploration can be found in the final chapter as well. The following list presents books and professional organizations focused on Social careers to help get you started.

Books for Social Careers

Careers for Good Samaritans and Other Humanitarian Types by M. Eberts and M. Gisler, published by VGM Career Horizons, 1991

Careers in Child Care by M. Eberts and M. Gisler, published by VGM Career Horizons, 1994

Careers in Education by R. Edelfelt, published by VGM Career Horizons, 1993

Careers in Health Care by B. Swanson, published by VGM Career Books, 1994

Careers in Medicine by T. Sacks, published by VGM Career Horizons, 1993

Careers in Medicine: Traditional and Alternative Opportunities by D. Rucker and M. Keller, published by Garrett Park Press, 1990

Careers in Social and Rehabilitation Services by G. O. Garner, published by VGM Career Horizons, 1993

Careers in Social Work by C. Simpson, published by Rosen Publishing Group, 1992

Good Works: A Guide to Careers in Social Change by J. Cowan, published by Barricade Books, 1993

Graduate Programs in the Humanities and Social Sciences, published by Peterson's Guides, 1992

Handbook of Health Care Careers by A. Selden, published by VGM Career Horizons, 1993

Health Care Job Explosion: Careers in the 90s by D. V. Damp, published by D'Amp Publications, 1993

Nurses: The Human Touch by M. Brown, published by Ivy Books, 1992

Opportunities in Hotel and Motel Careers by S. Menkin, published by VGM Career Horizons, 1992

So You Want To Be a Doctor? by S. Zeman, published by Ten Speed Press, 1992

Professional Organizations for Social Careers

Below are organizations that can provide information about social careers. Consider contacting organizations that interest you. Be sure to include a self-addressed stamped envelope when writing to request information.

American Association for Adult and Continuing Education
1112 16th St., NW, Suite 420
Washington, DC 20036

American Association of School Administrators
1801 North Moore St.
Arlington, VA 22209

American Counseling Association
5999 Stevenson Ave.
Alexandria, VA 22304

American Federation of Teachers
555 New Jersey Ave., NW
Washington, DC 20001

American Hotel and Motel Association
Information Center
1201 New York Ave., NW
Washington, DC 20005-3931

American Nurses Association
600 Maryland Ave., SW
Washington, DC 20024-2571

American Society for Training and Development
1640 King St., Box 1443
Alexandria, VA 22313

Hebrew Union College (reform)
Jewish Institute of Religion
1 W. 4th St.
New York, NY 10012-3101

National Association of Social Workers
7981 Eastern Ave.
Silver Spring, MD 20910

National Association of Student Personnel Administrators
1875 Connecticut Ave., NW, Suite 418
Washington, DC 20009-5728

National Coalition for Church Vocations
1603 S. Michigan Ave., Suite 400
Chicago, IL 60616

National Council of Churches
Professional Church Leadership
475 Riverside Dr., Room 863
New York, NY 10115

National Educational Association
1201 16th St., NW
Washington, DC 20036

Reconstructionist Rabbinical College
Church Rd. and Greenwood Ave.
Wyncote, PA 19095

Society for Human Resource Management
606 N. Washington St.
Alexandria, VA 22314

The Jewish Theological Seminary of America (conservative)
3080 Broadway
New York, NY 10027

The Rabbi Isaac Elchanan Theological Seminary (orthodox)
2540 Amsterdam Ave.
New York, NY 10033

★★★ RALPH NADER

CONSUMER ADVOCATE

VER SINCE I WAS VERY YOUNG, I have been interested in public service work. My parents were a powerful influence in this, and a professor at Princeton was also influential through a course he taught about power in American society. At Harvard Law School, the influence was adverse. My reaction to the sterility and oligarchic quality of the law teaching was to become even more interested in a field like automotive safety and the law.

Once I asked a law professor why there was no course on *food* in the law. His response was that it hadn't yet matured to a level sufficient to provide an adequate intellectual challenge to the students as in the case of, say, the intricacies of the tax code.

In my work, funding has always been an issue. There should be more attention paid to systems of fundraising, like check-offs and so forth, which reach out to people in great numbers and avoid the loss of time that's involved in trying to always play catchup in fundraising in various groups and foundations. The Wisconsin consumer check-off concept is an illustration of an effective fundraising technique.

I think that as the citizen action movement matures, it offers more opportunities for different specialties, and certainly fundraising is one of the specialties. It's something that can be taught and also refined on the job. It's part of a citizen curriculum.

Anyone who is interested in the type of work I'm involved with will find that there is no clear career path. It's fine to work for the government or in the private sector for a while if you can get *out* of it eventually. If you're strong enough to just go in for some experience and then go into the citizen's movement—fine! But a lot of people yield to the call of big salaries and don't ever leave.

I think the citizen field is moving in the same trajectory—more groups, more full-time citizen careers, more innovations to make citizen work more effective on institutions. I think the big effort will increasingly become international. The movement to control the nuclear arms race, the infant formula struggle, and the world environmental struggles are examples. More and more, the U.S. is going to be known for its citizen leadership overseas. And a lot of people overseas will be learning as well as teaching us. I see young people coming along who are capable of directing a worldwide effort, but they've got to get some sort of resource support. There are far more people able and willing than there are structures to support them. My own plans are to do more of the same kind of work, quantitatively and qualitatively.

My goal is basically to deepen the fiber of democracy. That's what it's all about. Traditions, ethics, laws, standards, and institutions must all be geared toward increasing power and responsibility for the citizenry. You can't just have power if people aren't willing to exercise it. It's a cruel myth when the power brokers say, "See, you've got all this power—you can vote."… And then they go out and *buy* the election.

I do a little international traveling every year or two. I put together an international conference in Washington, D.C., on indigenous peoples and multinational corporations and had representatives from Australia—aborigines—and Brazil, Central America, Alaska, Canada, mainland U.S. Indians. I would like to do more of this kind of work. We want to try to link groups together around the world. Companies are sure linked together; governments are linked together; citizens have to be linked together.

People often ask me how I maintain such a high level of intensity. The question implies that there's a kind of pressure that has to be released, a kind of anxiety and tension—and there *isn't*. I mean, there's pressure when you're up against a bloc in Congress or General Motors—that's a pressure-cooker type activity—but if you enjoy what you're doing and you know what the alternatives are to *not* doing it, then you reach a kind of equilibrium. The main strains are trying to get the job done better. To do this, I typically work twelve hours a day.

I think the characteristic that has enabled me to persist is a kind of aversion. It's an ability not to be disappointed or disillusioned and an ability to accept failure or setbacks.

If you look at failure or losses as a reason to think through the process and become more effective—you know, your best teacher is your last mistake—then the impact of a loss or failure in a particular area does not have adverse consequences. It becomes a stimulation to recover, rebound, be resilient, and generate better strategies and stronger ideas. So that's really the most important single trait I think people have to have in this work. I seem to have had these qualities all along.

Once I had a young woman come up to me at a college after I had given a talk about the citizen career, and she said, "You know, I used to have a lot of personal problems which were troubling me and causing me anxiety. But when I became involved in the women's rights movement, all these personal problems just dissolved. They just became totally insignificant, and I had a broader purpose in life." So when you look at a lot of obstructions to citizen involvement, namely, all the neuroses, and anxieties, and worries, and inhibitions, and hang-ups the young people have, then you see that involvement in civic, purposeful work tends to be a universal solvent for those personal problems. It's also possible in this field not to become consumed by your work. Most of us put in an honest week's work and have other lives to live as well.

It's important for people to realize that there's a very significant role for every citizen. If you're going to go into physics, you don't have to become an Einstein. Value systems and compassion and idealism and steadfastness are not monopolies of the few. There are opportunities for many of us that are going begging.

★★

★★★ RUTH SIMMONS

COLLEGE PRESIDENT
SMITH COLLEGE

ALWAYS ADVISE YOUNG PEOPLE of the importance of studying a broad array of courses, including some in literature and the arts; history, philosophy, and religion; science, technology, and mathematics; and the social sciences. This diversity of study will inevitably lead to a better preparation for almost any career one ultimately selects and will assuredly help any future leader—whatever their field of endeavor. Learning about the variety of methods and perspectives used in the organization and transmission of knowledge can provide not only an interesting and effective means of selecting a career but also an understanding of how to make use of those different perspectives to enrich efforts in one's chosen field.

It is very important for young people to remember not to pay attention to inhibiting stereotypes. When I was a child, the prevailing stereotype was that African-Americans could not achieve in certain fields. After segregation was abolished, the country came to understand better that one's degree of success is largely a function of education and training, hard work, and ambition. Young women today are still guided toward certain fields thought to be more appropriate for women and, to a certain degree, this is also the case for young men. I encourage every individual to resist such artificial constraints and to seek freely areas of endeavor that attract their interest and challenge their ability.

Young people are not the only ones who may become confused about the path to take. Many of the best choices I have made in my career were deemed inadvisable by others. Many adults, while drawn to different career paths, are reluctant to take steps to satisfy their interests. Their reluctance may be based on the economic risks of changing careers, the natural reluctance associated with striking out in new directions, or the fear that their peers may regard the change as irresponsible. Some are deterred for many years from making a change that could bring them much happiness and peace of mind. Delaying the fulfillment of one's goals can be debilitating. I have found that when I am seized by the idea that a change in direction would be good, it is useful to create a plan that addresses the main obstacles—financial as well as personal. Often, in working out the plan, one's goals become clarified and one's determination to achieve those goals is revealed as lacking or more manifest.

My own experience tells me that the most important element of achieving success in any endeavor is having a strong interest in and commitment to the direction one chooses. It is hard work and a firm commitment that accomplishes most of what people achieve. I have often found in teaching that many of my students believe that if they have a certain level of aptitude, that is all they need. Others believe that success is a function of having the proper friends or material trappings. The truth is that there is no substitute for hard work. I have seen many of the students of highest aptitude fail and many of lesser ability achieve great success. Conscientiousness, hard work, and a commitment to quality are surely the best attributes to cultivate if one seeks a life of accomplishment.

★★★

SHEILA MEHTA

SOCIAL WORKER

Sheila was introduced to social work after volunteering at a shelter for battered women during her senior year at college. At the time of this interview, she was working as a social worker for a nonprofit private organization that provides alternative programs in education and social services for troubled youths.

I AM A SOCIAL WORKER, currently working for a nonprofit private organization. Where I work, we have about twenty clients, either in foster homes, or living with their parents, or living on their own. We make daily contact with these clients, both male and female, whose ages range from twelve or thirteen through age twenty-one. All of these kids are in the care of the state; some are in trouble because they don't go to school, some are in trouble with the law, and others are on probation. Some aren't in any trouble, but their families are not functioning well.

Ever since I was a child, family and friends had told me that people liked to talk to me, and that I actually listened and was interested in their conversation. I liked that people were attracted to me, and I knew at an early age that I wanted to be working with people in some capacity.

I went to Brown University, where I received a liberal arts education and majored in religious studies. I was interested in pursuing a career in counseling, and at that time I seriously considered going to graduate school for clinical psychology. But before I made a commitment to another four to five years of school, I wanted time and some concrete experience to help me decide if that was what I wanted to do. I had already taken a number of psychology courses, and for a number of reasons I decided against going to graduate school.

In my senior year, I volunteered at a shelter for battered women and also staffed its hot line, which was the first time that I was able to use my counseling skills. This experience helped me develop a vague idea about the direction in which I wanted to take my people skills.

I started job hunting the summer after graduation. I was looking for work that would give me time and flexibility to think about what I wanted to do. For the first six months after graduation, I was working two, sometimes three part-time jobs that were not related to social service, but I was spending a lot of time doing informational interviews and going to a career library and using its resources. These interviews were helpful, but I realized later on that they would have been much more beneficial if I had first narrowed down my interests. Not having a few concrete career choices in mind before the interviews overwhelmed me. Then I received word that there was an opening in a non-profit social service organization, which is my current employer. I consider myself very fortunate to have this position. If I were to apply for this job today, I would probably not be accepted, because I do not have a degree in human services, which is a new requirement at all social service agencies. There is also a lot more competition, and agencies are looking to satisfy the educational requirements of the position, sometimes at the expense of the applicants' personality and people skills. I strongly believe that personality is far more important in this kind of work than certifications and requirements. Empathy and the ability to listen well are definite qualities of success in this field.

A typical day for me would include picking up a client and his or her parent and taking them to court for a six-month's court review. This could take up my whole morning. My afternoons usually include a meeting with a school guidance counselor or vice principal to discuss one of the clients' troubles in school. I go on a lot of house visits, and I drop in frequently to clients' places of employment. I might also take a client to a doctor's appointment. In between all of this is lots of paperwork. The other day, I was in my office doing paperwork and got a call that one of my clients wasn't in school. I had to drop everything and find out why he wasn't. What I learned when I arrived at the school was that he was getting kicked out altogether for a variety of reasons, so I had to immediately try and get him into an alternative program. All of this activity is not unusual during any given day in my position.

Having hectic days like the one I just described doesn't leave much energy or time for a personal life or leisure activities. But I have been willing to compromise my personal life for my first year on the job. I would rather compromise now and not later in my career; besides, all in all, I love what I do. Social work has definitely lived up to all my enthusiastic expectations.

What we do as social workers in my agency is best learned through on-the-job training. My agency provided me with excellent training over a four-month period, through workshops. But because the workshops were staggered, there was a lot of time when I was working without having been formally trained on the topic. But I know now that even if I had gotten all the training immediately in the first two weeks, undoubtedly situations would pop up that I would still be totally unprepared for.

Perhaps the absolute best part of my work is the reward I feel when I know I have helped someone: A client got a good job that he or she had been trying for and was able to keep it; another client found an apartment they liked and moved. The goal of the residential program is to get the kids out on their own. When you succeed, there's no greater feeling.

The downside of my work is when you know you are trying really hard to help someone and you can't see results, or you see them getting worse. What's most difficult for me is having to try to break up physical confrontations between clients and not be intimidated by your client.

Anyone who wants to "save the world and everyone in it" should not pursue this field. Social work takes a lot of energy; it's hard work and often quite draining. And you are not doing your client any favors by wanting to rescue him or her. That's up to the client. We are only there to help.

Eventually, I would like more professional independence, which would require an advanced degree. I still have not ruled out graduate school for clinical psychology, which would allow me to enter private practice. I have also considered the ministry, which is a related field. I want to have a career with variety. I have also contemplated doing research and teaching in a university. All of these would require an advanced degree.

The best advice I can give anyone trying to make a career decision is talk to as many people as you can—not just formal informational interviews, but talk to the guy sitting next to you on the train. Ask everyone about their careers—what they're doing, why they're doing it, and what they like about it—and go from there.

~~~ RANDY CHARLES

MINISTER

Randy has been an ordained minister since 1976. He grew up in the political and social climate of the sixties. He graduated from Sewanee University in 1969 and worked in its alumni office for three years. He then entered the General Theological Seminary in New York City. For eleven years, he served as pastor at St. Paul's Episcopal Church, an inner-city parish in Newport News, Virginia, and, at the time of this interview, was the senior pastor of the Church of the Epiphany in Washington, D.C.

THROUGHOUT MY CHILDHOOD and adolescence, the church had always been an important part of my life. I am sure that it was a factor in directing me into ordained ministry because it was part of my day-to-day routine. Being a high school student in the 1960s furthered my interest. The political and social climate of that decade awakened in me an awareness of social issues, peace, and justice, and furthered my sense of right and wrong in our society and culture—and I connected all of that to the church.

I was a well-rounded student in both high school and college. I was involved in athletics and academics, as well as student government and social organizations. This variety of activity has proved to be invaluable, as I truly believe it prepared me to handle the diversity of my work as an ordained minister. I was especially interested in my English classes in high school, and I majored in English in college. I was encouraged in these classes to look for the spirit beneath the work of literature, which is akin to seeking God's spirit and presence in us all. I think this was clearly a preparation for ordained ministry—looking for the creative word, which some people can express better than others, and is part of the human experience. I was also encouraged in high school and college to look for my creative self, which was a second element that prepared me. I think there is a close connection between spirituality and creativity, and I am fortunate to have had the academic experience that prepared me for the world of ordained ministry, which is really to dwell in the world of creativity.

I was hired by a governing board and they pay my salary and I am accountable to that board. But my work is not only a job, and I hesitate to categorize it as a "career." The church uses the word *call*. When we talk about our work in the church, the element of God's calling and God's action is the more important element. In other words, it would be difficult for me to say that I chose the ministry. More correctly, I was "called" to it.

I was ordained in 1976. The road to ordination is not an easy one. It begins with at least a year to a year and a half of work before seminary, and while you are in seminary, you are working with a commission on ministry. The purpose of this process is to confirm, or not to confirm, a "call" to the ordained ministry. Even though a person feels really excited about being a priest and feels "called," the ultimate decision comes from the diocese, who may decide that you haven't been called. Most of the mainline denominations have this process of community confirmation, or lack of confirmation, of the call.

The most important characteristics an individual who feels called should possess include people skills, a strong sense of compassion, administrative skills, an openness to the mystery of creation and God's presence, and deep faith not only in God but also that God is working through the person, and, of course, remaining faithful to the call.

I graduated from a small-town South Carolina high school, with a graduating class of one hundred. I then attended and graduated from Sewanee, the University of the South, which is an Episcopal college and was all-male at that time. I then worked for three years at Sewanee, first in the alumni and development office raising funds and managing alumni activities, and then as the director of admissions for Sewanee Academy. I then attended the General Theological Seminary in New York City and was ordained a deacon and then a priest.

There are many different types of church congregations and church situations. My parish is located three blocks from the White House and has a grand history. The building itself is beautiful and large—it can hold about eight hundred people. It has a fantastic music program and an amazing history of social awareness and consciousness. It has been a leading parish in this diocese and a leading church in downtown Washington. But what I find the most challenging about being here is that we are rebuilding. Our average Sunday attendance is about 125, and we have money problems and challenges and building problems and challenges. But the church is downtown, in the center of activity, where we experience both the pain and the joy of the human community. I am excited to be in a place that is historical and at the same time looking toward a new future. It excites me that we are racially, culturally, and socioeconomically diverse, as well as diverse in sexual orientation. This congregation, although small, has a large number of highly committed, faithful, and skilled laypeople. I find it exhilarating to be the leader of a congregation that is facing some tough challenges. We've had a $100,000 deficit for the past six years, but we, the church, are living in the real world and are excited about our future. Being honest and hopeful about where God will lead us and being willing to act on that direction is the environment that excites me. This means rebuilding and looking for new ways to live out our lives as a faith community.

Being an ordained minister is a challenge in itself because there are so many different skill and time demands. Even though I like a high degree of activity and enjoy being a part of people's lives at important points in their lives, as well as being an important part of a congregation, it is a challenge to make decisions on how to use my time and where I might be needed most. I have to constantly listen to God's direction. It is a blessing and a curse. I am on call twenty-four hours a day. I have a tendency to work too much, and that's a challenge to correct. Effective and appropriate time management is the greatest challenge of ordained ministry and the most frustrating aspect of it.

I am motivated by being a pastoral part of people's lives when they are at a significant point, which is also a tremendous responsibility. Doing pastoral counseling with people who really need it is also a challenge, but it's very satisfying. I also enjoy working with diverse groups of people—the congregation, the vestry, the commission—all the time looking toward the future. I enjoy planning with them, and determining what is God's will for us as a group and what their needs are as individuals, and carrying out that work. I also enjoy working with this parish in making a difference in the world and in the city of Washington, D.C. We work not only to proclaim our faith but also to reach out to people in need throughout the world, trying to make a statement of hope in the center of a city that is filled with pain. It is exciting for me to wrestle with these questions because it touches on why we are here.

I am also a single parent of a fifteen-year-old and an eleven-year-old. My typical day is morning breakfast, kids off to school, then prayer time, at home or at church, which is personal prayer time. At 9:30 A.M., I meet with the office manager for a few minutes to talk about the day and ongoing projects. At 10:00 A.M., I will either prepare my sermon or have other meetings scheduled for the rest of that day. But one day a week is dedicated to preparing my sermon. I have lunch meetings almost every day with somebody. I leave at 2:30 P.M. and pick up my son from school, and do some calls from home. Several times a week I return to church in the evenings for other meetings. I try to take Saturdays off as a family day and Friday off as a personal day. But this is usually my greatest challenge. There is some flexibility in that I can take an hour or two during the week to do family stuff. Even though I don't get a block of time to do something for myself, right now it really meets my personal and family needs, providing stability at home and enabling me to get some personal things done in the afternoon. It's a strange kind of schedule. I put in loads of time for the church and for my family. I am able to get home on Sundays by 2:00 P.M. for the day. Many churches, especially suburban churches, have evening activities and other groups that meet at night.

There are a lot of other opportunities that exist within ordained ministry and in related fields. Within the ordained ministry, a person can choose to be on staff—a clergy team member in a congregation—and move to a multistaff position. Another possibility is some sort of chaplaincy, either with a school or with a hospital, or to be a chaplain in a helping agency, such as AIDS organizations. Outside the ministry, counseling is an option. A parish priest might decide that he or she has had enough but still wants to do similar and related work. These priests can leave the ordained ministry or the parish ministry to become a pastoral counselor or therapist, which provides short-term counseling to satisfy an immediate pastoral need. Some have also moved into helping agencies, not as a pastor but as a director. In all these cases, the connection is still that you are making a difference in the world, that you are helping people in need and are also still using people skills, which is an essential part of being an ordained minister.

I think there will be plenty of opportunities available in the near future to anyone called to the ministry. Over the past twenty years, many changes have happened. As the baby-boomer clergy members age, there are going to be lots of retiring clergy. As a result, there will be slots for new clergy to fill. On the other hand, many churches are becoming more realistic about how many clergy they can hire, and more realistic about their budgets. I think our church and the Episcopal church in general is starting to grow again. The really rough statistics about church attendance decline that were floating around five or ten years ago are changing. We are all beginning to grow again, slowly, but everybody is leaner, the government included, and cutting back on personnel. Yet there is a growing interest in the church and more people are going to church, or at least becoming more serious about their faith. And it is also true, at least in the Episcopal church, that we are beginning to place an emphasis on recruiting, which is a strange term, indeed, but we are letting people plant the seed, at least in the minds and hearts and souls of young men and women who seem to have the gifts and call to be ordained ministers.

The pay scale for ordained ministers ranges according to experience. In my case, I am also given a housing allowance. Housing can also be supplied by the parish. A pension plan, health insurance, life insurance, and transportation expenses are also parts of the package.

~~~ CAROL ANN ALOISI

TEACHER

*Carol Ann knew she wanted to be a teacher in the eighth grade. She
majored in elementary education and minored in psychology as an undergraduate. She has been a member of the Big Brother/Big Sister organization and the Education Society, which provides the latest information on
teaching. At the time of this interview, she was a junior high school
instructor, teaching seventh- and eighth-grade science and eighth-grade
reading.*

THERE WERE TWO THINGS that made me decide to choose teaching as a profession. First of all, I was influenced by teachers I
knew as I was growing up. Second, I had many positive experiences in jobs I had taken in school settings, such as tutoring and substitute
teaching. Looking back, it was when I entered the sixth grade that I met the
man who was later to become my best friend, a teacher at a local high school.
Kevin's love for children and his ability to teach and touch others influenced
me greatly. By the time I was in the eighth grade, I knew I wanted to teach
and teach like him. During high school, I wanted to make sure I was really
capable of being a good teacher, and as a way of testing myself, I took jobs
tutoring during the school year and at summer schools. This work showed me
I had the ability to teach and that I really enjoyed doing it. This experience,
too, proved to me that I should study education in college.

I majored in elementary education and minored in psychology as an undergraduate. My education courses naturally helped me in my job, especially those
in discipline, curriculum, and practice teaching. My psychology courses gave
me some insight into why children do what they do and how people learn, and
I learned how to listen to and interact with people. I also took a course in public speaking, which showed me how to outline a topic and gave me confidence
in my ability to speak in front of groups of people. I was a member of a Big
Sister/Big Brother organization for needy children. This organization gave me
the valuable experience of working with inner-city children and allowed me to
become more familiar with streetwise youth. I was also a member of a volunteer
organization that gave tours of the campus and spoke with high-school students
about the college. I belonged to the Education Society, an organization which

provided the latest information on teaching and gave me the chance to share my own experiences with other people studying in the field, as well as with experienced teachers.

As a federal government clerk for two years, I got used to doing a lot of paperwork, something that I also found to be a big part of teaching. I also spent two years working as a supervisor at campus ministry at my college. This job involved scheduling work hours for student workers and running retreat programs. The work gave me organizational skills and helped me to learn how to work under time pressures, as well as to become comfortable in working and talking with groups of people. I also held odd jobs—baby-sitting, tutoring, and substitute teaching—all of which gave me time to work with children of all ages. I found the experience helpful later when I was thinking about what grade to teach. Substitute teaching gave me an opportunity to try out my own ideas in the classroom and to receive feedback from professionals with whom I worked.

A teacher needs to feel comfortable talking in front of groups of parents, children, and staff members. You need to schedule class time, write out lesson plans, prepare tests, correct papers, discipline students, and, most importantly, reach the students in your class and learn to understand them.

Job hunting was terrible. Teaching is a difficult field to get into. I decided not to send out résumés to any public schools, since so many teachers in my area were being laid off. Since I definitely wanted to teach, however, I decided to look into the Catholic schools. I knew the pay would be low, but felt I could get valuable teaching experience and then move on to private or public schools later. I began sending out résumés in late April to early May of my senior year. I did not find a job until early August, when I applied for a position as a part-time teacher's aide. I figured some experience is better than none, and, besides, I was planning to go on to graduate school full time to study counselor education. After being interviewed, I received a call from the school telling me they were impressed with my résumé and interview, and they offered me a full-time position as their junior-high science and reading teacher. Clearly, training in interviewing and résumé writing at my college placement office helped greatly in my getting this job. But it was also a matter of luck—I happened to be in the right place at the right time.

To be honest, unless one is willing to consider several locations, it is very difficult to get a job teaching in some areas. You have to really want teaching, and you have to devote a lot of time and energy to looking and interviewing for jobs. In certain areas, such as the South or West, jobs are easier to find; but even in those areas, there are not jobs for everyone.

In my current job, I'm responsible for teaching seventh- and eighth-grade science and eighth-grade reading. I will probably also teach seventh-grade religion. Besides my classroom responsibilities, I teach gym, watch students during the day, and have my own homeroom. I arrive at school by 8:00 A.M. During homeroom, 8:20 to 8:35 A.M., I take attendance and lunch count, lead morning prayer and the pledge, and complete other paperwork. Three forty-minute classes are held between 8:35 and 10:00 A.M. From 10:40 to 11:00 A.M. is recess. Two classes are held from 11:05 A.M. to 12:30 P.M. Lunch is from 12:30 to 1:10 P.M., and another class is held from 1:15 to 2:00 P.M. Homeroom is again from 2:00 until 2:15 P.M. During the day, I am responsible for at least two duties, either taking the children inside the school in the morning or then supervising recess or lunch. Free time is virtually nonexistent. Every day is the same except for Wednesday, when instead of classes I have science labs, which last about one and a half hours each. On Thursdays, I teach gym during the last period of the day. Some other responsibilities include level meetings, full-school meetings, report cards, permanent-record cards, class registers, and other paperwork.

The pressures of teaching are many: making sure the children understand what you are teaching, that you please the parents, that each week's lesson plan is conscientiously prepared, that papers are corrected, and that discipline is enforced. My first responsibility is to teach. I must also get along with and share information with the staff. As a junior high school teacher, I am also responsible for helping with graduation. As a science teacher, I am responsible for labs and the school science fair. I also help coach the eighth-grade girl's basketball team. This might seem like a grim picture—and granted, there is lots of work to do—but when you get acknowledgment from a parent or fellow teacher or especially from a student, it seems to make all the work worthwhile. The benefits are not in pay, and when you go home at night, the work does not stop, since there is always planning to be done; but a smile or a hug from a student, or a card of thanks, makes it all worthwhile.

Teaching is more work than I ever dreamed it would be. I also have found that I need to be more of a disciplinarian than I had thought would be the case. Other than that, teaching is pretty much what I had expected.

I think the training that I received was as good as I could have anticipated or gotten anywhere. I do wish we had done more actual classroom work with students, though. It was those classes that made me realize that teaching was really for me.

Everyone in the school is very supportive of one another. We give each other suggestions, and nobody feels threatened by what we say. Gaining the respect of a veteran staff member, parents, and students was a great plus for me. I was treated as a professional and not a rookie. The worst part of the year was learning how to get control of the class, learning the curriculum, and knowing how to manage time. They say it takes five years to finally feel comfortable with all there is to do in teaching. After this year, I believe it.

Teachers have to be patient and gentle with students and at the same time let them know who is boss. You must maintain discipline at all times. While you have a professional manner, you must always remain a bit of a child yourself inside. This you need in order to be able to understand your students, think up new ideas for teaching, and do creative things like making bulletin boards. Lastly, you need to be totally dedicated to what you do, and you have to be willing to work long hours. One of the most important things teachers need to remember is to never change their minds. If you make a decision about something, such as disciplining a student, stand by that decision. Don't change your mind. You have to feel that what you are doing is right, no matter which parents or which students turn against you.

I use organizational skills in my work. I need to do paperwork, manage my time extremely well, and manage groups of people. Public speaking skills are also very important for teachers.

My principal last year was previously a master teacher. He was a strict disciplinarian, and he helped me a lot. He gave me suggestions, but most of all he allowed me to use and develop my own style of teaching in the classroom and to formulate my own curriculum. This certainly helped me grow as a teacher. I felt very comfortable asking what he thought about my teaching. He helped me to see my potential as a teacher, and I appreciated it greatly.

In the future, I will get a master's degree in counselor education. I will then need to make a decision about whether to stay in teaching, or to go on to counseling exclusively, or to educational administration.

My plans for the future have changed since I began working. I am a person who needs to move, to get ahead and grow. Although I can do that as a teacher, I have seen too many teachers who are in a rut, doing the same thing year after year. I know now that I will have to move on to other aspects of teaching, especially after five years have passed.

I had planned to live on my own, but have found that it is not possible because of my salary. I live at home with my parents and older brother. Leisure time is infrequent. I spend most of my nights either coaching, taking classes, or doing paperwork that is necessary for my job. It is very important, though, for teachers to set aside at least one day (I find Friday nights and Saturdays good) just for themselves. This helps to prevent burnout.

Summers are needed to restore myself. Although I do teach summer school three days a week, I use the rest of my time for reading, relaxing, socializing, and being alone. The summer seems to fly by, and in mid-August, it is again time to prepare bulletin boards and set up classrooms for the coming year.

If you are considering the teaching field, you should be aware of the limitations of the job. You should take tutoring and teaching positions to see if you really want to teach. If you want to teach, be prepared for long hours, little pay, and sometimes little gratitude for what you do. Take a variety of courses in college. You need to know a little bit of everything, since you will probably end up teaching any and all subjects. Learn to be a good listener as well as a good teacher, and learn to be loving, caring, and patient with your students. Last but not least, if you like what you are doing, don't let anyone discourage you. Teaching can be a very rewarding experience if you let it be.

The social service field is similar to teaching in the qualities it requires of a person. With further study in psychology, a person could easily move from teaching into the social service field and counseling.

It takes time and a lot of effort to become a good teacher. If you like it and are willing to work hard, however, it is a very rewarding experience to reach out to children and teach them. By giving them knowledge, you can influence in a great way the future of your country; and that is a big responsibility and a great gift.

~~~ STEPHEN JOHANSSON

COUNSELOR

At the time of this interview, Stephen was the director of the Career Counseling and Placement Office at Middlebury College. He graduated with a liberal arts degree from Bates College and has a master's degree in education with a strong management curriculum. He was originally hired by Bates as an admissions counselor. He was soon promoted to assistant to the president, and after three years became the associate director, then director of the career counseling office.

URING MY SENIOR YEAR IN COLLEGE, I decided that Christmas vacation was going to be the time when I decided on a career. In a flash of lightning, I determined that I really wanted to be college admissions officer. While I was seeking information about the field, the director of admissions at Bates asked me if I would be interested in working for him. A few months later, I was hired as an admissions counselor. After three years in that job, the college president invited me to join his staff as an assistant. I spent three years working with him, doing a number of different tasks, and then switched to career counseling. I started as the associate director, became acting director for one year, and was named director of the office.

My initial decision to become a college admissions officer was not made in any systematic way. As an undergraduate, I conducted tours of the college and enjoyed my association with the people in the admissions office. My decision to go to work in admissions was based on my relationship with those people as much as anything else. And it seemed like fun to interview people, to visit high schools, and to talk about a place that meant a lot to me. On the whole, it was a very enjoyable job. The only really negative thing about it was that it got to be very repetitive, especially during those times of the year when we conducted one interview after another. Reviewing admissions folders also became extremely tedious.

My duties as director of career counseling and placement change, depending upon the time of the year. I have administrative responsibilities for managing a full-time staff of five and supervise a number of student workers. I administer a fairly good-sized budget, and I am responsible for planning and carrying out programs during the school year. One of the things that I really like about my job is that I get a chance to utilize a number of different skills in a lot of different ways. I also have responsibilities as a counselor to undergraduate and more advanced students.

I view career counseling and placement primarily as a student service, in that all of our activities revolve around the needs of undergraduates. Secondly, I view myself as a member of that part of the administrative team within the college, including the alumni office, the admissions office, and the development office, which is responsible for marketing and public relations. We present the college to a number of publics, including our alumni; graduate and professional school admissions officers who come to recruit students; and employers who come to give information and to seek students for entry-level positions in their organizations.

During the semester, the day typically starts at about 8:30 A.M., when I clear my desk of things that need to be read, return phone calls, write memoranda, and meet with the staff. I take one-hour appointments with students from 10:00 A.M. until noon, and then again from 1:30 P.M. through 3:30 P.M. By 3:30 or 4:00, I turn my attention once again to projects, memos, and phone calls until the end of the day, which is usually 5:15 or 5:30 P.M.

My day often starts by having coffee with other administrators. This usually generates a very lively discussion about what's going on at the college and what's happening in this small rural community. When the students are away, there is a lot more unstructured time, there's no demand for counseling, and it gives me a good chance to complete some projects that have been put off. During January, February, and March, when the recruiters are on campus, my day typically starts earlier. I like to make sure that visitors to the campus are welcomed by me personally before they see students. At noontime, I entertain interviewers for lunch, and then usually stay for the end of the interviewing schedule. Generally, recruiting visits by employers are preceded by an information session, which occurs the evening before the day of interviews. Since I am relatively new at the college, I attend most of these sessions, which means entertaining in the evening, generally for drinks and/or dinner.

During the summer, I have limited counseling responsibilities. I deal with students who are generally older and are seeking advanced degrees. My workday is shortened, allowing plenty of time for athletic activities, gardening, and just generally being outdoors in this wonderful setting. My work environment is delightful. The Career Counseling and Placement Office is housed in an old frame building on the top of a hill on a small, rural New England campus. My office overlooks farmland and, in the distance, snow-covered mountains. Another nice thing about working in this college atmosphere is that many of my peers are interested in athletics, which means lunchtime usually includes either a run, a game of tennis or squash, or some other form of exercise.

I have a fair amount of autonomy and support in developing programs to provide the best services that I can for undergraduates. One of the best features of my job is also one of its greatest weaknesses: I operate pretty much in a vacuum. I am responsible to the dean of the college, as is true for the other directors of student personnel departments. But while my boss is very supportive, he does not really have a great comprehension of the kinds of things we're trying to do. The director of the college counseling center and a number of other student personnel administrators and faculty members fill that void, and I enjoy that very much.

There are a number of different kinds of people in the field of career counseling and placement. Some spend most of their time counseling people and don't have responsibilities in administration, budgeting, and marketing. As associate and assistant directors, they have a great deal of student contact and some programming interests. The people at the director level, on the other hand, are involved in counseling and programming, and are quite interested in promoting their own institution as well as making sure that they are developing skills in the staff members they supervise. I think it's important that a person who directs a career counseling office have good administrative skills, good common sense, the ability to lead and manage others, the ability to communicate effectively, and a cultivated skill carried over from counseling: the ability to listen to what others in the office are saying and to take criticism constructively.

There is no particular type of educational background that is most effective for work in this field. I have a liberal arts background and a master's degree in education. In my master's program, I took a number of management courses. I wanted my master's degree to give me the kinds of management skills used in higher education, and also which could be applied to any other field that I decide to enter in the future.

A person in this field must have a willingness and fondness for dealing with people who are eighteen to twenty-one years old and who are, for the most part, pretty confused about what it is they want to do. Also, one must be interested in helping clients with their own growth. One of the most rewarding aspects of my job is dealing with students on a year-to-year basis, seeing them make up their minds about what they want to do upon graduation, and then maintaining a relationship with them after they leave the college to see how their lives develop.

One of the most surprising aspects of what we are doing outside the field is the extent to which we deal with personal issues. A counseling session with eighteen- to twenty-year-olds deals with career issues and the question, "What do you want to do after you leave college?" It is not unusual or inappropriate to ask questions about careers tied in with finances, what's happening in college, what's happening in academics, and what's happening in personal, social, and family life. And, more often than not, decisions about career fields are really a subset of other personal issues. A person who is considering entering the counseling field should be familiar with those issues and not be surprised to face them and any other questions that impact a student's decision-making process.

Every spring, there are always job openings in the career counseling and placement field. There are also a number of career-entry job openings every year. Private, selective colleges tend to be the most flexible in the types of people they hire to fill these positions.

The career planning and placement field has changed drastically in the last five to ten years. Ten years ago, many colleges had placement offices where students met with employers and recruiters and generally walked away with an entry-level position. Within the last ten years, the emphasis has changed from a placement operation to one that includes career counseling. And a number of very able younger people have become interested in the field. I think as the profession matures, there will be more and more people who start out as career counselors or assistant directors, move up through the ranks to assistant and associate, and then director of career counseling and placement in colleges and universities. There are also fields within education that are related to career counseling and placement. For example, professionals in college counseling offices do very similar work. There are also people in other student personnel areas and in alumni relations doing similar work and using the kinds of skills that one uses in career counseling and placement.

I've known people who have moved from career planning and placement offices into development and fund-raising activities. There has also been a fair amount of movement from career counseling and placement on the college side to college relations and personnel work in corporations, mainly for better salaries and benefits. Another natural move from career counseling and placement is into an executive search firm. The same kind of skills—administrative, counseling, and marketing—clearly are utilized in executive search.

I don't have a five-year or a ten-year plan for what I want to be doing. The remainder of my career will undoubtedly be affected by lifestyle issues. I am not married, I have no family, and my present rural location places certain limitations on my social life. The opportunities for social contact here are limited, and this will have an effect on what I decide to do and where and when I decide to do it.

I always thought that having a house and having a new car and a lot of creature comforts—good vacations and so forth—was something that I would never have to worry about. I'm finding out, however, that the kind of salaries paid in higher education may put a house and some other things out of reach. It may be necessary to leave higher education for the private sector in order to achieve these goals.

Working in higher education, and working at liberal arts colleges in particular, has provided me with stimulating work, a pleasant lifestyle, and opportunities to meet interesting and talented people. If I had it to do over gain, I would not hesitate to make the same choices.

～～～ MARY YAKABOSKY

COMMUNITY SERVICE ORGANIZATION DIRECTOR

At the time of this interview, Mary was the program director for the Women's Opportunity Center in Burlington County, New Jersey. The center, which she founded, provides guidance and counseling to women in transition, specifically those who have lost financial support, either through death of their spouses or divorce, and are looking to enter the workforce. She has an MBA in management and is a licensed and certified social worker in the state of New Jersey.

AFTER GRADUATING FROM COLLEGE with a degree in education, I taught for six years at a private business school. Many of the students I taught were women and men going through major transitions in their lives, resulting from a variety of factors, including divorce or death of a spouse, and were looking to enter the workforce either for extra money or to establish a career. A lot of them had barriers to cope with, such as finances, lack of skills, or personal problems. I found myself referring them to community resources and finding out information for them on how they could best overcome these barriers. I soon realized that I had a strong interest in helping this adult population. When a position became available as a job developer for the displaced homemaker program at my local community college through the county YMCA, I jumped at the opportunity, and, within two months of being hired, I was promoted to coordinator. I have since been promoted to program director.

I have always had an interest in helping people. In college, I took a variety of psychology courses, as well as geriatrics, family life, and marriage courses. I have since received an MBA in management, and I am a licensed and certified social worker in the state of New Jersey.

In my current position, I wear many hats. One of my functions is to counsel these women, either in person or over the phone, and make appropriate referrals to community resources. I am also involved in planning activities such as community education workshops and community outreach seminars that enable these women to achieve their goals. There is a tremendous amount of community outreach, which helps others to get to know our program and helps me get to know what community resources are available to our program. I also recruit volunteers. Because we are grant funded, we operate on a very strict budget. There are only two paid staff members, including me; the other paid member is the job developer. So we rely heavily on volunteers.

Much of my time each day is absorbed by administrative paperwork, which includes word processing, preparing a monthly newsletter, and handling all of the program's finances, but I am also involved in case management; interaction with our regional, state, and national chapters; and regular meetings with our job developer to discuss which clients are job-ready. There is a diversity of tasks, and certainly no two days are alike.

What I enjoy most is assisting people in planning and working toward achieving their short, intermediate, or long-term goals. There is a tremendous sense of satisfaction when former clients call back and tell us of their successes. Most of the women, when they first come to our center, have low self-esteem and lack self-confidence. Watching their goals fall into place is very rewarding. I also enjoy going out into the community and networking to develop special events and life-skills training seminars.

What I don't like about my work is not knowing each year whether the program will be re-funded. Because we are grant funded through state money, our program works on a yearly contract. This means having to spend a lot of time each year writing proposals and grants. So far, we have had the good fortune to have been re-funded every year since the program began, and I think this is because we have such a great program and so many women benefit from it. What we do here really does make a difference in our clients' lives.

My leisure time and my family are very important to me. I am a firm believer in not bringing work home. Occasionally, I will have to attend evening activities that may include speeches, advisory board meetings, or legislative activities. But otherwise I can schedule my own hours, which usually varies from thirty-five to forty hours per week, not including evening commitments, and I make sure I never work on weekends.

Related fields, with my academic background and work experience, would include management, outplacement, career counseling, community liaison or special events coordinating, life-skills training, and anything to do with program development.

I have several goals for the next five years. Because I am the founder of our program, starting it from nothing, I would like to try to expand the center and secure more staff. I am currently looking into endowments to fund our expansion, so we don't have to rely so heavily on state grants. I would also like to develop a program geared toward high school students that teaches them the importance of gaining skills in the event of a marital failure.

There are a variety of ways to best break into this kind of work. Unfortunately, there is a very low turnover rate in our program statewide, and because the programs are state funded, there are even fewer paid positions. However, some recommendations would be cold-calling and letter writing to agencies with your résumé attached, answering ads in the newspaper, and a lot of networking, such as attending public meetings on different advisory boards and commissions related to vocational education. Most community service programs are grant funded—which means you are never going to know for sure if the funds are going to be available in the state budgets on a consistent basis. This is why networking is so important—to get your face and name out there. The best recommendation, in my opinion, is to volunteer in a social service agency, a college counseling service, or a local telephone hotline, even if it's just for a couple of hours a week. If a job opening should become available, most agencies would rather hire someone they know than someone from the outside. I had a client who volunteered for Contact-We-Care, and now she is their community services director.

A successful person in my field is someone who can handle a multitude of tasks at one time, prioritize those tasks, and be geared for interruptions while trying to carry out those tasks. Listening skills are important, as well as empathy for people going through very dramatic times in their lives, confidentiality, friendliness, openness, and genuine interest in people.

Salaries vary from agency to agency, especially grant-funded agencies. In general, an entry-level college graduate can expect an annual salary in the low- to mid-$20K. The highest salaries are usually in the $35K to $40K range, depending on funds available and merit increases.

My college experience has been the most important foundation in my life, because I not only took my core courses, but I also used my electives for a variety of interests, and I literally attended every activity I could on campus. Whether it was participating in sports or art appreciation, I tried to get as well-rounded an education as I could, so I had definite ideas about what I liked and didn't like.

~~~ JON CARROW

NURSE

Jon has been an army nurse since 1979. He was introduced to nursing as an navy corpsman in the mid-1960s, after earning a bachelor's degree in sociology and working in army intelligence. He earned both a bachelor's and master's degree in nursing. At the time of this interview, he worked in infection control at the Walter Reed Army Medical Center in Washington, D.C.

I'M VERY COMFORTABLE WITH NURSING. I enjoy it. I enjoyed it when I was doing it as a hospital corpsman in the navy when I was in Vietnam for the first time. It's very fulfilling, although it also can be frustrating. I must say I do it because I like to help others; it's exciting and it's nice to be able to get close to people you work with.

I like the way my job makes me feel. I feel that I'm helping somebody. It's fulfilling for me emotionally, gives me a good sense that I have accomplished something meaningful not only to myself but to others as well. As I've done different things or different types of nursing, there's been a renewed sense of personal accomplishment each time I've done a different job.

What I do now, by its very nature, is a quality-assurance type of program. One of my tasks is to monitor the patients in the Medical Intensive Care Unit and the Surgical Intensive Care Unit. These are considered to be the sickest or some of the sickest patients we have. I look at infections that are acquired by patients in the hospital. About 5 to 8 percent of all patients who are admitted to any hospital or hospitals nationwide will acquire another infection or an infection while they're in the hospital. My job is to watch the rates of those infections and to see if they are rising or falling and to identify trends and so forth and try to keep those things under control.

We have Centers for Disease Control (CDC) guidelines that we use. Is it an infection, is it not? Believe it or not, it is not as easy to answer that question as you may think. I apply CDC guidelines, monitor patient lab work every day, and read their charts every day, or try to read them every day. Monthly, I prepare a report that I present to the Infection Control Commission. I'm pretty much independent. I'm here between 6 and 6:30 in the morning. I do other things—teach classes, go to meetings, serve on committees, and all the other usual stuff.

There are three ways you can get a basic nursing education these days in the United States. You can still get what is known as a diploma from a hospital program. This was the traditional program we had before we had baccalaureate programs. There aren't as many hospital programs operating as there used to be. You can get a bachelor's degree, a four-year bachelor's degree, or you can get a two-year associate degree. All three of those routes prepare the individual to take a state board examination to be licensed.

That has been a problem within the profession because there are so many ways of being prepared and people have been utilized in a variety of ways by hospitals. I can certainly get a nurse with an associate degree cheaper than I can get a four-year-degreed nurse.

There are lots of different types of nurses. It's not all just direct patient care by any stretch of the imagination, though the vast majority of nurses are probably involved in a direct bedside job. That's really what we all do ultimately. All of the other jobs that I've done, the administrative-type jobs, really should be focused on facilitating the staff nurses' ability to deliver care. That's what administration is supposed to be all about, although sometimes I think people lose sight of that.

I think there are downsides to just being a nurse, one of which is that sometimes you feel like you're being drained of everything. It's kind of hard to explain to someone who doesn't understand. I think you give, give, give, and when you leave, people want you to give some more physically, emotionally, and in every other way.

By the nature of this profession, we deal with a lot of human suffering. When people are suffering, many are not rational. You get all of those emotional things with people dying, people sick, and you see all of that and you're swept up in it. You experience people's anger and frustration through no fault of your own, and that can be wearing after a while.

The pay scale definitely depends on the area of the country you're in and, of course, the cost of living. The problem with nursing salaries has been traditionally that the difference between the salary of the brand-new graduate and the salary of the ten-year experienced nurse has not been wide.

I think people should be very careful about coming into the profession in the first place. For some, it can be very unrewarding and frustrating. People considering nursing really should know exactly what it entails. I think there are a lot of people who don't really realize what nursing is or should be until they get into it, and then sometimes they're bitterly disappointed.

I would never advise anyone to get any less than a baccalaureate degree in nursing. I also think you need to figure out early on what you want to specialize in and get the additional education or credentials, a master's degree, even if it takes awhile. If you want to do research or teach in some fields, you need to get a Ph.D. You need to have a plan early on if you want to go anywhere.

◤◢◤◢ Some Things to Think About...

Now that you have an understanding of Social careers, here are some things to consider:

1. What insights about Social occupations have you gained from these interviews?

   _____

   _____

   _____

2. Which characteristics, abilities, and personal qualities discussed in the interviews are similar to your own? Which are different or in contrast to your own? How might the similarities or differences affect your satisfaction with your possible career choices?

_____

_____

_____

3. Ask yourself the following:

   * Do you like working with people? _____

   * Do you like helping people? Do you find fulfillment in helping others?

   _____

   * Do you feel the need to make a contribution to society? _____

   * Are you a good listener? Are you empathetic?_____

   * Do you have strong interpersonal skills? _____

   * Do you work well on a team?_____

   * Do you consider people's feelings and values to be the most important factors when making decisions?_____

   How might your responses to these questions suggest satisfaction with a Social career choice?_____

   _____

4. Which interviews held your interest? Why? _____

   _____

5. Which interviews were not what you expected? Why? _____

   _____

6. Which occupations are you going to investigate further? How?

   _____

   _____

   _____

   _____

CHAPTER SIX

Sell Yourself on an Enterprising Career

ARE YOU AN ASPIRING Donald Trump, Janet Reno, or future president of the United States? Could you convince an Alaskan to purchase an air conditioner? Do you swear by Dale Carnegie's *How to Win Friends and Influence People?*

If so, you may be on your way to a successful future in an Enterprising career. Read on, you might be convinced!

〜〜〜 What Are These Careers and Where Can I Find Them?

Of all the Holland types, Enterprising people are probably the most likely to be found in a true business environment. Enterprising work is usually focused on achieving bottom-line results in a hard-driving, results-oriented environment. In this area there is concern with producing high-quality products or services that will generate high income potential. Typically, Enterprising occupations are those that are related to sales, management, supervision, politics, and leadership. Enterprising opportunities can be found in a full range of business settings: large corporations, financial institutions, small businesses, government, retail stores, restaurants. A representative sample of many job titles that fall into the Enterprising realm are listed in table 6 below. For a more complete listing of Enterprising careers, consult *The Dictionary of Holland Occupational Codes* or the appendix.

TABLE 6
EXAMPLES OF ENTERPRISING CAREERS

Computer salesperson	Lobbyist	Purchasing agent
Investments manager	Wholesaler	Realtor
Corporation executive	Athletic director	Financial planner
Media director	Interior decorator	Buyer
Life insurance agent	Marketing executive	Travel agency manager
Human resources director	Communications consultant	Foreign exchange trader
Investments manager	Ski patroller	Park superintendent
Employment manager	Elected public official	Stockbroker
University business manager		

You may notice that some careers, such as chef, are also classified under other Holland types. A chef may own his or her business, handling customers, vendors, and bookkeeping, in addition to preparing food. When a person is focused on the bottom line, no matter what the job title, she or he is considered enterprising in the true sense of the word.

～～～ Who Are These People and Am I One of Them?

What types of people are drawn to and do well in Enterprising occupations? What are their characteristics, values, and interests?

Stereotypic images of the eager used-car salesperson or the slick politician may come to mind when one pictures what an Enterprising person is like. Although some Enterprising types might actually have a hidden agenda, most know it pays to be scrupulously honest in the business world or the political arena.

Generally, Enterprising people perceive themselves to be self-confident, assertive, and social, possessing speaking and leadership abilities and lacking in scientific abilities. They enjoy using their social skills to influence people toward the achievement of economic or political gain. They tend to be adventuresome, persuasive, and highly energetic. Because they are drawn to power and are usually status conscious, Enterprising people can sometimes come across to others as superficial. But due to their strong ambition and high degree of self-confidence, they are often oblivious to the image they may portray to others.

Enterprising people have strong interpersonal skills and are generally considered outgoing and strong communicators. Like Social types, Enterprising people enjoy human relations, but, unlike Social types, their goal is often not service but sales or promotion. Enterprising types work hard at getting along with others, especially when achieving a particular goal is what is at stake. However, the goal may not always be for personal gain. The Enterprising individual may also use his or her skills and energy to benefit t   he community or a charity.

Enterprising people are probably the networking kings and queens of the world. Maintaining active contact with their large network of professional and personal colleagues and friends is of the utmost importance to Enterprising types. They are undoubtedly the least likely to burn any bridges. You never know when paths may cross again.

★ ★ ★ ★ *"You continue to grow by exposure to new problems and new material that you have to try to master. At each juncture in my career, I was listening to my inner voice. At each one, I heard people telling me to go elsewhere. There were many voices of authority advising me to do one thing or another, and I ultimately did something different. So the key is to develop a sense of your strengths and weaknesses over time and, despite failures now and then, to act on your own hunch about what's the best path to follow."*

BILL BRADLEY
U.S. SENATOR FROM NEW JERSEY

∿ ∿ ∿ So, Willie Loman You're Not...
Or, Should You Avoid This Field?

If you're only out to make a quick buck and are not really concerned whether the customer is satisfied, you probably won't last long in an Enterprising career. In addition to making a profit, people in Enterprising occupations need to respond to their customers' needs and be willing to compromise to ensure customer satisfaction. Retaining customers is the key to a successful business.

Other red flags to alert you that an Enterprising career is probably *not* for you include:

* *You spend as much time managing your budget as you do clipping your toenails.* To be successful, most people in Enterprising careers must devote ample time and energy to money management and producing bottom-line results. Many have strong mathematical abilities.

* *You're not comfortable being the center of attention and clam up in front of crowds.* Many Enterprising occupations entail lots of verbal communication and often include public speaking as part of the routine.

* *You couldn't sell a life preserver to a drowning person.* The art of persuasion is extremely important in most Enterprising occupations. Basic sales skills are usually a plus.

* *You prefer to be a follower rather than a leader.* Leadership roles are often part of the package in a number of Enterprising careers. Comfort with influencing and leading others is necessary.

~~~ How Do I Get Started?

It usually takes ambition, self-confidence, and energy to get started and become successful in an Enterprising career. Those aren't necessarily skills or traits that can be learned, but they can usually be detected early on and developed. The kid with the most successful lemonade stand on the block will probably be the one to go on to a fruitful Enterprising career.

Formal training or education is not always necessary to enter the Enterprising fields. However, the more sophisticated a person is in finance, marketing, and human relations, the more competitive and successful she or he can be. Preparation in math and social skills are critical for most Enterprising opportunities. A bachelor's degree has generally become the minimum educational credential required to become marketing, advertising, and PR managers; property and real estate managers; purchasing agents and managers; underwriters; wholesale and retail buyers; merchandise managers; insurance agents and brokers, manufacturers' and wholesale representatives; real estate agents, brokers, and appraisers; and securities and financial services sales representatives.

It's become more and more common for MBAs or other related graduate degrees to be required to enter and/or advance in many of the business-related Enterprising careers. An advanced degree is needed to compete for jobs as financial managers, general managers, top executives, management analysts, and management consultants.

Of all the Holland types, Enterprising people are probably the most comfortable selling themselves to a potential employer. However, in today's competitive job market, the more related experience and activities on a person's résumé, the better his or her chance of making the "sale." Extracurricular activities and part-time or volunteer work are important avenues for developing social skills and learning more about yourself and the kinds of situations in which you might succeed. Keeping score for athletic events, serving as president or treasurer of a club, joining the debate team, selling ad space for the school paper, working on a political campaign, and fund-raising for a charity are all ways to gain experience and get exposure to Enterprising fields.

~~~ What's It Like Out There?

Those who have a strong, eye-catching résumé and excellent networking and interviewing skills will be the most competitive in today's Enterprising job market. The outlook is good for Enterprising people who can deal with increasingly complex problems. Additionally, Enterprising types often have the skills and the foresight to create their own opportunities.

According to the *1994–1995 Occupational Outlook Handbook*, Enterprising occupations that will have average growth through 2005 include retail managers; funeral directors; underwriters; insurance agents and brokers; and real estate agents, brokers, and appraisers. Those occupations with faster than average growth include services sales representatives; real estate managers; property managers; lawyers; marketing, advertising, and PR managers; and securities and financial services representatives. Occupations that will grow much faster than average include management analysts and consultants; opticians; and travel agents. General managers and top executives; manufacturers and wholesale representatives; purchasing agents and managers; judges; government chief executives; and legislators will experience little or slower than average growth.

Geographically, those interested in working for financial institutions and larger corporations will probably have to settle in larger, more populated cities or regions. Those who are entrepreneurs and want to start their own businesses are less geographically constrained but will need to carefully consider market factors and customer demand when selecting a location.

◢◥◢◥ Where Do I Find Out More About Enterprising Careers?

The best way to learn more about what Enterprising people do is to talk to them directly. People generally like to talk about themselves and what they do. In fact, at the end of an informational interview with an Enterprising person, you'll probably be convinced that you've found the perfect career! Conducting informational interviews will give you the best picture of what a career is like, what's required for the career, how to prepare for it, and whether you'll enjoy the work.

We've started the process for you by conducting informational interviews with people in Enterprising careers; these comprise the remainder of this chapter. Continue by conducting additional interviews on your own. Refer to the final chapter in this book, What's Next?, for specific steps on doing informational interviewing.

Researching and reading about Enterprising careers is also key in your career exploration. Information on how to do career research and other tips on A list of books and organizations geared to Enterprising careers is presented below to get you started.

Books for Enterprising Careers

America's Top Office, Management, and Sales Jobs by M. J. Farr, published by JIST, 1994

Careers for Travel Buffs by P. Plawin, published by VGM Career Horizons, 1992

Careers in Accounting by G. Gaylord and G. Ried, published by VGM Career Horizons, 1991

Careers in Advertising by S. W. Pattis, published by VGM Career Horizons, 1990

Careers in Business by L. Stair, published by VGM Career Horizons, 1992

Careers in Finance by T. Ring, published by VGM Career Horizons, 1993

Careers in Marketing by L. Stair, published by VGM Career Horizons, 1991

The Insider's Guide to the Top 20+ Careers in Business and Management by T. Fischgrund, published by VGM Career Horizons, 1993

Marketing and Sales Career Directory by B. J. Morgan, published by Visible Ink Press, 1993

Opportunities in Business Management Careers by I. Place, published by VGM Career Horizons, 1991

Opportunities in Human Resource Management Careers by W. J. Traynor and J. S. McKenzie, published by VGM Career Horizons, 1994

VGM's Handbook of Business and Management Careers by C. T. Norback, published by VGM Career Horizons, 1993

Working in TV News by C. Filoreto and L. Setzer, published by Mustang Publishing, 1993

Professional Organizations for Enterprising Careers

Below are organizations that provide information on Enterprising careers. Consider contacting organizations that interest you. Be sure to include a self-addressed stamped envelope when writing to request information.

American Association of Advertising Agencies
666 Third Ave., 13th floor
New York, NY 10017

American Bankers Association
Reference Librarian
1120 Connecticut Ave., NW
Washington, DC 20036

American Bar Association
Information Services
750 North Lake Shore Dr.
Chicago, IL 60611

American Financial Services Association
919 18th St., NW
Washington, DC 20006

American Management Association
Management Information Service
135 West 50th St.
New York, NY 10020

American Marketing Association
250 S. Wacker Dr.
Chicago, IL 60606

American Society of Travel Agents
1101 King St.
Alexandria, VA 22314

Board of Governors
The Federal Reserve System
Human Resource Management Division
Washington, DC 20551

Council of Sales Promotion Agencies
750 Summer St.
Stamford, CT 06901

Council of State Governments
P.O. Box 11910
Iron Works Pike
Lexington, KY 40578

Financial Executives Institute
Academic Relations Committee
P.O. Box 1938
Morristown, NJ 07962-1938

Institute of Real Estate Management
430 N. Michigan Ave.
Chicago, IL 60611

Manufacturers' Agents National Association
23016 Mill Creek Road, P.O. Box 3467
Laguna Hills, CA 92654

National Association of Home Builders
15th and M St., NW
Washington, DC 20005

National Association of Life Underwriters
1922 F St., NW
Washington, DC 20006

National Association of Purchasing Management
P.O. Box 22160
Tempe, AZ 85285

National Association of Realtors
875 N. Michigan Ave.
Chicago, IL 60611

National Retail Federation
100 West 31st St.
New York, NY 10001

Sales and Marketing Executives International
458 Statler Office Tower
Cleveland, OH 44115

Securities Industry Association
120 Broadway
New York, NY 10271

Society of Chartered Property and Casualty Underwriters
Kahler Hall
P.O. Box 3009
720 Providence Road
Malvern, PA 19355-0709

The Council of Consulting Organizations, Inc.
251 Fifth Ave.
New York, NY 10175

The National Association of Counties
440 First St., NW
Washington, DC 20001

★★★ DIANNE FEINSTEIN

U.S. SENATOR FROM CALIFORNIA

WHEN CHOOSING A CAREER, young people should follow their strengths and their hearts. It's important to select a profession that one feels passionate about—whatever that is. Otherwise, it is too difficult to do the hard work necessary to succeed.

My father was a physician and he very much wanted me to follow in his footsteps. Of course, I tried, slogging my way through biology and other science courses at Stanford University. But my heart wasn't in it.

Then I took some history courses, and one in particular, "American Political Thought," really sparked my interest.

But my first exposure to politics had actually come years earlier when a favorite uncle took me to city hall to watch what he called the "Board of Stupidvisors." My uncle was a working-class man who had given up his own education to help send my father to medical school. I was an impressionable fifteen-year-old school girl and this early experience really made its mark. My uncle used to say, "Dianne, you get an education and you do this job and do it well."

I can't tell you exactly why, but that stuck. I knew that someday I wanted to be a city supervisor and I wanted to be a good one.

At Stanford I studied history and politics. I participated in a lot of activities and volunteered for a variety of jobs—doing scut work as well as work that allowed me to take a leadership role.

After college I was selected as in intern for the Coro Foundation, a fellowship program in public affairs. This was a pivotal experience. Through hands-on training I discovered that significant change could be effected through the political process and my commitment to a career in government had begun.

But no matter what career one picks, it is important to have a sense of commitment and caring—enough to be willing to start at the bottom and work one's way up to positions of responsibility. Don't be hesitant to start as a clerk or a typist, if that's the job that needs to be done. Such work will serve you well in the long run as you hone the skills and develop the expertise you will need throughout your professional career.

One thing I would caution for anyone choosing public service as a career, however, is to have a strong ideology, to know why you are going into the governmental arena. There are many who are in it for the wrong reasons: self-gratification, a sense of theater, ego.

But the best reason to choose a career as a public servant is to serve people. I chose government because I felt that the political process was an effective way to contribute to my community, bring about significant change, and to try and make a better life for those who need our help most. Government can be a brutal arena, but entered for the right reasons, it can also be tremendously rewarding.

★★

∼∼∼ W. ANDREW MCGURK

STOCKBROKER

At the time of this interview, Andrew was a stockbroker with a small firm in New Jersey. His interest in stocks began in a high school economics class. He began as a runner and plans to specialize in retirement planning for small-business owners and employees.

THE PRIMARY PURPOSE OF A BROKER is to place customers in a proper investment based on their needs and, of course, their personal income level, be it retirement, growth and equity, income products, or possibly one that is very, very high risk.

The day typically begins with checking financial periodicals, the *Wall Street Journal*, investment business dailies, and Dow Jones news wires for information pertaining to any positions in which you currently have or are initiating coverage. Then, basically, if there's any breaking news or news that you want to relay to customers, you contact your customers throughout the day or when it's convenient, passing on the information in either print form through the mail or verbally over the phone.

A good portion of your day will be involved in prospecting. Prospecting can be done in a number of ways, through what everyone fears and loathes, and that's through cold-calling. Prospecting can also be done through direct-mail advertising. The best source of prospecting is through referral. And that's the constant ongoing job of a broker: to constantly get new referrals and to get customers for a number of different investments or investment strategies.

My first experience with investments was in a high school economics class in which I enjoyed the correlations between the economy and the development of a company—social, economic, political, and financial. That's what brought me to this area originally.

I actually went into economics in college and then came through the ranks as most people do. It's paying your dues. You start as a clerk somewhere—as a runner, as it's sometimes referred to. And you learn the business and you try to make your contacts that way.

After working in operations for a number of years, I went to what is called a trading desk, and that is where you actually take products that have been delivered by customers and you try to find the best possible price using whatever sort of parameters the customer may instruct you. You just try to do your best job in getting the best price at the best time for the particular customer or institution that is looking at the financial product.

Then I went into retail, which is bringing customers to an appropriate financial investment vehicle of their choosing.

From here, several brokers make what is called a niche in the market. Some brokers are specifically equity investors, some are fixed-income investors, some are tax-free investors. Other brokers, such as me, are independent retirement coordinators—setting up small corporations, small businesses, which might not be going to a larger financial institution for their retirement needs and, hopefully, directing them into something that will protect employees' and employers' money over a period of time against taxes. I believe it's the basis of many, many brokers' businesses, and, if not, it's something that everyone obviously is concerned with—preserving capital for retirement, their heirs. You know, the rainy-day policy.

I enjoy most the constant influx of current information and the excitement of watching developing companies grow, watching the development of my customers. Several times you'll meet customers who start on a very, very small level and they grow into their careers and into businesses and you grow with them. So it's the constant change.

It's always a challenge, and it is by no means a repetitive business. You are constantly changing, you are constantly trying to stay aware of the financial markets and the changing political and even the social atmosphere of your community and the customers that you have in particular investments.

The downside is that there is a tremendous amount of competition out there, and competition comes in several ways. First of all, you have discount brokers. You also have a lot of full-service brokers.

You have competition in the sense of perceptions. Many times people will look at a broker and they will look at the industry from a very, very narrow view and see a broker as somebody who is your Gordon Gekko type of Wall Street, who is trying to take a company, rip it apart, sell it for his own personal profit.

Typically, what you need to do is establish yourself in some way with a reputable firm. And that's not as hard to do as some people may think. You have to become licensed through the National Association of Securities Dealers and pass a test, which is called Series 7. It's a rather difficult test and typically takes six months to pass.

Most firms do like to take someone who has some college education; however, that's not a prerequisite for the job. You will find brokers who come from every facet of life. There are brokers who were once lawyers, doctors, dentists, reporters. There are brokers who never graduated from high school.

There are many prerequisites you can put upon yourself. However, all a college education will prove is that you can complete something. It is always good to have general knowledge of areas of business and social environment. Several brokers come from the liberal arts area of the curriculum, bringing in a fresh attitude and knowledge.

Generally, people who succeed in this business are those with Type A personalities—someone who can take rejection very well, someone who understands the value of time (which is very important) someone who will bring a customer to an idea or bring a group of employees to an idea and be able to build that over time.

The people who are generally the best in this business are the ones who can take risks. The risks they are taking are not with customers, however, they're taking the risks with themselves because they have to believe in themselves. They are coming into a situation where they are going to face a lot of competition, they are going to face a lot of down days. You don't have down days in careers in which your income is steady and you have a very stable environment. However, you have to learn how to overcome every aspect of that to try to become successful.

As a first-year broker, the pay typically is on the very, very low end. The idea is that it takes approximately two years for a typical broker to build a book, a customer base, with a comfortable income level. So there is often a need for some sort of financial base or at least financial backing. However, it's not always necessary. There are several firms that offer arrangements in which you will be able to finance your career and get started in your business. And that's exactly how you treat it, as your own personal business.

In terms of salary, you have complete control over that, since you can give yourself a raise in many ways. It's just to what extent you're willing to dedicate yourself.

I think it is best for anybody starting out to have a very realistic attitude. People come into the business and they think in their first year they're going to make a phenomenal salary. It just doesn't happen that way. As in anything else, dues have to be paid. You need to look for reputable firms, feel comfortable with the people you're working with, and know that you're going to have to dedicate yourself. This is not the kind of job where you're going to go in at a set salary and start getting cost-of-living increases and merit bonuses. You have to have a little bit more drive, and a strong desire to pursue success.

~~~ JOHN O'CONNELL

SALESPERSON

At the time of this interview, John was a sales representative for Aetna Life & Casualty in the company's Employee Benefits Division. Working through a network of independent insurance agents, financial consultants, and brokers, he markets Aetna's group insurance and investment products to prospective clients.

LIKE MOST COLLEGE SENIORS, I went through the on-campus interview process in the spring of my senior year. What I first attempted to do was outline my strengths and weaknesses and target job opportunities that I felt would mesh. I think it is important to look at yourself with a critical eye and figure out the type of situations that you seem to do best in. I had always been a people-oriented person. Therefore, sales positions were the job category I was looking for. The insurance industry appealed to me because you are not selling a tangible item. Your product and your sales rely on your ability to create a feeling of trust and confidence between your client and yourself. Yet probably the biggest influence on my decision was the impression made by the various companies with which I had interviews. I tried to analyze the people who made up those companies and to judge how I would work as their peers. The people at Aetna Life & Casualty seemed to have similar backgrounds to my own and I saw myself as being one of them. The decision to work at Aetna, a place where I would be comfortable with the other employees, was an easy one for me.

My academic record in college was not great. I was very much involved in extracurricular activities, in most cases, in a leadership position. The lessons I learned outside of the classroom in leadership positions were of great assistance in developing the confidence necessary to be successful on the job. Skills such as public speaking, delegating work assignments, and running meetings are intangible skills that I use every day in my present position. My outside activities during college helped me develop skills that also helped me when I attempted to enter the workforce.

My job-hunting strategy consisted of using the career counseling office. I interviewed with as many companies on campus as possible. I think the Christmas vacation is a great time to begin arranging interviews with firms other than the ones that visit the campus. Again, once you analyze in general terms the type of job you want, your time can be split between talking with firms that visit the campus and those that do not. In my case, I got an interview with Aetna through a referral from a career counselor.

The position I now hold is very competitive. In my training program, for instance, we had twenty-two men and women from all over the country. In selecting these people, Aetna interviewed approximately a thousand candidates nationwide. These twenty-two people, who left the training program last summer to enter various field offices, now are part of a field force of three hundred sales representatives who, in one year, generated over $2 million in new business.

My job is to sell group insurance and pension/investment products to clients. I work through a network of independent insurance agents, financial consultants, and brokers to convince them that Aetna products should be recommended to their clients. In addition, I service an existing "book of business" for Aetna policyholders. Most of my week is spent on the road, where I meet with agents and brokers and assist them in presentations to a prospect. I am in the office approximately two full days a week, to handle paperwork or administrative chores. I am judged primarily on my sales efforts. Therefore, it is imperative that I spend a great deal of my time in "live" situations, convincing agents/brokers/consultants and their clients that Aetna is the way to go. Because I sell both group insurance and pension plans, the time demands in my job are tremendous. To be successful, one must be extremely organized and time efficient. Because I am on the road so often, learning to use a secretary and delegating responsibility to others are skills that must be mastered very quickly. What I like about this position is that I am my own boss. What I do with my time, how I delegate responsibility, and how I structure my relationship with clients is entirely up to me. With this freedom, of course, goes the pressure of being successful. We are paid quite well, and the feeling of losing in a highly competitive situation is difficult to accept. The responsibilities early on in one's career are quite large, but I much prefer this situation to one in which you are nurtured for a long period of time before your responsibilities are measurable.

I had expected a position with more structure. As I mentioned before, the use of my time is up to me, and I much prefer that situation to a rigid timetable. I also had not expected the level of responsibility I currently have. But I love a situation in which you are constantly "in the fire" and have many more things to do than you could possibly have time for.

The training I've received has been outstanding. I attended a two-month classroom program during the summer after I was hired. I was assigned to a field office, where I had an opportunity to learn the business firsthand. I returned to the training site nine months later, for further specialization in product knowledge. I'm sure Aetna is not unique in demanding a high level of expertise from its representatives, and a large dose of dedication is necessary during the initial training period.

As I review my past year with Aetna, my best times were seeing myself improve in my level of expertise. Of course, as a salesperson, there is nothing quite as thrilling as closing a sale. The most difficult times were when, as a newcomer to the business world, people judged me to be too inexperienced to help them in what they were doing. There is nothing more frustrating than giving a presentation to a group of older prospects and being asked a difficult question that I can't answer with my limited experience. Of course, the only solution to this problem is time and more exposure.

In my business, the most successful people are extremely adaptable and are capable of split-second situation analysis. And good organizational skills and time management translate into more selling time. Successful sales representatives are very outgoing.

The skill I use most often in my job is public speaking. Whether it be during a formal presentation/slide show to a million-dollar pension prospect or explaining group insurance benefits at a union hall, I must be very flexible and understanding of my clients' needs. Therefore, I must be an outstanding listener. Overall, communication skills are most important. A close second is the ability to manage others. Learning to delegate tasks and the ability to motivate others enable me to use my time wisely.

During the next five years, I intend to remain where I am. I am going back to school in the fall, but I haven't decided whether to work for an MBA or a CLU (Certified Life Underwriter) designation. The nature of my work requires that I be transferred whenever a promotion is in line. Therefore, I anticipate an exciting few years of constant changes and new environments.

Many people start work in one city and stay there for forty years. I will never have that luxury. If I am to advance, I must go where I am told and do my best there. I am unmarried now, so being single allows me flexibility.

I live in an apartment in Buffalo, New York. I enjoy being in the city, as it is not far from the office and has all the convenience—and drawbacks—of big-city life. I spend a fair amount of my day entertaining clients, but it is nice to know when you leave the office that you do not have to worry about something until the next morning.

In college, you have the constant pressure of academics. Now that I am free from that, I can structure my time differently. I structure my workweek to accommodate what I feel is most important. Therefore, if I want to take an afternoon off to play golf with prospects, I have the flexibility to do it. My leisure time is much different from that of someone who is sitting behind a desk from 9 to 5 each day.

Before anyone enters my line of work, he or she should be aware that there is a large amount of pressure to perform. You need to be sure that your strengths match up to those of successful people in the profession. Many people would not like the kind of flexibility that I have, but I enjoy the feeling of being my own boss.

I would say that anyone wishing to enter the employee benefits market must be able to relate well to others, be very self-motivated, and have a high degree of flexibility. There is also a level of maturity necessary, as you are dealing with people of all ages and occupations, and you must be understanding of each particular need that you address. Most people in this line of work have relatively large egos and need the constant pressure and competitiveness of this field. There are three hundred sales reps working nationwide to sell my company's group and pension products. To back up this field force, there are approximately twelve thousand employees in various departments. Therefore, it is very easy to hang an "elitist" tag on this position. I am the type of individual who enjoys having twenty-five hours' worth of work to do each day. I enjoy being in front of people, and I enjoy the benefits that come from living at a rather frantic pace. That's why I feel it is so important for a job seeker to analyze the job and him or herself to come up with a successful match.

RANDALL HOLDEN

CONSULTANT

Randall entered the job market when he was twenty-seven years old, after graduating from college with a BA in history and serving three and a half years in the navy. He worked for four years as an account manager-consultant for a private firm, where he was responsible for several client projects involving telecommunications.

AFTER GRADUATING FROM COLLEGE with a BA in history, I spent three and a half years as a navy officer. As a result, I was almost twenty-seven years old when I entered the job market. I took a management training position with New York Telephone and remained there for seven years, primarily in sales. Although I learned a lot about my field, I probably stayed too long with New York Telephone. That is my only career regret to date. I joined my present firm four and a half years ago as an account manager, where I am responsible for several client projects. Since that time, my responsibilities have increased as the company has grown from 20 to 105 people.

I am responsible for all consulting projects undertaken by my firm. I also manage the consulting personnel who work on these projects. My job, therefore, requires two primary skills: consulting expertise in telecommunications and management skills in supervising and training personnel—twenty-seven people altogether.

I spend the majority of my time in management and less and less in actual consulting. However, since my firm is a small one and our field is technical, fast-growing, and innovative, I have to stay as knowledgeable and conversant as possible in my field. To accomplish this, I read trade publications and technical information provided by vendors and suppliers in the telecommunications industry. I also accompany our consultants to client meetings to keep up to date on our clients' concerns and needs, and how we can best respond to them.

Any consulting career requires prior knowledge and experience in the field. My firm used to be able to make consultants out of college graduates with no track record or experience. However, the industry has become so technical and sophisticated that successful consultants must have previous technical education and experience. In addition, consulting requires excellent communications skills, because the only product is what is transmitted verbally, or in writing, to the client. The information presented must be understandable, pertinent, concise, and easily converted to formats such as slides or transparencies. Most telecommunications consultants deal with people like financial managers, data processing managers, telecommunications managers, administration managers, and engineers. Learning to be a good listener and developing good interviewing skills are essential. When I began my career, liberal arts majors did best in consulting. Today, an accompanying computer science or other technical education is becoming more and more essential for a meaningful career in a technical consulting field such as telecommunications.

Although our firm is relatively large for a telecommunications consulting firm, it is still a very small company. Therefore, the working environment is intimate, relatively unstructured, and results oriented. Although we have official working hours, ours is not a 9-to-5 day. We must meet deadlines, and it is not unusual for staff members, including those at the junior level, to work late into the night and on occasional weekends to complete a report. This type of environment breeds an esprit de corps and cordiality that are personally appealing. However, the relatively unstructured environment may not be appealing to everyone, particularly someone who is just coming into the workforce and may be more comfortable in a more regulated environment.

Telecommunications—telephones, video, data communications, and satellite communications—is one of the fastest-growing industries. The entire field of information processing, office automation, and global networks is concerned with telecommunications. In addition, data processing and telecommunications have merged to form an incredibly powerful force in the marketplace. Since the Bell System, long the dominant force in the industry, was deregulated by the FCC and forced to split up by the courts, the environment has become very competitive. These changes in the industry, as well as incredible technological advances, have created and will continue to create incredible opportunities for new small firms to provide essential telecommunications products and services. The job market offers entry-level positions for those with a technical education in computer science, mathematics, or electrical engineering. From this background, moving into a consulting firm within telecommunications becomes attractive. The number of suppliers and new technologies in the industry have made the choices and options available to the business community confusing and staggering. The need for consultants to assist in decision making has dramatically increased.

Career fields related to mine include telecommunications management in a large firm, telecommunications equipment selling, data processing management, and other areas of management consulting. Movement is relatively easy, since experience gained in telecommunications is in great demand.

My most important career-related decision was to leave a huge, well-structured company, which provided absolute security, in order to go to a small, young company with little security. I knew telecommunications was the field for me, and I had great confidence in the future of the industry. My primary reason for leaving the Bell System was my conviction that the large-company environment was beginning to suffocate my initiative and was providing me with little opportunity for personal growth.

The former Bell System provided an excellent training ground for the telecommunications industry, and for many people it offered an excellent career as well. Outside the Bell System, career paths were less clear, since most of the other companies in the industry at that time were relatively small. I decided, however, that a more entrepreneurial environment was best for me. Today, many of the firms in the industry, such as MCI, Sprint, and Northern Telecom, are huge corporations in their own right.

The primary factor that has hindered my career is my lack of technical or data processing background. Although my background has provided me with communications and management skills, I would have preferred more direct education and/or experience in computer science and related areas. I do not believe I could have attained my present position if I were starting out today. A technical background has become critical in this field.

I spend as much time with my family as possible. Despite long working hours, I don't find that my job interferes with my family obligations. I don't have to travel often, and this has improved my family situation considerably. I have made a conscious decision not to be a joiner. I feel my working hours are long enough and that it would be unfair to my family to spend time with clubs, groups, or associations. I do spend time playing golf, tennis, and watching sporting events, but keep these activities to a minimum.

The former Bell System was to provide the salary range for our industry. Today, because of the fast-growing nature of the industry, experienced telecommunications professionals are in great demand, and this has kept salaries in the industry competitive. In many cases, compensation, particularly in smaller firms, is tied to incentive and performance plans.

Unless you have specialized training, either professional or technical, the most important factor for someone entering the job market for the first time is the industry and *not* the position. Getting into a growth industry such as telecommunications provides so many opportunities that a job, in any capacity, even one that is not of particular interest to the individual, will enable that person to gain experience, evaluate other areas within that industry, and then make advantageous moves.

~ ~ ~ CAROLE PURKEY

NATIONAL ACCOUNTS REPRESENTATIVE

At the time of this interview, Carole worked in sales as a national accounts representative for a major national book distributor, serving accounts in the southeastern territory of the United States. She works from her home in Nashville. The books she promotes range in topics from technical science to leisure time recreation.

MY FORMAL EDUCATION has been in liberal arts. I majored in communications and have a master's degree in education. Although I did not set out to work specifically in those areas, or even in sales, this background has greatly enhanced the required skills essential to my field. In sales, communication is of the utmost importance because what I am doing is educating and communicating with my customers. I have been a teacher in public education and at the college level, which has also greatly contributed to my sales expertise. I have also worked as an instructor for computer training, where I learned and used a lot of technical skills. That position helped me land a job as a technical book buyer for a large wholesaler, and I went on from there to become a sales representative for general audience books. Through the connections and the networking that I cultivated while working in these capacities, I was able to qualify for my current position.

As a national accounts representative, I present, promote, and sell to consumers, retailer bookstores, and small wholesalers of books, the products that publishers have completed. I am currently representing several small publishers, who produce, write, edit, and bind books but need someone to go out and sell their books. I sell to a particular territory, specifically large accounts in the southeastern United States. I make presentations about the books I am selling and tell my customers, the bookstores and book buyers, just what a particular book is about and how that subject is presented in the book. I must present the book to my buyers in the context of why the end-user—the consumer—will want to buy this book.

As a salesperson, I need to know about my product, but I don't need to be intimate with my product. For instance, I don't have to read every book I sell. I love books, and I love to read, but it would take forever to read every book I promote. I am given tools by the publisher, mainly encapsulated information about the book, such as why it was written, information about the author, the subject matter, and how it is presented. I need to know enough about the book, without reading it cover to cover, so I do not misrepresent it.

One of the many advantages to what I do is that it is very much like running my own business. I have my own territory and can decide what it is I should do to make that book, or those books, sell in my territory. Occasionally, I go back to the publisher and ask for advertising, if I feel the book would appeal to a particular population. The door is really wide open for me to be as creative as I want in coming up with ideas to promote those books. The publishers also come up with ideas, but it is a lot of fun to be able to sit and think, What will sell this book in this place?, and What is it about this place that would make it need this book or want this book? For example, I spend a lot of time traveling around the Southeast. I make it a point to watch local television shows and read local papers to see just what it is about that place and what it is about that book that would fit in that region.

Working from home, I have the advantage of allowing myself a very flexible schedule. I decide when and how to get to the places I have to go. Where I go and who I go to see, however, is dictated primarily by the needs of my accounts. For instance, if there is an autographing scheduled by an author, I have to make sure the materials they need to promote the event get to the right location at the right time. The work involves a lot of coordinating, but it's also a lot of fun, because you see it all fall together.

I spend a lot of time away from home, which, for me, is an enjoyment. I am single and do not have any family or children, so a traveling career is easy for me. It is a solitary existence most of the time, so you have to be a person who doesn't mind being alone. You also have to be an enterprising individual. Unexpected car troubles, for example, will force you to readjust your schedule, or if someone takes advantage of your time, or, worse, simply doesn't show up for an appointment. The work involves a lot of packing and unpacking, and a lot of different hotels on a lot of different nights, but the publishing business is seasonal. There are busy periods, in the spring and the fall, and slow periods that make up for all the schlepping I must contend with during the busy seasons.

My typical workday and my typical workweek are atypical. There are a few daily responsibilities but, for the most part, there is no normal day or week.

Spending a great deal of time on the telephone with my accounts, or driving three or four hours to an account and back again in the same day, or getting on a plane in the morning and returning home that evening, are weekly events that I would call typical. And I love every minute of it.

Selling skills are selling skills. The products may change, but the skills do not. When you are in sales, and you are good at it, if you work at it, the opportunities are limitless as far as other sales opportunities. Relocating, however, is often a part of advancing yourself in sales. Advancement for me would mean a management position or directing a field sales force. I am not interested, at this time, in any advancement, not because I am not motivated or ambitious, but because I really do enjoy selling. Selling, to me, is what's fun.

Other opportunities that would exist for someone with my experience and background would be to start their own company, representing publishers or people in other fields. It can be a very lucrative business, but you have to be willing to work strictly on commission. Most book companies have a lot of opportunities for upward mobility. I have worked my way up from territory representative to my current title of national account representative, which means I deal with the larger accounts that are considered to have a national effect on my company.

I used to work in the computer business, where I spent hours and hours in the same office each working day. One Saturday, I caught myself thinking that if I didn't have that job, I wouldn't know what to do. It was at that moment that I decided that I did not want to live or think like that. Selling has given me a great balance of work and leisure, where I can plan my work schedule around social activities with friends. I am out of town frequently, but I can plan activities around those times, which allows for a relaxed lifestyle. There is pressure in any sales position, such as struggling to meet your quotas and other things, but if you work hard when you are at work, then you can relax. You work out your own balance.

Most companies looking for sales representatives want people with experience, but product knowledge and knowledge of the field is also very important. I meet a lot of young people working in bookstores who want to do what I do. I tell them to keep doing exactly what they are doing right now, until they get out of school. Knowing about your product, working in a bookstore, is the best on-the-job training you can get. And get a broad education. Having a liberal arts background has really helped me understand the well-rounded subject matter of the books I promote, but I can see where liberal arts would help in any sales capacity.

Success in sales requires more than a formal education. You have to be a self-starter, self-disciplined, and intrinsically motivated. Developing self-starting skills and learning to be persistent but not annoying are also essential. When I see buyers, I am certainly not the only sales representative they see, because buying a book to them is so sterile and they buy so many. I have to make sure that after they buy my book, they are going to promote it. Honesty is also essential, because you sell your credibility to your accounts. If I feel a book they might want to purchase would not do well in their market, I express that to them, and they remember me for that. There are bad days, but most days are good days. But you have to want to work every day, and a lot of that comes from inside.

The pay scale for sales representatives varies from publisher to publisher. I have a master's degree, which edges your salary up in any career field. What works the best is an open-ended bonus, which means you are paid a percentage for sales in your territory. With this kind of bonus package, it is possible to double your salary.

We all have dreams about what a job should be like, but the actual working, the nitty-gritty of it, is important to know up front. After you know that, choose a career that you know you will really enjoy. For example, I have very broad interests. I really enjoy literature and books, but I also like more technical things, like computers and marketing. My job is a classroom in and of itself, because I am always finding out things about all kinds of different subjects. Money can be misleading, although it is very important, especially for someone like me who is single. Know what kind of lifestyle you want to lead, and take the cost of that lifestyle into consideration. Students should also be aware of the benefits certain jobs offer. For instance, I am given a car allowance. That certainly gives more mileage to my salary. Last, but certainly not least, a career should be chosen based on whether or not you are a people person. If you are not a people person, sales is not for you. Because people skills are so important in sales, you really need to know who you are and be honest with yourself about what you are good at.

~~~ CHRIS CAVALIER

MARKET RESEARCHER

Chris managed a health and fitness facility for several years before deciding to attend college. At the time of this interview, he had worked for Procter & Gamble as a market researcher for two years. He was also cultivating his own business with a partner in the Cincinnati area.

AFTER GRADUATING FROM HIGH SCHOOL, I worked for a number of years before deciding to go to college. I decided to focus on the field of business because I thought my work experience, which included managing a health and fitness facility in Miami, best suited me to be a business major. However, the diversity in Miami made me interested in the field of international relations. In fact, I switched my major and decided to transfer to Georgetown University's School of Foreign Service.

I have been with the company almost two years now, where I am a market research supervisor. While I knew nothing about market research when I graduated, the transition has not been too difficult. I think the skills you develop in academia prepare you well for market research. We are involved in defining appropriate business questions, conducting research to answer those questions, analyzing information, drawing what we hope are intelligent conclusions, and presenting our findings to others, both verbally and in writing. I think the work is pretty analogous to what is done in academia. In fact, if a person can do well in school and scholastics fit well with their personality, I think they can do well in the entry levels of market research.

The market research function at Procter and Gamble is somewhat unique in that all of our clients are other people within the company. While some companies source out their research to outside companies, we feel it is a competitive advantage for us to have an internal research department. I know so much about our company's internal operations, as well as the products I work on, that I am able to address my clients' questions better than someone else who doesn't have that knowledge.

Currently, my clients within the company are people in the area of what Procter & Gamble calls Brand Management. These are people who serve as project leaders to get our products in the market. While these Brand Management people work with many people within the company, they come to me when they have specific questions that deal with what consumers think about our products or ideas.

In the end, market research at this company tries to serve as the voice of the consumer. What we are trying to do is understand, or estimate, what the "truth" is in the marketplace. By "truth," I mean what the people in the marketplace think or feel about our products as well as the products of our competitors. We use a number of different methodologies to try to ascertain this "truth" with a particular level of confidence. To do this, we run tests among a sample group of people who we have determined to be representative of a larger population and extrapolate the findings to the larger universe. That larger universe may be the total U.S. population or some other geography where one of our products or ideas may be expanded into. However, in the end, since the company cannot afford to sample our products with everyone in the larger universe, we still run the risk—albeit a small risk—that the hypotheses we formulate from our testing may be incorrect. That is why it is so important that we not only use the data we compile from our testing but we also use our judgment to make the best decisions possible.

Personally, I like being part of a function whose aim is to be the objective truth seekers. I have the freedom to look at things objectively without being dictated by a predetermined purpose, like trying to get a product into the market. In market research, we are trying to solve a puzzle, which is the consumer, and we try to do it objectively.

While I enjoyed my studies at Georgetown, I realized toward the end of my collegiate career that I wasn't interested in public service at that juncture of my life. It was at that point that I noticed Procter and Gamble's Brand Management Division was recruiting on campus. Feeling that I could expand my skills a lot more in market research than in sales, I accepted an offer in the company's Market Research Department.

On the other hand, I must admit that I do not like the fact that I am not directly involved in making final decisions about our company's initiatives. We are a staff, or support function. While I am becoming more influential in the decision-making process since my recommendations are becoming more valued by my clients, the bottom line is that the market research function is not responsible for making final decisions. While some people prefer not to have that kind of responsibility and the pressure that comes along with it, I personally would like more of it. In fact, there are no real tangible measures of my efforts which, at times, can be frustrating. I'm also not real big on bureaucracy, and in this company, which has been around for over 150 years, bureaucracy is fairly prevalent. Even with the company downsizing from 103,000 to 90,000 employees, there are still a lot of layers of management. You have to get accustomed to getting things approved before you do them.

What motivates me most is the satisfaction of knowing that I helped the company make appropriate business decisions. When I see an initiative go into the marketplace, and I know that I was instrumental in helping make the best business decisions to get it there, it's a nice feeling. I am also motivated by the fact that I am working with many highly intelligent and highly motivated people who constantly challenge me to put forth my best. In that kind of environment, it would be difficult not to be able to continually improve yourself.

On a typical day, I start out spending some time reading interdepartmental and electronic mail. I also spend a lot of time meeting with clients who come to me with specific questions. While it is my job to help answer their questions, I also find that I can add tremendous value by even helping to define exactly what the question is. You can do all the research you want, but if you are not attempting to address the right question, you aren't going to get the type of answers that can truly help you succeed in the market. Once the question is defined, I then design the research that will help answer the question.

My leisure time is spent cultivating my own business in sports-related collectibles. Market research is a field where you can find a comfortable balance between work and leisure time.

I began my job search at the beginning of my senior year and solidified my job offer in January of my graduating year. The best advice I can give to students of any discipline is to start your job search early, because the process takes time. Take the time to be introspective and find out what drives you and what things are important to you. Before I started working for Procter & Gamble, I read a lot of literature about the company and felt that I would fit well within it. When I started working at Procter & Gamble, a co-worker advised me that a career is not a sprint—it's a marathon, so pace yourself. Take your time and find the things that you enjoy and do them because life's too short to spend it doing something you don't like.

A successful person in market research is one who demonstrates leadership abilities, although it's not necessarily a requisite to fulfill the responsibilities in an entry-level position. Since leadership skills become instrumental when you begin to progress, being able to demonstrate leadership from academic experiences will aid a person in getting a position in market research. In addition to leadership, the Market Research Department at Procter looks for people who demonstrate strong initiative, follow-through, and good problem-solving skills.

Any student considering market research should take classes that help in understanding human behavior. Introductory psychology classes helped me tremendously, and any classes that deal with understanding consumer behavior can only be beneficial. Statistics would be helpful since we do statistical analyses in market research. I had absolutely no background in statistics when I started at Procter, so I had to learn everything on the job.

In making a career decision, I would suggest that you surround yourself with people who you admire and that you believe have integrity. Look for these people in your current environment so that you can continue to elevate yourself and get valuable perspectives to aid you in your decisions. As you begin to explore a career, don't hesitate to talk to people already working in that field. There are professionals out there who are more than willing to help you and give you advice. I will never forget the people who helped me along the way, and I would never hesitate to try and help someone else looking for help.

~~~~ LISA CORVESE

RESEARCH ANALYST

Lisa decided on a career in finance after taking a nine-month leave of absence from Boston College to work for Merrill Lynch at their corporate headquarters in New York, where she worked in fundamental analysis. At the time of this interview, she was a research analyst for Data Resources, where she was responsible for financial consulting of very diversified markets, such as trading and corporate finance.

I DECIDED ON MY CAREER during my second semester of my senior year of college. My background was in linguistics, computer science, and economics. Linguistics was not going to put a roof over my head or food in my mouth, so I focused in on computer science and economics and started spending time at the career planning and placement office at Dartmouth. I went through the decision process by going through the brochures they had available on different companies and decided what positions were available and whether or not they met my needs. Then I started sending out my résumé with a cover letter using mass mailing lists. I had the career planning and placement offices at my colleges look at my résumé to be sure that it complied with the standards in the business world.

I had also attended four different universities. I started out at Boston College and graduated from Boston College. In between, I had gone to Middlebury College for languages and Dartmouth College and New York University for computer science. I also attended Languard University in the then-Soviet Union.

I was extremely involved in school. I worked with the college radio station as a hobby, mostly doing radio discussions on women's issues, and developed an underground network for the women's movement in Cambridge. I was also involved in curricular activities, especially "My House," which was a commuter resident house where commuters attending Boston College could hang their hats during the day or stay overnight if they got stuck at the college. We coordinated social events, invited guest speakers, and led group discussions. My House was pretty much a full-time job, with a full budget to manage and about five work study students to coordinate.

Previous work experience is really what helped me land my current job as a research analyst for Data Resources, Inc. (DRI). Prior to coming to DRI, I had worked for Merrill Lynch as a junior analyst in their International Research Department. I had taken a nine-month leave of absence from college to work for Merrill Lynch. It was there that I got the idea that I wanted to go into finance. I acquired a pretty good financial background from those nine months. I worked in fundamental analysis, which helped me decide what companies I should look at and what type of job I was looking for when I went back to school.

Most financial companies today are looking for students whose backgrounds are extremely diversified. Job candidates have to have quantitative skills, so their major has to be in computer science, economics, or mathematics, but at the same time, they have to have strong interpersonal skills to be able to interact with clients and co-workers. They have to have a high energy level and must be well-rounded in their interests and work experiences.

One of the most important aspects of my job as a research analyst at DRI is learning to work with the clients. Each of us has a client base we work with, and we learn to work in a team environment. There are co-workers who work with us on the same level and managers who are above us on a senior level who direct. It is basically on-the-job training, and the work is extremely diversified.

A typical day includes answering phones, learning a new proprietary computer language, learning to interface with clients, and during your first year (typically after about three months), working with the clients directly, not only at DRI, but also at the client's site. DRI moves you fairly quickly. The usual course is six months as a research analyst, then associate consultant, and, finally, consultant, after you have been there about a year and a half.

The days are long. A typical workday is about ten hours, and that is a conservative estimate. I end up working anywhere between fifty and seventy hours a week, depending on the work I am involved in. There are a lot of pressures, mainly to perform and make revenues grow. Every analyst has direct account responsibility after about six months, so even though we are working in a team environment, I have got to set an autonomous role, because it is up to me to develop my own work schedule.

What I like best about working for DRI is that the company is a young company and everybody who works there is young. The median age is probably about twenty-five to twenty-six, so it's new and unique to be working in a peer environment where even the senior-level people are very close to your age. What I like least has been getting used to the amount of work that is expected of me and having to do it in a very short period of time.

Possessing a high energy level is extremely important in this field. A candidate must be willing to put in the hours and like what he or she is doing. Being able to learn quickly and being able to think quickly are also important. Strong interpersonal skills are essential, because you have to be able to interact with people. If I do not know the answer to a client's question, I must get back to the client as quickly and as gracefully as possible. I also have to know the market I am dealing with, because as a financial consultant, I deal with mostly very diversified financial markets, such as trading, corporate finance, and fundamental analysis, which are all very different. There is no way to be an expert in all of them, but I am expected to know a little bit about every one of them.

I am using all of the skills that I learned in college, especially my computer science skills. I have often wondered what it would be like to go back to my computer science classes; I would probably sleep through them because the amount of information that I have learned since then is incredible. I have learned to take the theory of economics and, realizing that theory does not always work on the street, translate it to the practical side of economics, where I am drawing from theory. I have also used my finance education and I have also learned an incredible amount more about finances through my work experience.

During my first year, I had several bosses. My first boss was one of the reasons I joined DRI. I felt very comfortable with him during my interview, and I felt that we would have a good relationship. I knew that I would have to have on-the-job training, so I knew that I wanted to have somebody I could trust. After that, my relationships with my bosses have been somewhat tenuous. I do not always feel I am getting the superior direction that I believe I should be getting. However, the head of our office, the group vice president, has just recently given me a great deal of guidance in setting a career path for me. I do not want to be a consultant forever, and he has allowed me the opportunity to explore marketing, which I find interesting.

There are a couple of things anyone considering this field should be aware of. My career field is very diversified, which means I do not do the same thing all the time. It is very difficult to become an expert in one area, so two years down the road, if you are looking to be very credible in one particular subject, it may be difficult because you are spread over the whole board. Other considerations are the long hours and high energy level, which is essential in this field.

Other fields I could move on to would include anything to do with Wall Street, especially the financial markets. It would be very easy for me to move from DRI to any of the Wall Street investment houses. The problem with this is the fact that New York is the hub for finance, and if you are considering relocating, you may find yourself somewhat constrained in the type of work you can go into. However, as an industrial consultant at DRI working with corporate companies, you're much more mobile.

My advice to anyone considering finances as a career is make sure you want to do a lot of different things. Make sure you do not mind setting your own schedule and sticking to it. Being flexible in the amount of hours and the time of the day that you are doing work, as well as weekends, should not bother you.

The things that stimulate, satisfy, and motivate me most about this work are probably the diversification. I like doing a lot of different things. And, I think when you are young and you really don't know what you may want five or ten years down the road, the best thing you can do is expose yourself to everything that is out there.

~~~ JOE FOYLE

PERSONNEL MANAGER

At the time of this interview, Joe was manager of compensation and bene-fits for the Semiconductor Division of the RCA Corporation, where he worked for a number of years. He was originally hired as a training repre-sentative, then was promoted to the administrator of organization develop-ment and training, then to administrator, salary administration, personnel manager for one of RCA's plants, and, finally, to his current position.

A T THE SEMICONDUCTOR DIVISION, we have five domestic plants with approximately 2,500 hourly and 2,000 salaried employees. My major responsibilities are to ensure that these domestic salaried employees are compensated competitively and that the compensation and benefits programs are administered consistently across our division. Typical responsibilities include surveying local industries to ensure our salaries and benefits are competitive. Twice a year, I meet with my counterparts in the semiconductor industry who also conduct surveys to swap stories, compare survey findings, and develop our skills. I design a merit increase program each year, meet with management to communicate the program, project increases for all employees, and administer the program throughout the year. My staff includes three exempt employees and one secretary.

After college, I worked in sales for Campbell Soups. I was then in the army for three years, stationed in Germany and Vietnam as a noncommissioned officer. I then worked in a placement agency, finding jobs for engineers and computer programmers. RCA was a client of ours. Business wasn't good, so I accepted a job at RCA. I have been with RCA twelve years.

My other duties include designing and implementing incentive plans and recognition programs, and ensuring that people are in the correct occupations and that job descriptions are correct, and that appropriate salary grades are established. I direct my staff and give them performance counseling and feed-back. I am also responsible for preparing and monitoring the operating budgets for our industrial relations function. I am also the industrial relations representative to our division's marketing group and the MIS and quality organizations. This means that I sit in on their staff meetings and serve as their industrial relations contact, regardless of the problem.

Typical skills utilized are common sense, problem-solving techniques, empathy, listening, and, generally, just good interpersonal skills. Depending on the problem, technical skills, which involve a knowledge of benefit and compensation, are also required from time to time.

The physical surroundings are quite pleasant. Our facility is the division headquarters. It is located on about twenty-two acres and is made up of four interconnecting buildings. My typical day starts at 7:30 A.M. I generally leave the office for home at about 5:30 P.M. So my average workweek is about forty-five hours.

The pace is usually quite hectic but often depends on the time of the month and year. It is always more hectic when we are processing the monthly merit increases; when we are doing the yearly salary planning from October through December; and whenever we're in a layoff mode.

What I enjoy the most about my field is the recognition I get for doing a good job; the people I work with in an exciting environment; and, of course, my salary and compensation. What I enjoy the least in the semiconductor industry is its tendency to be unpredictable, with minimal overhead staffing. This can create a hectic pace and pressure to get things done quickly and, oftentimes, with insufficient help. More specifically, the salary/merit planning part at the end of the year is always filled with confrontation and pressure.

I think a person would do well in personnel or in compensation and benefits if they had a good ability to problem solve, that is, take two opposing opinions and compromise without having either party feel like they have lost. A candidate for this field should be analytical and conscientious, be able to meet commitments, have a good sense of humor, and possess good written and verbal communications skills.

In general, the best industrial relations or personnel people I have come in contact with have had liberal arts undergraduate degrees, such as psychology, sociology, and history. Master's degrees are helpful in industrial relations, human resources, or business administration.

Personal qualities should include absolute honesty, good ethical standards, integrity, a sense of fairness, comfort with details, and a desire or at least a willingness to confront. Employees rely on personnel to be the conscience of the organization. For example, you have to be helpful to management without usurping their authority. There's a tendency for management to try to delegate to personnel all people-related issues. It takes guts and confidence to help managers see when things are really his or her responsibility as managers.

Personnel, besides being an educator, adviser, and sounding board of management, is also a service function. You will only be successful if your clients are pleased enough with your service. I tend to look at my job as my own business and want to make sure it is as successful as possible. This does not mean that you have to become a rubber stamp, but rather have to take some risks, stand up for what you believe is right, and give honest reactions in a timely and thorough manner.

I would tell people who are considering personnel or industrial relations as a career path that there is a lot more to these fields than hiring and firing, including employment, labor and employee relations, benefits, safety, organization development, security, training, career planning, and compensation. I would also tell them that it is a growing field that gives one the option of being a specialist or a generalist. There are excellent opportunities available in this field, and the salary and rewards are good.

I believe good personnel people could move into many functions within another business, specifically, sales, purchasing, accounting, education, and counseling. I think the movements would be relatively easy, depending on your industrial relations discipline and education.

~~~ Some Things to Think About...

Now that you have an understanding of Enterprising careers, here are some things to consider:

1. What insights about Enterprising occupations have you gained from these interviews?

   _____

   _____

   _____

2. Which characteristics, abilities, and personal qualities discussed in the interviews are similar to your own? Which are different or in contrast to your own? How might the similarities or differences affect your possible career choices?

_____

_____

_____

3. Ask yourself the following:

   * Are you concerned with high quality goods and services? _____

   * Are you interested in high income potential? _____

   * Are you business oriented with a concern for the bottom line? _____

   * Do you have strong verbal communication skills? Can you converse easily with others? _____

   * Do you have good sales ability? Are you competitive? _____

   * How would you rate your self-confidence? _____

   * Do you have strong leadership abilities? _____

   How might your responses to these questions suggest satisfaction with an Enterprising career choice? _____

   _____

4. Which interviews held your interest? Why? _____

   _____

5. Which interviews were not what you expected? Why? _____

   _____

6. Which occupations are you going to investigate further? How?

   _____

   _____

   _____

   _____

CHAPTER SEVEN

Invest in a Conventional Career

DOES COUNTING SHEEP keep you *up* at night? Can you spot a needle in a haystack? Are you the one your friends would trust with their lives? Can you turn chaos into order?

If so, you may want to consider a career in the Conventional fields. Read on and *count* the possibilities!

~~~ What Are These Careers and Where Can I Find Them?

Conventional work environments generally provide structure and order with clearly defined rules and policies. The work typically involves the systematic manipulation and organization of data. Often, Conventional occupations entail the control or expenditure of very substantial amounts of money. Attention to detail and quality and accuracy of work are critical in Conventional work. Frequently, deadlines and other pressures are part of the scenario. Conventional people generally need the aptitude to read financial statements and quantitative data as well as the ability to write and present reports. Typically, Conventional occupations are those related to accounting, business, finance, office support, and administration. Conventional jobs are usually found in office environments in all sizes and sorts of organizations. A representative sample of many job titles that are considered Conventional include those listed in table 7 below. For a more complete listing of Conventional careers, consult *The Dictionary of Holland Occupational Codes* or the appendix.

TABLE 7
EXAMPLES OF CONVENTIONAL CAREERS

Accountant	IRS agent	Employment manager
Paralegal	IRS tax auditor	Business education teacher
Actuary	Mathematics teacher	Small business owner
Financial analyst	Credit manager	Computer operator
Banker	Certified public accountant	Nursing home administrator
Business programmer	Production manager	County welfare worker

Quite a few Conventional occupations entail a great deal of responsibility and offer high prestige and income potential. That can make a field that seems a little dull and drab sound pretty good. Conventional people are critical to any successful business, government, or institution and often hold quite challenging and important positions.

～～～ Who Are These People and Am I One of Them?

What types of people are attracted to and do well in Conventional occupations? What are their characteristics, values, and interests?

Thoughts of a Conventional person do not tend to conjure up images of a Mr. or Ms. Excitement. On first impression, the description of a Conventional person may seem a little on the dull side. Images of the meticulous accountant or the stone-faced IRS agent may come to mind. But after further examination, it is clear that Conventional people are more appealing than their stereotype might suggest.

Dependability, self-discipline, and a strong work ethic often make the Conventional individual one of the most invaluable employees in any organization. Mature and conscientious, Conventional types tend to exude confidence. Their persistence, precision, and attention to detail leads them to turn chaos into order. Conventional people perceive themselves as conforming, orderly, and as having clerical and numerical ability. On the one hand, Conventional types tend to be careful, efficient, and practical. On the other hand, they can sometimes be defensive, inflexible, and inhibited.

When stressful or catastrophic situations arise, a Conventional person is definitely the one you want around. As more flamboyant types start to become unglued, Conventional people stay on track and remain focused and goal oriented. Their analytical skills are an excellent resource for assessing and reviewing situations. The Conventional individual can act as a balance for impulsive types and bring them back down to earth. She or he can modify unrealistic ideas and plans so that they really can "make us millionaires!"

On the interpersonal side, Conventional people tend to be quiet and reserved. Because of their precise nature, Conventional people usually measure their words very carefully. Often, they rely on their work to communicate for them. Because they tend to resist change, Conventional types develop new relationships slowly. They are likely to have a small group of long-term close friends with whom they have much in common.

Conventional people can be the most trustworthy and straightforward of the Holland types. Confidential information is safe in their hands. You can feel relatively certain that they will be discreet. Similar to the Enterprising types, Conventional types value business and economic achievement, material possessions, and status. Unlike Enterprising people, Conventional people prefer stability and security over risk taking and tend to avoid fast-paced environments.

★ ★ ★ *"I think my success has been based upon a couple of things. First, I am a hard worker, and I try to ensure that the hours I spend working are well spent. It is not just that I work a lot of hours. I seem to have an appetite for nearly everything that comes along. In theory, everything comes across my desk— everything that the federal government does, practically, because everything has some budget effect. There is some sorting out of the magnitude of things, and everything is necessarily judged on the dollar-volume basis. Clearly, analytical and quantitative skills, a good sense of structure of the budget, and attention to programmatic detail are critical. The understanding of what is behind the programmatic detail is even more important."*

DAVID STOCKMAN
FORMER BUDGET DIRECTOR

～ ～ ～ Can't Balance Your Checkbook... Or, Should You Avoid This Field?

If you crave variety, action, and ambiguity, it's probably best if you steer clear of the Conventional careers. Conventional work generally takes place in orderly, structured environments where precision and routine are valued. No "flying by the seat of your pants" or "que sera, sera" attitudes are found in the Conventional world.

Other red flags to alert you that a Conventional career is probably *not* for you include:

* *You can't seem to get the hang of the computer or other office machines.* An aptitude for computers is generally required for Conventional careers. Most administrative and financial work is now done on computers.

* *You get antsy at the thought of being chained to a desk all day long.* Because of the nature of Conventional work, most of the workday is spent in an office at a desk.

* *You'd rather hire an accountant than be an accountant.* An affinity for numbers is needed in many of the Conventional occupations.

* *You consider reading the IRS tax preparation guide to be the perfect cure for insomnia.* Reading and digesting quantitative data and reports is often part of the package for Conventional careers.

~ ~ ~ How Do I Get Started?

Conventional occupations generally need serious, mature, intelligent individuals and often call for substantial educational background and training. Frequently, people aspiring to Conventional careers need to be serious about their careers during their early years of college. Becoming an accountant is not something you decide late in your senior year on the way to the career planning and placement office.

Bachelor's degrees are needed to become accountants, auditors, budget analysts, adjusters, and cost estimators. Coursework in accounting, finance, economics, and computer sciences encompasses the core of the curriculum required. Supplemental work in human resources management and written and verbal communication is often suggested. Movement into supervisory and management positions generally requires an MBA. To advance, accountants generally need to take licensing exams to become certified (e.g., certified public accountant, or CPA).

Four-year college degrees are not always necessary for Conventional careers in the clerical and administrative areas. Bank cashiers, secretaries, and administrative clerks may need a high school diploma only, but additional training or experience with computers is usually a plus. Some college is often now preferred for many secretarial positions, especially for those that may lead to clerical supervisor or manager positions. Courtroom stenographers and court reporters usually require postsecondary training in court reporting/stenography.

In addition to formal education and training, it is critical to have extracurricular activities and prior experience in order to successfully compete in today's Conventional job market. Serving as president or secretary of a club, helping others with taxes, proofreading the school yearbook, and typing reports and papers for others are ways to gain skills that are needed for Conventional careers. A part-time or summer job in an office environment can be an invaluable opportunity to gain exposure and experience in the Conventional fields.

⌐⌐⌐ What's It Like Out There?

The outlook for Conventional careers does not tend to fluctuate as sharply as in other fields such as manufacturing, high-tech, and marketing. There is a need for Conventional people in almost any type of organization. Conventional job opportunities are among the most abundant for college graduates.

According to the *1994–1995 Occupational Outlook Handbook*, Conventional occupations that will have average growth through 2005 include financial managers, budget analysts, adjusters/investigators/collectors, and clerical supervisors/managers. Those occupations with faster than average growth include accountants, auditors, and cost estimators. Occupations that will grow much faster than average include health services managers, food service managers, and paralegals. Employment of credit analysts, bookkeepers, secretaries, and administrative services managers is expected to have little change or slower than average growth. Occupations that will experience a decline in growth due to automation include bank tellers, court reporters, and stenographers.

There are virtually no geographic limitations to pursuing a career in Conventional fields. Most organizations, whatever and wherever they may be, need Conventional people to handle administrative and financial details.

⌐⌐⌐ Where Do I Find Out More About Conventional Careers?

The careful and practical Conventional person will want to know what she or he is getting into before starting down a career path. The best way to find out about Conventional careers is to talk directly to people in those careers. Conducting informational interviews with people whose careers interest you can give you the best picture of what it's like, what's required for a career, how to prepare for it, and whether you'll enjoy the work.

We've done some of the initial investigating for you by conducting informational interviews with people in Conventional careers; these comprise the remainder of this chapter. You'll need to continue the process by getting out there and doing some interviewing of your own. Refer to the final chapter of this book, What's Next?, for some specific steps on doing informational interviewing.

Researching and reading about Conventional occupations is another important step in your career exploration. Information on how to do career research and tips on career exploration can also be found in the final chapter. A list of books and professional organizations related to Conventional occupations is shown below to help get you started.

Books for Conventional Careers

America's Top Office, Management and Sales Jobs by M. J. Farr, published by JIST, 1994

Careers for Number Crunchers and Other Quantitative Types by R. Burnett, published by VGM Career Horizons, 1993

Careers in Accounting by G. Gaylord and G. Ried, published by VGM Career Horizons, 1991

Careers in Business by L. Stair and D. Domkowski, published by VGM Career Horizons, 1992

Careers in Computers by L. Stair, published by VGM Career Horizons, 1990

Careers in Finance by T. Ring, published by VGM Career Horizons, 1993

Careers in Government by M. E. Pitz, published by VGM Career Horizons, 1994

The Insider's Guide to the Top 20+ Careers in Business and Management by T. Fischgrund, published by VGM Career Horizons, 1993

Opportunities in Food Service Careers by C. Chmelynski, published by VGM Career Horizons, 1992

VGM's Handbook of Business and Management Careers by C. T. Norback, published by VGM Career Horizons, 1993

Professional Organizations for Conventional Careers

Below are organizations that provide information on Conventional careers. Consider contacting organizations that interest you. Be sure to include a self-addressed stamped envelope when requesting information.

Administrative Management Society
1101 14th St., NW, Suite 1100
Washington, DC 20005

Alliance of American Insurers
1501 Woodfield Rd., Suite 400 West
Schaumburg, IL 60173-4980

American Bankers Association
Reference Librarian
1120 Connecticut Ave., NW
Washington, DC 20036

American Institute of Certified Public Accountants
1211 Avenue of the Americas
New York, NY 10036-8775

American Society of Professional Estimators, Inc.
6911 Richmond Hwy., Suite 230
Alexandria, VA 22306

Association of Record Managers and Administrators
4200 Somerset Dr., Suite 215
Prairie Village, KS 66208
1-800-422-2762

Institute of Management Accountants
10 Paragon Dr.
Montvale, NJ 07645

Insurance Information Institute
110 William St.
New York, NY 10038

National Association of Legal Secretaries
2250 East 73rd St., Suite 550
Tulsa, OK 74136

National Association of Public Adjusters
300 Water St.
Baltimore, MD 21202

National Court Reporters Association
8224 Old Courthouse Rd.
Vienna, VA 22182

Professional Secretaries International
10502 NW Ambassador Dr.
Kansas City, MO 64195-0404

The Institute of Internal Auditors
249 Maitland Ave.
Altamonte Springs, FL 32701-4201

U.S. Office of Personnel Management
1900 E St., NW
Washington, DC 20415

~~~ PAULA CARR

BANKER

At the time of this interview, Paula was a credit analyst for a commercial bank responsible for in-depth reviews of companies applying for loans and how they relate to current markets and the industry in general. Her work involves extensive writing and a great deal of customer contact.

IN MY JOB, I assist the bank's loan officer. Before my bank gives a company a loan, it is my responsibility to take an in-depth look at the company, the industry, and the market. I call agencies and compare numbers, and take the company's numbers and analyze them. I write up a report, which is usually about twenty pages long, and then present the report to the loan officer. I am often included in the loan decision. There is also a great deal of customer contact in my job.

When I was in college, I was a European history major, with concentration in English history. I had to write a junior and senior thesis, which are actually the two things that prepared me the most for my current job because of the writing skills that are required for them. I also took some economics courses.

I knew I wanted to get into something business related, and I decided that I wanted to go into commercial banking after going on several research interviews and talking to a professional in commercial banking.

I entered a training program after I was accepted into my current position. The program was more academic than I had expected, and I was considered a trainee for one year. But I would encourage anyone considering commercial banking to enter a training program like this one. It offers good exposure to the business world and helps establish a competitive edge. While there is more writing than I had anticipated, my academic background helped to prepare me for this unexpected requirement.

I currently work from 8:30 A.M. to 6:00 P.M., Monday through Friday. Longer days, however, are not uncommon. Weekends are usually work free, and I enjoy seeing the sights of New York, and also getting away.

Commercial banking is a very competitive field. There are many qualified people out there, so anyone considering this field has to keep competitive.

Exceptional people in my field possess an ability to talk to people at any level—whether they be friendly or hostile—and they must be inquisitive. One of the best aspects of my work and what motivates me the most is the people I work for and the people I meet at the bank.

I consider myself very fortunate in that I have a boss who is very thoughtful and concerned, especially with the younger people in his office. His door is always open to us to ask questions and discuss problems.

Other fields related to commercial banking that I would consider transitioning into would be something in industrial banking and/or financial analysis. I am presently deciding whether to make a commitment toward pursuing an MBA. My decision will depend on whether I plan on staying in banking or changing industries.

I would strongly suggest career counseling courses to anyone trying to make a career decision. Figure out what you want to do first, then go out into the world and ask the professionals what it is like.

～～～ ALLEN GOLDSTEIN

ACCOUNTANT

At the time of this interview, Allen was an accountant specializing in the formation and execution of mutual funds. He chose the profession after taking the Strong Interest Inventory as a college sophomore. The test results suggested that he had the attention to detail and affinity for numbers required for the field. He was working for a Big Six accounting firm in New York.

WHEN I FIRST JOINED Price Waterhouse, my first client was an investment company, which is like a mutual fund. The person I was working for took a liking to me and thought that he'd like to have me work with his clients, which were mutual funds.

I then left the business altogether to do something else for three or four years. I went to Washington, D.C., and worked for United Nuclear Corporation. They were a growing company that had been mining uranium and had some power plants. They were growing very rapidly and I thought there were opportunities there for financial people. It existed for a very short time because we had Three Mile Island. That put a cap on the country's interest in nuclear power plants. I then came back to New York to work with a company that had some mutual funds and needed somebody with some expertise in that area.

Accounting at first had a great appeal to me: It was logical, it dealt with numbers, it seemed to be very useful, and I did enjoy taking the courses.

What I enjoy about it now is the interaction with people, helping people. Yes, I enjoy the logic of what I do. And I think I enjoy the challenge of doing something new and helping people out.

I work on a project basis. Generally, there are two or three projects going on at a time. I have people working for me on different projects, who are dealing with different clients. They usually have finite deadlines that have to be met and we work toward those deadlines and then move on to another project.

The first thing that you have to recognize is that accounting is the language of business. And, therefore, depending on the discipline, the drive, and the energy level you have, you can use that as the basis for doing investment banking and commercial banking. I'm thinking of people who I know who are successful in each of those areas. There are investment people who came out with accounting backgrounds. There are people who run companies who have accounting backgrounds.

What you have to add on to the accounting background is the vision of where you want to take your company and how to make decisions. Accounting gives you a tool you can use in just about any business. For that matter, it's not limited to business. It's something that I think people in government could use and I guess I've always thought that people other than lawyers might be able to make a contribution in government.

My interests have changed somewhat since I first started out. Compared to the time before I became an accountant, I am more interested in dealing with people and working with people and am somewhat open to thinking objectively about what is good for people. I think that comes from the nature of the work that I've been doing, public accounting, for which you have to be a certified public accountant, which puts you in an arena where you are trying to be objective and make judgments about whether things have been fairly presented in terms of the accounting procedures.

The downside of the job is that you're at the beck and call of your client. Your hours are not your own. There are demands. It's not a 9-to-5 job.

Right now in the public accounting arena, there's a lot of change taking place. There is more emphasis on marketing, developing relationships with people, and networking than there is on technical capability, which used to be the strong suit of the profession.

If you're a freshman in college thinking about studying accounting, I think you have to get into an accounting program. Or you may want to consider a broader-based program of business and then moving into accounting in your junior or senior year, and then going on for a master's degree. You have to be thinking about what type of accounting you're interested in. Are you interested in public accounting, private accounting, corporations, or governmental accounting, a whole different area?

When I was in school, the thrust was to go into public accounting, become a certified public accountant, and then decide where you wanted to go. I would say that probably is still a good path to follow. It gives you the broadest possible options.

However, I think the public accounting profession is looking for very good people. It's an outstanding area. It runs in cycles. In the next five or ten years there is going to be a lot of pressure on the public accounting profession to get very good people into the profession and make sure the profession is continuing.

Salary depends on the region of the country in which you're looking to work. And also the size of the accounting firm. I think the major accounting firms, referred to as the Big Six, are very competitively priced in different regions of the country. In the higher-cost areas of the country, of course, they pay more money.

The nature of the public accounting profession has historically been "up or out." However, that's changing. For example, someone like myself, who has gained expertise in a particular industry, is considered valuable. Although I cannot go up all the way to partner, which is the ultimate, there now is a position called director, which is in many respects considered to be like a partner. It demands technical competence and involves dealing with clients, but doesn't have all the requirements of being a partner. So I think the profession is changing in that it recognizes that the "up or out" philosophy has prevented firms from retaining people with certain expertise that their clients need. But for most people, I think the profession has continued to be an "up or out" kind of road.

Today, public accounting firms are all moving in the direction of specialization. What's happened is that there are more accountants coming out of school, so you have more accountants going into corporations, and you have more trained accountants throughout the whole economy. The public accounting profession found that these corporate people were as knowledgeable about the general rules of accounting as the people they had. So now the public accounting firms have to add something of more value. And the way they do that is having specialized knowledge in industries. Most people in the public accounting firms are now trying to identify the industries that in ten and twenty years are going to be commanding the most of their service. The accounting firms are interested in finding people who are specialized in those industries.

The type of person who succeeds in accounting is a person who is, I think, somewhat of a perfectionist, wanting to be technically very good at what he or she does. I think, increasingly, you have to be a driven person because thereare a lot of demands put on you by the profession. Also, if you want to have an outside life, you have to be a person who can achieve balance.

I think the third characteristic is getting along well with people, developing relationships, and networking. I think that's going to be a very important criteria.

If you're breaking into accounting, you should expect that the business is going to be changing. It is a highly competitive business today, and it will be increasingly competitive. One piece of advice that I had gotten when I first started was to stay current on the subject, the body of knowledge, the profession. I think it's increasingly difficult to do that because the body of knowledge is growing so rapidly. It's going to require specialization so that you can pick out a portion of the subject and really become knowledgeable in it.

I think accounting is an outstanding profession for someone who feels he or she has very high ethics. The competition is going to be fiercely keen. I think there are a lot of very good accountants out there, and if you want a profession in which you feel very good about yourself and what you do, I think accounting works.

DONNA CLAIRE

ACTUARIAL CONSULTANT

At the time of this interview, Donna was an actuarial consultant. After she demonstrated strong math skills in high school, her teachers recommended actuarial science. She did a co-op program with New York Life Insurance Company throughout college and worked for the company for seven years. After working a couple of years for a different insurance company, she opened her own consulting business.

ACTUARIES WORK IN THE INSURANCE FIELD. They are insurance mathematicians trying to measure the value of a company on both the asset and liability side.

I have my own consulting firm, and one thing companies hire me for is to go in and tell them what they should invest in.

I enjoy the independence of consulting. I enjoy picking my own customers, theoretically making my own hours, and the variety of projects I work on. I have a variety of different clients, normally simultaneously. I will go out to their place, talk to the investment people, talk to the manager of the company, and try to add value to their company.

I also enjoy helping write the insurance regulations, the insurance law. I've given testimony to some congressional committees and also to state insurance departments.

At least half of all actuaries work in an insurance company. The advantage of an insurance company is you have a steady paycheck, a health insurance plan, and a pension plan. What they do, for example, is figure out what you should pay for auto insurance or how much you should pay for health insurance, pension plans, or whatever.

There are also actuaries in similar fields to mine who assist in explaining what types of investments insurance companies have. And others do basically financial-type work, figuring out if the company is making money.

It's heavily statistical, it's a little bit like operations research, it's a little accounting. Actually, we have a process in which, through a series of exams, you learn accounting, economics, investing, insurance pricing—all mathematically based fields.

Right now there is a series of exams. The latest claim I've heard is that it takes seven years to go through the entire series. However, while you're taking exams, typically you're working for an insurance company or consulting firm. If you're working for an insurance company, they will give you study time, in general during work, but you will also have to put in your own time, and they will usually increase your pay for each exam you pass.

The exams go by a 350 credit system, which is thirty-five hours' worth of exams. You'll take maybe four to five hours at a time and they offer exams every six months. It is very much like college, without actually attending college courses, although you can attend review courses for some of the exams you'll take.

It's easier to start taking exams in college. I actually finished the entire exam series two years after college. Seven years is just an average. You can do it a heck of a lot faster than that.

There are a lot of opportunities for actuaries, but it's not a guaranteed job. Probably for the first time there are now some unemployed actuaries, although it's a lot smaller percentage than most other fields at this point. But there is not a guarantee that just because you have those exams you will have a job.

Other things that matter are things that matter in all business professions: how well you communicate, how well you write, and whether you have basic business skills.

The exam process is probably a big turn-off for a number of people. It is heavily mathematical, to begin with. However, a lot of actuaries eventually go into management. In fact, there are presidents of insurance companies who are actuaries.

The downside to actuarial consulting is probably the same downside that exists in any other type of consulting. The hours can get rather grueling. In fact, this weekend I put in an all-nighter on Sunday night. This year, I will be on the road a little over one hundred days.

There is a way to keep regular hours, especially if you're within an insurance company. There are also a lot more women in the field, and a number of insurance and even consulting firms have created part-time jobs. It's mostly women who take that option, although I do know one man who has taken a part-time position. You're still getting a very decent salary, but you will work out of your home or perhaps come into the office one or two days a week.

I would strongly recommend talking to other actuaries. The insurance companies that have actuarial programs are very much willing to have people come in and see if they enjoy the profession. You do have to like mathematics and you do have to have some discipline. But other than that, it's a wide-open field and I would highly recommend it.

～～～ Some Things to Think About...

Now that you have an understanding of Conventional careers, here are some things to consider:

1. What insights about Conventional occupations have you gained from these interviews?

   _____

   _____

   _____

2. Which characteristics, abilities, and personal qualities discussed in the interviews are similar to your own? Which are different or in contrast to your own? How might the similarities or differences affect your satisfaction with your possible career choices?

   _____

3. Ask yourself the following:

   * Do you like working in a structured environment? Do you like to follow rules?_____

   * Are you detail oriented, accurate, and/or organized?_____

   * Are you good with numbers? Are you comfortable with statistics and data?_____

   * Would you consider yourself to be dependable and self-disciplined?

   _____

   * Are you proficient with computers, calculators, or other business machines?_____

   * Are you looking for high prestige and income potential?_____

   * Do you tend to stay calm and focused in a chaotic environment?_____

How might your responses to these questions suggest satisfaction with a Conventional career choice? _____

_____

4. Which interviews held your interest? Why? _____

_____

5. Which interviews were not what you expected? Why? _____

_____

6. Which occupations are you going to investigate further? How?

_____

_____

_____

_____

CHAPTER EIGHT

What's Next? Getting Where You Want to Go

BEFORE WE MOVE ON to begin talking about what's next, let's first briefly go over what you've had the opportunity to do so far. Up to this point, you've:

* Looked at a model for career decision making

* Learned about Holland's theory of career choice and six themes of people and work environments

* Had a chance to assess yourself against the Holland themes

* Read interviews with people in careers that correspond to the Holland themes

* Probably come up with some possibilities for yourself but still may be thinking, What should I do next?

As helpful as all of this may have been, you may still need to do more self-assessment and career exploration. Instead of vaguely alluding to those tasks, we're going to give you some specific details and steps to get you started.

～～～ More About You

Self-assessment should be an ongoing process, not just a onetime event. Self-knowledge is the key to successful career decision making. Each time you learn and experience something new, you need to assess the outcomes and/or changes in yourself. Engaging in continual self-evaluation allows you to be ready each time you are faced with a career transition. Your core values and competencies may remain fairly stable over time, but some changes may occur because of ongoing growth and development. Additionally, external factors may create changes in your values and interests. For example, family commitments may not impact your career decisions now but may play a large role in the future. Or, perhaps, after being exposed to your organization's new computer system, you may develop a new interest in learning and developing computer skills and knowledge. Take computer consultant Charles E. Rauch who is profiled in chapter 3, for example. When his company decided to computerize its work processes, Rauch went to the library to read up on computers and then let it be known that he wanted to work on the project. Subsequently, he went on to a successful career in information systems and computer consulting.

Taking a look at yourself now is integral to your career decision making in the present. But what you find out now may not still apply in three to five years, or even tomorrow. So, it's important to *reevaluate* yourself and your situation each time a new opportunity or career transition crops up!

Now let's look at some areas to cover in your continuing self-assessment.

Interests

This book has primarily focused on your career interests in the context of Holland's six themes—Realistic, Investigative, Artistic, Social, Enterprising, and Conventional—and how your interests can influence your career decision making. We recommend that you take the *Strong Interest Inventory* (*Strong*), described earlier, or another Holland-based instrument such as the *Self-Directed Search* (SDS), if you have not done so already. Contact your school career planning and placement center or a career counselor for more information on taking the *Strong* or SDS.

Even if you haven't taken one of the interest inventories, you should be able to make an educated guess about your Holland theme code from reading the preceding chapters. Chapter 1 in this book provides an overview of Holland's theory and the *Let's Make a Deal* exercise to assist you in determining your theme code. The subsequent chapters on each Holland theme gave a more in-depth picture that should help you see similarities and differences between yourself and each theme.

》MY HOLLAND THEME

Record your three-letter Holland theme code in this space:

_____

Understanding your interests can help you in choosing a career that fits. Wouldn't it be great if you could get paid for doing what you really like to do? As you've read, being truly interested in your work can positively influence your levels of career satisfaction and success. Do you like tinkering in your workshop, writing short stories, researching investment opportunities, helping other people with their problems?

Stockbroker Andrew McGurk, who is profiled in chapter 6, was interested in economics and the development of companies when he was in high school. He parlayed those interests into a career in investments.

» MY TOP THREE INTERESTS

Think about what you truly love to do or your favorite topics, then list your top three interests below:

_____

_____

_____

Values

Values are another area to investigate in your self-assessment. According to Howard Figler, author of *The Complete Job Search Handbook*, values are "the enduring dimensions or aspects of our work that we regard as important sources of satisfaction." Clarifying your values and determining which ones are the most important to you can help you assess which careers will best meet your needs. Values are generally reflections of your underlying needs—what really motivates you.

The more your chosen career is in line with your values, the stronger your commitment to the career will be. Sometimes you will have to make trade-offs when choosing between your values and your work. Also, your values may change over time, causing you to reassess your situation. The goal is to come up with a balance between your values and your career that allows you to feel personally satisfied *and* committed to your work.

Values assessments are often in the form of card sorts or checklists. Two examples are *The Values Scale* and the *Rokeach Values Survey*, which both must be administered by a qualified counselor. Check with a career planning and placement center for more information. Values that influence career decision making include adventure, creativity, flexibility, family time, health, achieving wealth, teamwork, independence, indoor/outdoor work, prestige, and variety.

» MY TOP THREE VALUES

What are the three values that are most important to you at this point in your life? What values must be satisfied in your work? List your top three values below:

_____

_____

_____

Skills

Skills identification is also an essential part of self-assessment. Of all the attributes that you might assess, your skills are the most likely to change over time because of ongoing learning and development. Skills are a set of abilities that you use to accomplish your goals and get things done. Assessing your skills and your potential to develop a skill can help you determine how well you'll do in a particular career. Skills can be natural or acquired, as well as developed or improved.

Sales representative John O'Connell felt it was important to look at himself with a critical eye and then look for the type of situation in which he'd do best. Before he began his job search after college, he outlined his strengths and weaknesses and targeted job opportunities that would mesh with his profile.

Reflecting on your past accomplishments can help you identify your skills. The word *accomplishment* can sometimes be daunting to people—they may say, "But I've never done anything that's an accomplishment!" Accomplishing something doesn't necessarily mean that you had to have won an award, gotten promoted, or done something earth-shattering. Accomplishments are situations in which you've done something that you felt good about—something you achieved when you were enjoying yourself. An accomplishment could be organizing a bake sale, completing a difficult school project, or teaching a student in a literacy program how to read.

The idea is to analyze your accomplishments to determine what skills you used in achieving the outcomes. A good method of doing this is to write down your accomplishments in detail and then go through a list of skills and check off the ones you used in each situation. There is an excellent, in-depth skills identification exercise available in Richard Bolles' *What Color is Your Parachute?* that employs this method.

Clarification of skills can also entail just simply going through a skills checklist or card sort and indicating whether or not you possess a skill and/or whether the skill needs to be developed. Whatever method you choose, identifying your skills and discovering which are most important to you and your satisfaction, well-being, and success is a key piece of self-assessment.

》 MY THREE MOST IMPORTANT SKILLS

Come up with what you think are your three most important skills and record them in the space below:

A More Subjective Approach

Sometimes formal assessment instruments may not give you all the information you need for your career decision making. Engaging in a more subjective approach to assessment is an excellent way to complement the objective perspective gained from more formal assessments such as inventories and card sorts. The value of life experience as a source of information about career preferences should not be underestimated. Integrating past experience recollections with your *Strong* or other formal assessment results provides a clearer, more complete basis from which to identify your career interests.

In *Career Development: Theory and Practice* (Montross and Shinkman, 1992), Mark Savickas described a subjective approach to self-assessment that employs an autobiographical technique in which past experiences are described and evaluated to look for common themes and meanings. By asking yourself questions, recounting past experiences, and analyzing life stories to identify themes and connections, you can uncover clues to what you might like and what you might not like about certain careers.

❯❯ MY LIFE EXPERIENCES

Begin your subjective self-assessment by answering the following questions:

Remember a significant experience. What was rewarding about it? What was frustrating? _____

_____

Think about an important decision you made. What were the considerations you made that led to the decision? _____

_____

What are your favorite topics or school subjects? _____

_____

Who are your role models or heroes? Why? _____

_____

What do you like to do? How do you spend your free time? _____

_____

What are the characteristics of past jobs and actitivies that you found challenging and rewarding? What was boring?_____

_____

How could your extracurricular activites and/or part-time jobs be related to possible career options?_____

_____

Where would you like to live?_____

_____

What are you doing when you lose track of time? _____

_____

What do people compliment you on? _____

_____

What do you do that makes you feel good about yourself?_____

_____

Evaluating your own life experiences will help you learn to appreciate your own perceptions and reactions. Trust your instincts! The way you felt about a certain activity, task, or subject in one environment will no doubt carry over into other environments in which it is encountered. In other words, if you really winced at the sight of blood while working as a candy striper, you might want to think hard before pursuing a career in medicine. Or maybe you can detect a common thread in your experiences: You lose track of time while you're doodling, you loved designing the fliers for the annual rummage sale, and people always compliment you on your flair for color. Remember, self-assessment should continue as you experience and examine your possible career options.

After examining your expressed interests and past experiences, develop a list of characteristics that made those things rewarding as well as a list of characteristics you found boring and/or want to avoid. You'll be able to determine more effectively whether a specific career will be interesting, rewarding, and challenging for you or not. People who begin their career exploration by analyzing what they have learned from past experiences are better prepared to realistically evaluate possible career options.

Roadblocks to Progress

You can do all the self-assessment you want, but if there are roadblocks to your moving forward in your career planning—internal or external—it will be to no avail. Besides assessing yourself, it is important for you to assess potential external or internal barriers.

External barriers might include lack of finances, lack of time, or an unfavorable geographic location. Often external barriers can be removed, but not always. At least becoming aware of the potential blocks that can't be changed gives you an opportunity to work around them. For example, in her profile in chapter 4, architect Page Goolrick relates that women in the field of architecture often have to prove their knowledge a little more than men in the field. She comments that men on the construction sites or in the trades tend to put women through a "testing" period on every single project. Being aware of the behavior allows her to prepare for and work around this potential barrier.

» MY EXTERNAL BARRIERS

What external barriers might be standing in your way?

_____

_____

_____

An inventory of *internal barriers*, blocks within yourself that can sabotage your own progress, is a must. The blocks can run the gamut from attitudes, behaviors, and beliefs to fears, misinformation, and deficits in skills. Perhaps you're a perfectionist and are too hard on yourself, or perhaps you hold stereotypic beliefs about what careers are "appropriate" for men and women. Goolrick's example could also have been an internal barrier if she held the same stereotypic beliefs as the people she encountered on the project sites. An internal lack of confidence in her own ability as an architect could have prevented her from dealing with the "testing" period.

Identifying your internal blocks allows you to change or at least manage the barriers and move forward.

What internal barriers might be blocking your progress?

_____

_____

_____

If you find it difficult to deal with or get around your barriers, it may be advisable for you to seek career or other suitable counseling. One point to remember is that barriers to one type of work environment may not be barriers in another environment. So don't get discouraged, and keep looking for the right fit!

The Big Picture

Once you have a clear picture of yourself, you'll be able to realistically assess yourself against the qualifications and requirements of the career options you might be interested in. Examining how your interests, values, skills, and personality mesh with a particular career or work environment is key to finding a good match. Review the results you got from assessing your interests, your values, your skills, and your experiences.

» WHO AM I?

In the space that follows, write a two-paragraph description of who you are. Be sure to discuss any themes or patterns you might have picked up on by reviewing your self-assessment. Use extra paper if you need to.

I am _____

_____

_____

_____

_____

_____

_____

_____

Now that you've got a handle on the big picture, you're ready to delve into some of the finer details. Read on for more on exploring your career options.

~ ~ ~ Hunting for Career Options

Exploring career options entails conducting thorough research on the world of work. The knowledge you gain through your own research is more meaningful than knowledge that is simply handed to you by other people. There are basically three ways to explore career options: by reading books, journals, and other resources; by conducting informational interviews; and by obtaining direct experience.

Poring Over Volumes

By delving into relevant books, magazines, professional journals, newsletters, and newspapers, you can discover a multitude of valuable information such as:

* Which jobs you may want to find out more about

* How others with your interests have built satisfying careers

* Names of associations to contact for assistance

* Industries you might like to work in

* What companies you should contact

You've taken the first step by picking up this book and reading through it. Make sure you refer to the appendix in the back of this book listing some additional careers categorized by Holland codes. Remember to check under all combinations of your code (refer back to your list on p. 8) for careers you might be interested in. This should give you a great start by providing you with a solid list of jobs to find out more about.

You can most likely do a lot of your career research for free with the help of a reference librarian at your local public or college/university library. At the end of each chapter on a Holland theme (see chapters 2 through 7), we suggested various references that were specifically geared to that theme. You'll probably be able to find many of them at your local library or, if not, at your local bookstore.

We'd also like to suggest some general career references here that can be found in most libraries or bookstores to help you in your career exploration.

Books for Career Exploration

Career Anchors: Discovering Your Real Values by E. H. Schein, published by Pfeiffer and Co, 1993

Career Planning and Development for College Students and Recent Graduates by J. Steele and M. S. Morgan, published by VGM/NTC Publishing Group, 1991

The Complete Guide for Occupational Exploration by M. Farr, published by JIST, 1993

The Complete Job Search Handbook by Howard Figler, published by Henry Holt & Co., 1988

Dictionary of Holland Occupational Codes, 2d ed., by G. Gottfredson, J. Holland, published by Psychological Assessment Resources, 1989

Do What You Are by P. D. Tieger and B. Barron-Tieger, published by Little, Brown, & Co., 1992

Graduating into the Nineties: Getting the Most Out of Your First Job After College by C. Carter and G. June, published by Noonday Press, 1993

The Harvard Guide to Careers by M. P. Leape and S. M. Vacca, published by Harvard University Press, 1991

Improved Career Decision-Making in a Changing World by J. M. Ettinger, published by Garrett Park Press, 1991

Making Vocational Choices: A Theory of Careers by J. Holland, published by Psychological Assessment Resources, 1992 revised

The 1995 What Color is Your Parachute? by R. Bolles, published by Ten Speed Press, 1995

Occupational Outlook Handbook 1994–1995 Edition. Washington, DC: U.S. Department of Labor Bureau of Statistics/U.S Government Printing Office.

Professional Careers Sourcebook by K. M. Savage and J. M. Palmisano, published by Gale Research, Inc., 1994

Researching Your Way to A Good Job by K. Crowther, published by John Wiley & Sons, 1993

Starting Out, Starting Over by Linda Peterson, published by Davies-Black Publishing, 1995

The Three Boxes of Life, and How To Get Out of Them by R. Bolles, published by Ten Speed Press, 1981

The 21st Century Careerist by Robert J. Ginn, published by Macmillan & Co., 1996

The Whole Career Sourcebook by R. M. Kaplan, published by AMACOM, 1991

Plan to spend anywhere from a day to a week in the library doing research, but don't get carried away. The supply of information is virtually endless. You could make a career of researching career options, and actually some people do. But the point is that your time and resources are not limitless, so you'll need to cut to the chase and hit the pavement for informational and/or job interviewing. Of course, this may be difficult for some of you, especially for Investigative people who might have to pry themselves away from the research process. But onward you must go.

Speaking of Hitting the Pavement

Informational interviewing—no, not job interviewing—requires you to get out there and talk to people directly about their careers and their experiences. It's a way of conducting research face-to-face and the best avenue for finding out the most up-to-date information on a variety of fields and industries. Informational interviewing brings research to life. People are usually flattered to be asked to talk about what they do and can provide more insight than any printed materials.

Social worker Sheila Mehta, who is profiled in chapter 5, spent a lot of time doing informational interviews when she was deciding upon a career. She felt the interviews were helpful but would recommend that people should narrow down their interests before embarking on the interviews. Not having a few concrete choices in mind before doing the interviews overwhelmed her. She also recommends talking to as many people as possible—not just in formal informational interviews. Ask everyone about their careers—even someone sitting next to you on the train.

The difference between an informational interview and a job interview is that in an informational interview, *you* make the contact, *you* make the appointment, *you* ask the questions, and *you* conduct the interview. The question you probably have is, How do I find the people that I am going to interview? First, start with the people you know—co-workers, other students, parents/relatives, friends, ex-co-workers/bosses—and build an initial contact list. Then ask everyone on your initial list if they have any additional contacts you might be able to talk to. You also might want to check with your career planning and placement office for names of alumni who are open to giving informational interviews and add them to your list. Informational interviewing can be a network-building experience as well as an information-gathering phase of career exploration.

❱❱ MY INFORMATIONAL INTERVIEW HIT LIST

Write down the names and phone numbers of everyone you know whom you might want to interview—relatives, friends, acquaintances, and co-workers. Use extra paper if you need to.

Name	Phone #	Name	Phone #

Continue the list by asking each person for the name of another contact:

Name	Phone #	Name	Phone #

Conduct practice interviews with people whom you know first and then move on to the others on your list. Offer to meet them in their office for twenty minutes—or, if they prefer, for breakfast, lunch, or coffee to minimize taking their time during their busy workdays. Reiterate that your purpose is to obtain information on careers, *not* a job. Make sure you have a set of *prepared open-ended questions* to ask. Here are some sample questions. Feel free to add more of your own if you need to.

How do most people get into your field?

How did you become interested?

What type of educational preparation is needed?

What does the future look like for this industry?

What skills and qualifications do you look for?

What attributes/qualities are essential for success?

What is a typical day/week like? What are the ups and downs?

What are the lifestyle considerations to keep in mind?

Which professional associations/organizations and journals should I look into?

What other jobs/careers might also be of interest?

Who else should I talk to?

May I use your name when I contact them?

Don't forget to send thank-you notes to *everyone* you meet with, even friends and relatives. The process of informational interviewing takes a lot of time and effort, but it's worth it. It's a good way to avoid getting stuck on the wrong track and building experience in a field that's not right for you.

TABLE 8
THE TOP TEN REASONS YOU SHOULD DO INFORMATIONAL INTERVIEWS

10. Find out about careers you did not know existed

9. Discover jobs that you want to build your goals around

8. Learn what types of personalities are best for the jobs you're interested in

7. Deepen your understanding of the world of work in a variety of settings

6. Rule out careers/jobs that won't suit you after all

5. Obtain the most up-to-date career information possible

4. Clarify areas/skills you may need to develop in preparation for your new career

3. Discover what motivates you—what your values are—what you can/can't live without

2. Test your perceptions with individuals actually working in the field— Conduct a reality check

And the number one reason you should do informational interviews...

1. Establish and build a professional network that will be an invaluable resource for years to come

Remember, this is not a job interview so don't offer your résumé unless you're asked for one. In fact, it's best not to even bring one with you at all. If the person asks you for a résumé, offer to mail it to him or her after the interview. The biggest stumbling block to informational interviewing is probably the fear of rejection, which is somewhat unfounded, since there really is nothing at risk. Again, it is not a job interview. All you should be seeking is information. Here are a few tips to ease your fears about the process:

If you encounter silence, just refer to your list of questions and ask one.

If you feel brushed off, the person is probably busy so leave early and thank him or her.

If the meeting becomes a job interview, restate that your objective is information gathering (unless, of course, you are extremely interested in the job!).

If you are asked for your résumé, offer to mail it or drop it off the next day.

For even more details on informational interviewing, check out Martha Stoodley's *Information Interviewing: What It Is and How to Use It in Your Career.*

Stepping Into the Real World

The absolute best way to get a real taste of a career is through direct experience —actually becoming immersed into the work environment/career that you are aspiring to. Here are some real possibilities for you:

Internships Paid or unpaid work experience obtained through your school's career planning and placement center or through your own "feelers." Internships often have specified start and finish dates and tend to parallel school terms or semesters.

Contact your career planning and placement center for help on finding an internship. Also, check with your career center library or local library for the following resources on internships:

The *National Directory of Internships* contains information on internships in nonprofit, government, and business settings. Opportunities in over eighty-five career fields are listed. (It's available from the National Society of Experiential Education, 3509 Hayworth Drive, Suite 207, Raleigh, NC 27609-7229 for $26.50.)

Internships 1995 pulls together information on over 1,700 organizations that offer paid and unpaid internships. (It's available from The Whole Work Catalog at 800-634-9024.)

America's Top 100 Internships covers the top 100+ programs in the country based on research from career development offices, employers, and interns. (It's also available from The Whole Work Catalog at 800-634-9024.)

Professional Organizations/Associations Many professional organizations and associations offer student memberships or discounted dues rates for students. Joining organizations can give you exposure to the career of your dreams as well as excellent opportunities for networking with professionals in the field. At the end of each of the chapters on a Holland theme, there is a listing of relevant professional associations and organizations to contact. Or, ask people who are working in your field of interest which organizations they recommend. Also, the *Encyclopedia of Associations*, available at your local library, is another resource that lists names of professional associations and organizations.

Volunteer Work Unpaid experience with organizations, associations, and companies. For example, during her senior year in college, Sheila Mehta, who is profiled in chapter 5, volunteered at a battered women's shelter and staffed its hot line. She had a chance to work on her counseling skills and get some direction about her career search in social work.

Contact those organizations that are related to your career interests and offer your services for free. Two books that might give you some ideas:

Volunteer USA: A Comprehensive Guide to Worthy Causes That Need You From AIDS to the Environment to Illiteracy. Where to Find Them and How You Can Help, by Andrew Carroll, published by Fawcett Columbine Books/Ballantine Books, 1991

Directory of Volunteer Opportunities, edited by Ellen Shenk, published by Career Information Centre, 1986

Shadowing Ask if you can "shadow" or follow one of your informational interview or network contacts on his or her job for a day or two.

Summer/Part-time Jobs Try to gear your summer and/or part-time job experiences to your career interests rather than an unrelated area such as waiting tables. Ted Beauvais, who is profiled in chapter 2, worked for the Forest

Service during the summer and, as a result, knew he wanted to work there after graduation. He gained solid, relevent experience and discovered the type of job that he wanted to go for.

Obtaining such employment usually takes advanced planning because the competition for career-related summer or part-time work is keen. Check with your career planning and placement center and put out your own feelers.

Summer Jobs '95 (published by Peterson's Guides) lists 20,000 summer job opportunities in hotels, resorts, businesses, parks, camps, government offices, and more.

Taking Courses Taking a few classes is a way to gain exposure and familiarity with a field before jumping into a long-term educational and/or employment commitment. Additionally, you may need to take courses to develop knowledge and skills prior to pursuing particular career interests. Local college and university course catalogs are usually available in the reference section of your public library.

A Few More Things You Can Do

Here are several other resources that you can pursue in your career exploration.

Visit a Career Planning and Placement Center Centers are generally found in public libraries, community colleges, and universities and are usually available at no cost. Services provided include reference/information libraries; self-directed and computer-based career assessment tools; formal career counseling; placement assistance and job leads; alumni networks; and workshops on interviewing, résumé writing, and networking.

The *Directory of Career Planning and Placement Offices* can help you locate a center near you. It's available from the College Placement Council, Inc., 62 Highland Avenue, Bethlehem, PA 18017, and at 215-868-1421.

Find a Private Career Counselor If you are seeking intensive, individualized attention, you might want to contact a career counselor who has a private practice. Unlike the free services at a career center, you will be charged a fee, but you should also receive more extensive assessment and counseling services. The following two organizations can refer you to qualified career counselors in your area:

International Association of Counseling Services, Inc.
5999 Stevenson Ave.
Alexandria, VA 22304/703-823-9800

National Board for Certified Counselors (NBCC)
5999 Stevenson Ave.
Alexandria, VA 22304/703-461-6222

Get Hooked Up With a Computer-Based Career Planning Tool   Computer systems such as Discover or SIGI are often available at career planning centers. Businesses often have systems such as CareerPoint available to their employees. These computer systems provide a self-directed career assessment approach, taking the individual through the career decision-making process via a computer program. The results usually should be interpreted with a qualified career counselor.

～ ～～ Some Parting Words

You may not have decided what career you want to pursue yet, but hopefully you're a lot closer as a result of reading this book. And remember, this career decision will not be your last. Most people make up to eight job changes and three major career changes during their lifetimes. So your decision is not set in stone. Also, don't forget that most people are combinations of two to three of the Holland themes, so being interested in and pursuing several different careers is par for the course.

The best advice is that each time you come to a crossroads in your life, take a good look at yourself, your interests, your values, and your abilities. Just as career decision making is no longer a one-time event, neither should be reading and using the information in this book. Pull out your copy and use it to help you examine and explore your career options; and make the decision that is truly in your best interest.

Additional Occupational Titles

Appendix A
Additional Occupations by Holland Code

REALISTIC OCCUPATIONS

THEME CODE	OCCUPATION	THEME CODE	OCCUPATION
R	Air force officer	RSI	Customs agent
R	Correctional officer	RSI	Special agent, customs
R	Union leader	REI	Aircraft sales representative
RI	Cartographer	REI	Environmental project manager
RI	Civil engineer	REI	Production planner
RI	Engineer	REI	Safety engineer, mines
RI	Forester		
RI	Mechanical engineer	REA	Marine service manager
RIS	Appraiser	RC	Army officer
RIE	Electronics engineer	RCI	Software technician
RIE	Facilities planner		
RIC	Optical engineer	RCS	Research assistant

INVESTIGATIVE OCCUPATIONS

THEME CODE	OCCUPATION	THEME CODE	OCCUPATION
I	Internist	IA	Clinical psychologist
I	Scientific researcher	IA	Language interpreter
I	Statistician	IA	Psychologist
IR	Astronaut	IAR	Physician
IR	Chemical engineer	IAS	Art appraiser
IR	Chemist	IAS	Counseling psychologist
IR	Chiropractor		
IR	Electrical engineer	ISR	Cardiopulmonary technologist
IR	Obstetrician	ISR	Paleontologist
IR	Optometrist		
IR	Pathologist	ISA	Physician assistant
IR	Surgeon		
		ISE	Photographic engineer
IRA	Geologist		
IRA	Physicist	ISC	Bursar
		ISC	Dialysis technician
IRS	Anesthesiologist		
IRS	Biochemist	IER	Project engineer
IRS	Curator	IER	Laboratory supervisor
IRS	Entomologist		
IRS	Geneticist	IEA	Land surveyor
IRS	Meteorologist	IEA	Quality control director
IRS	Neurologist		
IRS	Science teacher	IES	Occupational analyst
		IEC	Fire protection engineer
IRE	Archeologist		
IRE	Chief credit analyst	ICR	Navigator
IRC	Integrated circuit layout designer		
IRC	Medical technologist		

ARTISTIC OCCUPATIONS

THEME CODE	OCCUPATION	THEME CODE	OCCUPATION
A	Art museum director	ASR	Painting restorer
A	Author	ASI	Dance therapist
A	Entertainer	ASI	Television technician
A	Lawyer		
A	Librarian	ASE	Composer
A	Musician	ASE	English teacher
A	Opera singer	ASE	Playwright
A	Poet	AE	Advertising executive
A	Reporter	AE	Broadcaster
		AE	Public relations director
ARI	Architect		
		AER	Equestrian
ARS	Stage technician		
		AEI	Package designer
ARE	Photographer	AEI	Screen writer
AI	Anthropologist	AES	Account executive
		AES	Choreographer
AIR	Landscape architect	AES	Copy writer
AIR	Medical illustrator	AES	Corporate trainer
		AES	Creative director
AIS	Orchestra conductor	AES	Editor
AIS	Paper and prints restorer	AES	Industrial designer
AIE	Cryptanalyst	AEC	Photojournalist
AIE	Motion pictures set designer		
		ACS	Graphologist
AS	Writing teacher		

SOCIAL OCCUPATIONS

THEME CODE	OCCUPATION
S	Elementary school teacher
S	Guidance counselor
S	Public health nurse
SRC	Job development specialist
SI	Cardiac monitor technician
SIR	Orientation therapist for persons with visual disabilities
SIR	Podiatrist
SIR	Physical therapist
SIA	School psychologist
SIE	Correctional agency director
SIE	Head nurse
SIE	Medical records administrator
SIE	Nursing instructor
SIE	Psychiatric technician
SIE	School nurse
SIC	Index editor
SA	Social worker
SA	Speech pathologist
SAE	Food & drug inspector

THEME CODE	OCCUPATION
SE	Community service organization director
SE	High school counselor
SE	Parks and recreation coordinator
SER	Department store manager
SER	Hospital administrator
SER	School superintendent
SEI	Loan officer
SEI	Radio and TV producer
SEA	Dean of students
SEA	Occupational therapy aide
SEA	Social science teacher
SEC	Employment interviewer
SEC	Political scientist
SCI	Packaging engineer
SCI	Preparole counseling aide
SCE	Educational consultant
SCE	Eligibility worker
SCE	Interpreter for persons with hearing disabilities
SCE	Nurse, LPN

ENTERPRISING OCCUPATIONS

THEME CODE	OCCUPATION	THEME CODE	OCCUPATION
E	Life insurance agent	ESR	Airport manager
E	Realtor	ESR	Financial planner
E	Retailer	ESR	Museum director
		ESR	University business manager
ERA	Park superintendent	ESR	Urban planner
EIR	Foreign exchange trader	ESI	Estate planner
EIR	Industrial engineer	ESI	Securities trader
EIA	Communications consultant	ESA	College admissions director
EIS	Controller	ESA	Lobbyist
EIS	Training and education manager	ESC	Media director
EIC	Chief bank examiner	EC	Buyer
EIC	Industrial health engineer	EC	Corporation executive
EA	Marketing executive	ECR	Purchasing agent
EAS	Housing manager	ECS	Hotel manager
ES	Sales manager		
ES	TV announcer		

CONVENTIONAL OCCUPATIONS

THEME CODE	OCCUPATION	THEME CODE	OCCUPATION
C	IRS tax auditor	CE	Accountant
		CE	Banker
CRI	Business programmer	CE	Certified public accountant
		CE	Credit manager
CI	Actuary	CE	IRS agent
		CE	Tax preparer
CIE	Building inspector		
		CER	Budget analyst
CS	Surveillance system monitor	CER	Procurement engineer
CSR	Food and beverage controller		
		CEI	Customs inspector
CSI	Editorial assistant		
CSI	Financial analyst	CES	Business education teacher
		CES	Cost accountant
CSE	Systems accountant	CES	Food service manager
CSE	Title examiner	CES	Nursing home administrator
CSE	Underwriter		

OCCUPATION	THEME CODE	OCCUPATION	THEME CODE
Account executive	AES	Cardiac monitor technician	SI
Accountant	CE	Cardiopulmonary technologist	ISR
Actuary	CI	Cartographer	RI
Advertising executive	AE	Certified public accountant	CE
Air force officer	R	Chemical engineer	IR
Aircraft sales representative	REI	Chemist	IR
Airport manager	ESR	Chief bank examiner	EIC
Anesthesiologist	IRS	Chief credit analyst	IRE
Anthropologist	AI	Chiropractor	IR
Appraiser	RIS	Choreographer	AES
Archeologist	IRE	Civil engineer	RI
Architect	ARI	Clinical psychologist	IA
Army officer	RC	College admissions director	ESA
Art appraiser	IAS	Communications consultant	EIA
Art museum director	A	Community service organization director	SE
Astronaut	IR	Composer	ASE
Author	A	Controller	EIS
Banker	CE	Copy writer	AES
Biochemist	IRS	Corporate trainer	AES
Broadcaster	AE	Corporation executive	EC
Budget analyst	CER	Correctional agency director	SIE
Building inspector	CIE	Correctional officer	R
Bursar	ISC	Cost accountant	CES
Business education teacher	CES	Counseling psychologist	IAS
Business programmer	CRI	Creative director	AES
Buyer	EC	Credit manager	CE
		Cryptanalyst	AIE

OCCUPATION	THEME CODE	OCCUPATION	THEME CODE
Curator	IRS	Geneticist	IRS
Customs agent	RSI	Geologist	IRA
Customs inspector	CEI	Graphologist	ACS
		Guidance counselor	S
Dance therapist	ASI	Head nurse	SIE
Dean of students	SEA	High school counselor	SE
Department store manager	SER	Hospital administrator	SER
Dialysis technician	ISC	Hotel manager	ECS
		Housing manager	EAS
Editor	AES		
Editorial assistant	CSI	Index editor	SIC
Educational consultant	SCE	Industrial designer	AES
Electrical engineer	IR	Industrial engineer	EIR
Electronics engineer	RIE	Industrial health engineer	EIC
Elementary school teacher	S	Integrated circuit layout designer	IRC
Eligibility worker	SCE	Internist	I
Employment interviewer	SEC	Interpreter for persons with hearing disabilities	SCE
Engineer	RI		
English teacher	ASE	IRS agent	CE
Entertainer	A	IRS tax auditor	C
Entomologist	IRS		
Environmental project manager	REI	Job development specialist	SRC
Equestrian	AER		
Estate planner	ESI	Laboratory supervisor	IER
		Land surveyor	IEA
Facilities planner	RIE	Landscape architect	AIR
Financial analyst	CSI	Language interpreter	IA
Financial planner	ESR	Lawyer	A
Fire protection engineer	IEC	Librarian	A
Food & drug inspector	SAE	Life insurance agent	E
Food and beverage controller	CSR	Loan officer	SEI
Food service manager	CES	Lobbyist	ESA
Foreign exchange trader	EIR		
Forester	RI		

OCCUPATION	THEME CODE	OCCUPATION	THEME CODE
Marine service manager	REA	Pathologist	IR
Marketing executive	EA	Photographer	ARE
Mechanical engineer	RI	Photographic engineer	ISE
Media director	ESC	Photojournalist	AEC
Medical illustrator	AIR	Physical therapist	SIR
Medical records administrator	SIE	Physician	IAR
Medical technologist	IRC	Physician assistant	ISA
Meteorologist	IRS	Physicist	IRA
Motion pictures set designer	AIE	Playwright	ASE
Museum director	ESR	Podiatrist	SIR
Musician	A	Poet	A
		Political scientist	SEC
Navigator	ICR	Preparole counseling aide	SCI
Neurologist	IRS	Procurement engineer	CER
Nurse, LPN	SCE	Production planner	REI
Nursing home administrator	CES	Project engineer	IER
Nursing instructor	SIE	Psychiatric technician	SIE
		Psychologist	IA
Obstetrician	IR	Public health nurse	S
Occupational analyst	IES	Public relations director	AE
Occupational therapy aide	SEA	Purchasing agent	ECR
Opera singer	A		
Optical engineer	RIC	Quality control director	IEA
Optometrist	IR		
Orchestra conductor	AIS	Radio and TV producer	SEI
Orientation therapist for persons with visual disabilities	SIR	Realtor	E
		Reporter	A
Package designer	AEI	Research assistant	RCS
Packaging engineer	SCI	Restaurant manager	ECR
Painting restorer	ASR	Retailer	E
Paleontologist	ISR		
Paper and prints restorer	AIS	Safety engineer, mines	REI
Park superintendent	ERA	Sales manager	ES
Parks and recreation coordinator	SE	School nurse	SIE
		School psychologist	SIA

OCCUPATION	THEME CODE	OCCUPATION	THEME CODE
School superintendent	SER	Tax preparer	CE
Science teacher	IRS	Television technician	ASI
Scientific researcher	I	Title examiner	CSE
Screen writer	AEI	Training and education manager	EIS
Securities trader	ESI		
Social science teacher	SEA	TV announcer	ES
Social worker	SA	Underwriter	CSE
Software technician	RCI	Union leader	R
Special agent, customs	RSI	University business manager	ESR
Speech pathologist	SA		
Stage technician	ARS	Urban planner	ESR
Statistician	I	Writing teacher	AS
Surgeon	IR		
Surveillance system monitor	CS		
Systems accountant	CSE		

~ ~ ~ INDEX

water damage noted 1/14/99

MC